ARCHAIC
DESIGN

ARCHAIC DESIGN

CLAYTON ESHLEMAN

BLACK WIDOW PRESS
BOSTON, MA

BLACK WIDOW PRESS is an imprint of Commonwealth Books, Inc., Boston. All Black Widow Press books are printed on acid-free paper, glued and sewn into bindings.
JOSEPH S. PHILLIPS, Publisher
www.blackwidowpress.com

Cover Photograph: Grotte de Saint-Cirq (Dordogne) ©Michel Lorblanchet
Book Design: Kerrie Kemperman

ISBN-13: 978-0-9795137-1-8
ISBN-10: 0-9795137-1-5

Library of Congress Cataloging-in-Publication Data

Eshleman, Clayton, 1935–
    Archaic Design / Clayton Eshleman. — Black Widow Press ed.
    p. cm.
    ISBN-13: 978-0-9795137-1-8
    I. Title

Printed by Thomson-Shore
Printed in the United States

10   9   8   7   6   5   4   3   2   1

ALSO BY CLAYTON ESHLEMAN

❧ **POETRY** ❧

Mexico & North [1962]

Indiana [1969]

Altars [1971]

Coils [1973]

The Gull Wall [1975]

What She Means [1978]

Hades in Manganese [1981]

Fracture [1983]

The Name Encanyoned River: Selected Poems 1960–1985 [1986]

Hotel Cro-Magnon [1989]

Under World Arrest [1994]

From Scratch [1998]

My Devotion [2004]

An Alchemist with One Eye on Fire [2006]

Reciprocal Distillations [2007]

❧ **PROSE** ❧

Antiphonal Swing: Selected Prose 1962–1987 [1989]

Companion Spider: Essays [2002]

*Juniper Fuse: Upper Paleolithic Imagination &
the Construction of the Underworld* [2003]

🌿 JOURNALS AND ANTHOLOGIES 🌿

Folio [Bloomington, Indiana, 3 issues, 1959–1960]

Quena [Lima, Peru, 1 issue, edited, then suppressed by the North American Peruvian Cultural Institue, 1966]

Caterpillar [New York–Los Angeles, 20 issues, 1967–1973]

A Caterpillar Anthology [1971]

Sulfur [Pasadena–Los Angeles–Ypsilanti, 46 issues, 1981–2000]

🌿 TRANSLATIONS 🌿

Pablo Neruda, *Residence on Earth* [1962]

César Vallejo, *The Complete Posthumous Poetry*
(with José Rubia Barcia) [1978]

Aimé Césaire, *The Collected Poetry*
(with Annette Smith) [1983]

Michael Deguy, *Giving Given* [1984]

Bernard Bador, *Sea Urchin Harakiri* [1986]

Conductors of the Pit: Major Works by Rimbaud, Vallejo, Césaire, Artaud, & Holan [1988, 2005]

Aimé Césaire, *Lyric & Narrative Poetry 1946–1982*
(with Annette Smith) [1990]

César Vallejo, *Trilce* [1992, 2000]

Antonin Artaud, *Watchfields & Rack Screams*
(with Bernard Bador) [1995]

Aimé Césaire, *Notebook of a Return to the Native Land*
(with Annette Smith) [2001]

César Vallejo, *The Complete Poetry* [2007]

for Gary Snyder and Adrienne Rich

TABLE OF CONTENTS

Gustaf Sobin: "An Ars Poetica"

AN ARS POETICA
for Clayton Eshleman

...for the taut, overlapping ligature of the
muscles only serves to
en-
velop the smoke, withhold the roll of all that baroque

effluvia.   wedge, then, to
those narrow drafts, the slip of every
such disparate
in-

determinant: the 'abolished alphabet,' as you'd
called it, or a
once
pellucid script. that there, where even the vertebrae
get caught in the
coils of

that
vaporous emission, the
implicit might edge, in meted sections, towards

transmission.   blow, then, on
those
choked vocables.   tease

intention forth.   that each thing, once told, might
resonate, finally, with its
lost
luminosity: there, that is, where the
breath, at the very

end of
its
beaten pilgrimage, might, at long last, squirt gold.

—Gustaf Sobin

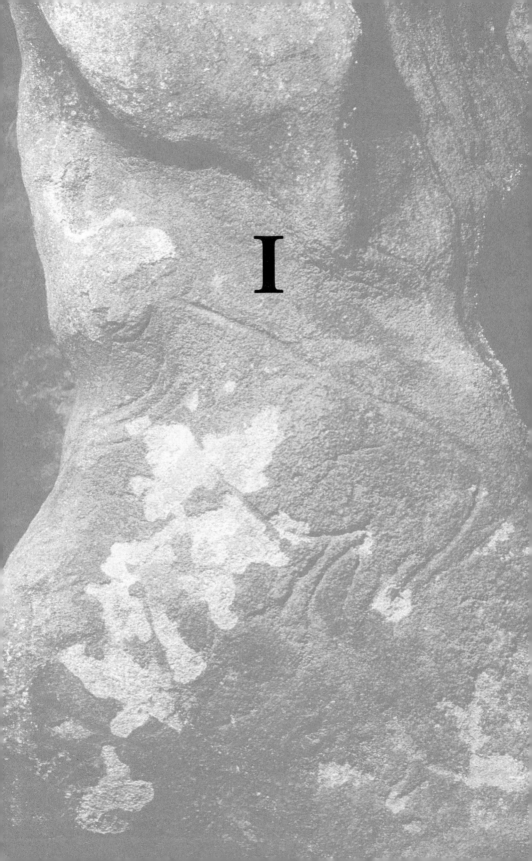

WHAT BROUGHT YOU HERE WILL TAKE YOU HENCE[1]

A Poetic Apprenticeship in Kyoto

I started writing poetry in 1958, as a student at Indiana University. By 1960, I had a sketchy sense of the contemporary poetry scene, partially through hours spent in the periodical section of the university library, where I discovered Cid Corman's magazine, *Origin*. Via *Origin*, I was introduced to the poets associated with Charles Olson and Black Mountain College (the first two issues featured the then-unknown Olson and Robert Creeley); *Origin* also had a generational range, publishing young poets alongside William Carlos Williams and Wallace Stevens. I became acquainted with a number of European poets, such as Antonin Artaud, Gottfried Benn, and Henri Michaux, whose work appeared there in translation. In short, *Origin* covered a lot of ground in its 64-page issues, and seemed to me to be a model of a poetry magazine.

My research revealed that Corman had started *Origin* in 1951, when he was 27 years old, with a $550 donation from a friend, while living at his parents' home in Boston (on an allowance of $5 a week). Corman went to Paris on a Fulbright Grant in 1954, and moved to southern Italy the following year (all the while continuing to edit *Origin*). In 1958, he took a teaching job at the Women's University in Kyoto, Japan. There he began to translate the famous haiku poets. When I first wrote to him, in 1960, he was back in the United States, living in a boardinghouse in San Francisco.

Along with my letter telling Corman how much I valued *Origin*, I included a few poems of my own. If he liked them, it would confirm that I was a poet. Corman's response (which came back almost immediately—I later learned that he always answered letters the day he received them) dismissed my poems as a waste of his and my time. He told me to get serious about poetry or do something else. His language was so cutting that my face flushed while reading it. It was a fascinating blow: It smacked me in the face *and* implied that there was a life commitment—indeed a commitment to life—in writing poetry.

Stimulated by his response, I arranged to meet Corman in San Francisco on my way to Japan in August 1961. I had accepted a position with the Far-Eastern Division of the University of Maryland, teaching literature to American Armed Forces personnel in Japan, Taiwan, and Korea. We met in his room, and he was kinder than I expected. He asked me to read a couple of poems from my first poetry manuscript, which I had brought to show him. I expected the worst and was surprised when he told me that some of my images were powerful and that I had great inventive potential. He then talked about his plans to start a new "series" of *Origin* magazine, which was published in four numbered sets. I had read the twenty issues that comprised the first series, 1951–1957, at the Indiana University Library. He was planning on building the second series, which eventually comprised fourteen issues published between 1961 and 1964, around Louis Zukofsky (1904–1978), the "Objectivist" poet whose work had been heralded by Williams and Pound but who had few readers at that time. Corman also discussed his publishing enterprise, Origin Press Books. In 1959 he had brought out the first twelve sections of Zukofsky's long poem, *A*, in book form, along with Gary Snyder's first book, *Riprap*. Corman informed me that he was returning to Kyoto the following year.

While I was teaching at Tachikawa Air Base, outside of Tokyo, in the winter of 1961, Gary Snyder visited on his way to India. He convinced me that I would be much happier teaching English as a second language in Kyoto than continuing to teach literature to GIs, so in the spring of 1962, my first wife, Barbara, and I moved to Kyoto. Based on Corman's positive remarks about my writing in San Francisco, I decided to look him up.

For over two years, once a week, I walked or motorcycled to the Muse, a coffee shop in downtown Kyoto, and spent several hours with Cid in his booth. He used the Muse as an office and as a place to meet friends and visitors. There he read, wrote letters, and edited *Origin*.

Cid's initial response to my visits fell somewhere between welcoming and putting up with me. He was not much for small talk and gave the impression that if I wanted him to talk with me I had to engage him. I prepared for these meetings with a mental list of things to discuss. As time went by, he warmed, somewhat. While he was diffident, circumspect, and authoritarian, he was willing to share what he was doing and what he knew. Corman became the first substantial literary person with whom I had an ongoing, reflective association.

Over the two years of these weekly meetings, Cid introduced me to an international range of writers, most of whom were appearing in *Origin*, generally in translation by Cid. It amazed me that in Kyoto (which had one English-language bookstore at the time, and no stores stocking French, German, or Spanish titles) he was able to keep up with contemporary European poetry. I recall his introducing me one evening to the poetry of Paul Celan, whom he had discovered in Paris in the mid-'50s and immediately begun to translate.

A couple evenings a week, Corman met with his Bashō co-translator, Susumu Kamaike, to work on Bashō's hike journal masterpiece, the *Oku-no-hosomichi* (which appeared in *Origin #14*, second series, as *Back Roads to Far Towns*). In *Origin #12*, Cid dropped a bomb by printing a statement attributed to Pablo Picasso, in which the celebrated painter claimed that art had become just another commodity, and that he himself, unlike Goya and Rembrandt, was only a "public entertainer." Picasso's opening sentence, "I came to see that art, as it was understood until 1800, was henceforth finished, on its last legs, doomed, and that so-called artistic activity with all its abundance is only the many-formed manifestation of its agony," made me reel, and I pondered it for years, in spite of the fact that Sir Herbert Read, upon reading the statement, wrote Cid to say that it was a bogus document, written by an Italian art critic, Giovanni Papini.

I watched Cid edit at least eight issues of *Origin* on tables at the Muse. He had taught himself to edit while doing the first series of *Origin* in the 1950s, and by the early 1960s, with the second series, he was a master. I discovered that he was a unique combination of relentless dedication, scholarly acumen, and word-by-word attention to anything he read. I learned this as we co-translated some poems by the Spanish poet José Hierro, and again when Cid went over some of my early versions of César Vallejo's *Poemas humanos* (which he published in *Origin #13*). His meticulousness as a writer brought home to me, in the realm of translation, the necessity to do absolutely accurate versions as well as versions that attempted to rise to the performance level of the originals. No translation theory was needed.

In Kyoto, I rarely saw Cid outside of the Muse. He never hung out in bars, came to the expatriate weekend parties (where poets Gary Snyder, back from India, and Joanne Kyger; stone lithographer Will Petersen; and various Australian potters would show up), or joined us for late night sushi and sake feasts along the Kamogawa River. In fact, his only social life seemed to be with Will Petersen (who helped him edit *Origin*) and Will's Japanese wife, Ami (a potter to whom Cid took his weekly laundry to do, gratis). If he was seeing his future wife at this time, I was not aware of it. His deep fascination with Japanese culture was odd, on one hand, as, to my knowledge, he never learned the modern Japanese language. Knowing his horror of cults of personality (personified for him, in America, by the Beats and confessional discharge), I think that Japanese reserve and attention to natural detail made him feel at home in Kyoto as he had never felt at home in America or in Europe. Besides doing the finest translating of haiku poetry ever, in my opinion, he studied *utai* (Noh singing) with one of the actors in a Kyoto Noh family. His knowledge of Noh plays influenced the structural elements in many of his books. For example, the five play category devised by the great Noh dramatist Zeami became a model for organizing a collection of poems into five sections.

The Muse took up the second floor of a small, Western-style building along an offshoot of the Kamogawa River. As I would mount the steps, I was never quite sure what I was going to run into, mood-wise, with Cid. For example, at some point I discovered the writing of Paul Bowles in a *New Directions* annual, a potent story called "Pages from Cold Point," in which a son seduces his own father. Without thinking about the effect of such a story on Cid, I enthusiastically mentioned it to him and loaned him the magazine. When I sat down the following week, his face turned to stone. "Why did you give me that story to read?" he demanded. I told him the truth: I thought it was one hell of a piece of writing! I then recalled that he despised Lenny Bruce and Paul Krassner (of *The Realist*) for their sexual explicitness. Did he think I thought he was gay? Did he think I had seduction in mind?

While Cid was only 11 years older than I was (in 1963, he was 39, I was 28), on a literary level there was a greater discrepancy in our ages, enough to create a relationship of mentor and apprentice, or even father and son. As a novice, I was struggling to emerge from the limbo that committing myself to poetry had thrust me into. When not translating Vallejo every afternoon at my coffee shop, I was reading William Blake, Northrop Frye on Blake, the *I Ching*, Joseph Campbell's tetralogy *The Masks of God*, or working on poems. In our 19th-century Japanese house, I sat on tatami, cross-legged, the typewriter on a low table before me. I would sit there for hours, staring at a single line, not knowing how to move beyond it into something that seemed to be my own. Squatting in the *benjo* one morning, I realized that I was in the position of Tlatzeotl-Ixcuina, the Aztec goddess of filth and childbirth, in a nephrite carving with a tiny god-infant projecting from between her thighs. I, too, wanted to give birth, but all that seemed to come out of me was shit.

Other than Vallejo, I spent more time reading Blake than any other poet. I was particularly struck by Blake's long, arcane "prophetic books," abysses charged with warring psychological states. While such works helped me dare to express my own turbulent fantasies, they were also supporting a kind of self-investigation that Corman did not believe was appropriate for poetic display. I was aware of this even as I was trying to write things that he would admire and publish. When writing, I could feel his presence, frowning over my shoulder at what I was struggling to articulate. And even though I was beginning to understand that the kind of poem I had to write would not fall within the realm of the acceptable for Cid, I was plunged into self-doubt when he rejected the poems I occasionally showed him. "Corman's Presence" was the part of myself that was stimulated by what he meant to me. Cid evoked in me the stern father that I was to my emerging son-self. I also had to acknowledge that, as poets, Corman and I were, in Blakean terms, "spiritual enemies."

Cid was friendlier in person than he would once again prove to be in correspondence. After returning to the States in 1964, I encountered a dictatorial rigidity on his part in our exchanges. Over the next decade I engaged him as best I could, which often meant sparring about this issue or that, without Cid, as I recall, ever giving way. In the fall of 1966, I moved to New York City, left my wife and baby son, and went into Reichian therapy. Reich's writings were a big discovery for me, so I wrote Cid a long letter about their effect on my life. His response was: "Reich is so thin he makes me wince."

I was asking Cid to accept me as a peer, to adjust what had been our mentor-apprenticeship. His refusal to do so was tied up with his own apprentice relationship in the early 1950s with Charles Olson, who was then in a similar position, in terms of age and experience, to Cid as Cid was to me a decade later. Olson lambasted Corman in correspondence (while offering him a lot of potent advice), in a way that evoked Olson's apprentice ordeal with the prose writer Edward Dahlberg in the late 1940s. Writers apparently pass along to the young what they suffered from their elders, creating generational chains of the paternal abuse of offspring. I am sure that I passed on some of my frustration to others during and after these years.

In 1972, while teaching at the California Institute of the Arts, in Valencia, I was able to invite Cid to give a reading there. He read impressively, after which he urged students to buy the books he had brought with him, proposing that they would be worth much more in the future than they were at the time. He also gave a reading at our house in Sherman Oaks to a dozen or so of my students. He read several of his Elizabeth Press books (sixteen tiny poems per book), then paused, and said: "A year from now, one of you may not be alive. With that in mind, I would like to read these poems to you a second time." As he did, and as dusk settled in, students sitting on the floor turned and looked at me as if to say: "What's with this guy?" My current wife, Caryl, left the room while the second reading was taking place. She later told me she had gone to the bathroom and vomited. She really literally couldn't stomach Cid! To give Cid the benefit of the doubt, perhaps he wanted the students to hear his death-centered poems with their own transience in mind. However, the impression was that he mentioned our mortality to make his poems more dramatic. Other than at a party the following evening, I never saw him again.

Cid published several short poems of mine in the second and third series of *Origin*, but they are slight pieces, chosen seemingly to complement his own poetic procedures. I sometimes had the sensation that my writing interested him more than he would acknowledge, so in the late 1970s, I decided to test out my feelings. I had written a collection of poems under the name of Horrah Pornoff (the whole story, as well as Horrah's poems, can be found in *Under World Arrest*, Black Sparrow Press, 1994), and I decided to submit "her" poems to some of the editors who had rejected my own work. I took out a P.O. box in West Los Angeles and sent a large selection to Cid. A reply zipped in immediately: "At last," he wrote, "there is a poet in Los Angeles!" He accepted twenty-four poems by Horrah Pornoff for *Origin #7*, fourth series. He also began to write to "her," and for a while I went along with it. We had a weird and funny exchange. At one point, he wanted to fix Horrah up with an elderly bachelor friend in Laguna Beach. I decided enough was enough, and stopped corresponding. Since the display in *Under World Arrest* let the cat out of the bag, I imagine Cid found out about it. If he did, he never mentioned it.

I published a lot of Cid's poems, translations, and essays in the magazines I founded and edited, *Caterpillar* (1967-1973) and *Sulfur* (1981-2000). He and I also wrote and published poems to or about each other. In such pieces, the ways we clashed showed their horns. From my viewpoint, in his several poems concerning me, it seemed that Cid took events of my life, or stories that I told him, edited out what did not interest him, and used the rest to show me in a negative light. For my part, in *Altars* (Black Sparrow Press, 1971), I published a brief poem that set out the difference between Corman's and Blake's effects on me while in Kyoto: "Cid said no / & Blake said yes." In *Coils* (Black Sparrow Press, 1973), in the poem "Origin," I worked up a burlesque of our mentor-apprentice association, drawing upon Blake's homemade mythic figures: I created Origin (Corman) as a master of Yorunomado (Eshleman), whom, in this context, I saw as a dog.

If one wanted to read a single collection of Corman's to get a solid sense of his achievement as a poet, I would recommend the first volume of *Of* (Lapis Press, 1990). However, I was shocked to find Cid's translations there—of Homer, Sophocles, Catullus, Tao Chi'ien, Montale, Villon, Rimbaud, Bashō, Mallarmé, Rilke, Ungaretti, Char, Celan, Artaud, and Scotellaro—treated as Corman poems. I wrote to him questioning such appropriation. He responded, evading the translation identification matter, by directing my attention to his claim of being "the most productive poet in human history."

Appropriation aside, this list of poets translated by Corman represents an extraordinary achievement as a translator—he did book-length collections of Char, Ponge, du Bouchet, Daive, Jaccottet, Denis, Celan, Montale, Zeami, Bashō, and Kusano. As far as I can tell, Corman was the first to translate some of these authors and, given the fact that most of these translations are still buried in *Origin* (with its print run of 300 copies per issue) or in out-of-print books, it would be most appropriate for some publisher to bring out a generous "selected translations by Cid Corman." For young poets, such a collection would be a landmark overview of 20th-century European poetry, with deep forays into the Japanese literary past.

𝖇

More than any other Western poet, Corman has "translated" the Japanese haiku tradition into resonant, brief American poems. As the poet Robert Kelly has written, "Nobody knows how to do so much with so few words as Corman." The core of his poetry is expressed by his self-coined word, "livingdying," a conjunction underscored by the opening poem in *Of*, volume one. In its entirety it reads: "You are dead. / Speak now." Corman's minimalism is permeated, contoured, and centered by dying and death ("as if death were my Torah," or "I'm not / the poet / of death I / *am* death"). This fixation may account for the monolithic brevity of thousands of Corman poems. Dying is so at one with the act of poetry that it curtails, in Corman's view, all the detours into mythology, psychology, eroticism, politics, and metaphoric arabesque that most of us employ to explore the psyche. The aim of Corman's poetry is to confront the reader with his own demise. This is not to say that Corman cannot marvel at natural synchronicity and serendipity:

> Rain nailing earth down
> Grass hammering back

or:

> Only an insect
> struck it alighting
> but the pond knows and

> reverberates to
> the edge and beyond
> and pulls together

Such poems are acutely perceptive and organized. Cid's best poetry sublimates the fact of death into a structure that evokes the rich transience of life. Here are two more that have stayed with me for years:

> gong gone
> odor of cherry tolling
> eventide
>
> ...
>
> I picked a
> leaf up
>
> it weighed
> my vision
>
> I knelt and
> placed it
>
> almost
> where it was

In retrospect, my distinction between Blake's "yes" and Corman's "no" is more complex than my 1971 poem probably registered. Cid's chronic withholding of himself from getting in over his head in experience expressed itself as the "no" in his character. However, the "no" in his poetry is sufficiently metaphysical to sound one of Kafka's aphorisms: "What is laid upon us is to accomplish the negative; the positive is already given." Corman's exploration of the negative bears comparison with Jabès and Celan, and is not only present as subject and focus; it collects (as rain collects in a cistern) in his use of the word *this*, which is endlessly cross-pollinated with *poem* and *death*.

Now, with Cid gone, I must take to heart his negation and his solace. He encouraged me as he resisted me, or let me say that the caliber of his resistance led me to convert it into something that was my own, to incorporate his resistance to the self-investigative and to political materials into my own imaginative system. Much of what I initially took as resistance—an alter-ego presence defying my own incipient poesis—turned out to be Cid's death obsession, which he constellated into a poetry genuinely his own. What offered me support—"what brought / you here will /take you hence," he once proposed—was an all-encompassing dedication and devotion to the art of poetry that he was willing to share.

He is an anomaly today, this socially-awkward loner who lived for the art in a way that makes many of our poets look as if their writing were, at best, a diversion, a hobby, or clever entertainment.

As I Live & Breathe

This is not my father's photograph but me
fading in the mirror—rummaging for
and picking on details—rags of wrinkles

at my several chins—implications
of grey hair gone to white—the empty stare
haunting a battlement suggesting bone

emptier yet. Poor Dad seemed small. I loom—
I bulk—I brim. This is clearly not my
day—but this is what I get for looking.

—Cid Corman, 1924–2004

NOTES:

[1] An earlier version of this essay appeared in Lucas Klein's *Cipher Journal*. This final version, edited by Therese Eiben, appeared in *Poets & Writers* magazine.

A TRANSLATION MEMOIR[1]

For nearly fifty years, I have been translating the poetry of César Vallejo. His writing has become the keelson in the ship of poetry I have attempted to construct. Here I would like to offer an overview of my lifelong evolving relationship with Vallejo and with translation, and to evoke some of the experiences that have come out of it. Finally, I would like to say what this companionship has meant to me, as a poet and as a human being.

While I was a student at Indiana University in 1957, a painter friend, Bill Paden, gave me a copy of the New Directions 1944 *Latin American Poetry* anthology. I was particularly impressed with the poetry of Pablo Neruda and César Vallejo. While I was able to make sense of Neruda's Latin American surrealism by comparing it to its French prototypes, Vallejo was something else: he had a unique imagination and a highly complicated style, and his images seemed to work on several levels. He wrote bitterly about Peruvian provincial life and passionately about the Spanish Civil War. I decided at that time to read Neruda first and, other than a few poems from his first book, hold off Vallejo for later.

I then discovered that Angel Flores had translated all of Neruda's *Residencia en la tierra*, and upon comparing his versions with those of H.R. Hays and Dudley Fitts in the anthology, I was intrigued by the differences. Without knowing any Spanish, I began to tinker with the versions. Doing so got me to thinking about going to Mexico City, which was then featured in the literary news as a mecca for the Beats and their followers. At the beginning of the summer of 1959, with a pocket Spanish-English dictionary and two hundred dollars, I hitchhiked to Mexico. The following summer, in order to improve my Spanish, I returned to Mexico, rented a room in the back of a butcher's home in Chapala, and spent the summer reading Neruda's poetry, as well as writing most of the poems that were to appear in my first book, *Mexico & North*, in 1962.

In 1960, I edited three issues of the English Department-sponsored literary tri-quarterly, *Folio*, where I printed some Neruda versions I had done with friends in Mexico City, and four Vallejo versions, co-translated with another graduate student, Maureen Lahey. Discovering the poetry of Neruda and Vallejo made me realize that poetry was an international phenomenon and that North American poetry was but one part of it. As a young aspiring poet, I had a hunch that I would learn something about poetry by translating it that I would not learn solely from reading poetry written in English.

I finished a Master's Degree in 1961, and took a job with the University of Maryland's Far Eastern Division teaching literature to military personnel stationed in Japan, Taiwan, and Korea. Before leaving, almost as an afterthought, I packed the copy of *Poesía de América #5: Homenaje a César Vallejo* that I had found in a Mexico City bookstore.

The following year, my first wife, Barbara, and I moved to Kyoto on the advice of the poet Gary Snyder who was studying Zen Buddhism there. For the next two years I studied and wrote, making a living teaching English as a Second Language at various Japanese companies. In 1962, having completed a small collection of Neruda translations (published in San Francisco by George Hitchcock's Amber House Press as *Residence on Earth*), I decided to investigate the Vallejo poems in the Mexican journal.

The first poem I tried to read, from *Poemas humanos*, was "Me viene, hay días, una gana ubérrima, política..." It was as if a hand of wet sand came out of the original and "quicked" me in—I was quicksanded, in over my head. Or was it a spar Vallejo threw me? In this poem, Vallejo was claiming that he desired to love, and that his desire for desire led him to imagine all sorts of "interhuman" acts, like kissing a singer's muffler, or kissing a deaf man on his cranial murmur. He wanted to help everyone achieve his goal, no matter what it was, even to help the killer kill—and he wanted to be good to himself in everything. These were thoughts that, had I had them myself, I would either have dismissed or so immediately repressed that they would have evaporated. But now I realized that there was a whole wailing cathedral of desires, half-desires, mad desires, anti-desires, all of which, in the Vallejo poem, seemed caught on the edge of no desire. And if so, what brought about these bizarre desires? The need to flee his body? His inability to act on desire? A terrible need to intercede in everyone's acts? I did not know, but trying to read him made me feel that I was in the presence of a mile-thick spirit. So I kept at it.

Soon I decided that I should not just try to read the eighty-nine poems in *Poemas humanos*, but I should also try to translate them. To do that meant an awesome commitment of psyche as well as time. In committing myself to such a project, was I evading the hard work of trying to find my way in poetry of my own? Or could I think of working on Vallejo as a way of working on myself? Possibly. But much of what he wrote seemed obscure to me. Did that mean my Spanish was so inadequate that I simply could not make sense of Vallejo's language? Or was it a combination of those things, plus my having tapped into something that was coherent, and instructive, but on a level I had yet to plumb?

In the afternoon I would ride my motorcycle downtown and work on translations in the Yorunomado coffee shop. I would always sit by the carp pond on the patio. There I discovered the following words of Vallejo: "And where is the other flank of this cry of pain if, to estimate it as a whole, it breaks now from the bed of a man?" In that line I saw Vallejo in a birth bed, not knowing how to give birth, an impression that led me to a whole other realization: that artistic bearing and fruition were physical as well as mental, a matter of one's total energy. Both in translating and in working on my own poems, I felt a terrific resistance, as if every attempt I made to advance was met by a force that pushed me back. It was as if through Vallejo I had made contact with a negative impaction in my being, a nebulous depth charge that I had been carrying around with me for many years. For most of 1963 and the first half of 1964, everything I saw and felt clustered about this feeling; it seemed to dwell in a phrase from the *I Ching*, "the darkening of the light," as well as in the Kyoto sky, gray and overcast, yet mysteriously luminous.

I also began to have violent and morbid fantasies that seemed provoked by the combination of translating and writing. More and more I had the feeling that I was struggling with a man as well as a text, and that this struggle was a matter of my becoming or failing to become a poet. The man I was struggling with did not want his words changed from one language to another. I also realized that in working on Vallejo's *Poemas humanos* I had ceased to be what I was before coming to Kyoto, that I now had a glimpse of another life, a life I was to create for myself, and that this other man I was struggling with was also the old Clayton who was resisting change. The old Clayton wanted to continue living in his white Presbyterian world of "light"—not really light but the "light" of man associated with day/clarity/good and woman associated with night/opaqueness/bad. The darkness that was beginning to spread through my sensibility could be viewed as the breaking up of the belief in male supremacy that had generated much of that "light."

In the last half of "The Book of Yorunomado," the only poem of my own I completed to any satisfaction while living in Japan, I envisioned myself as a kind of angel-less Jacob wrestling with a figure who possessed a language, the meaning of which I was attempting to wrest away. I lose the struggle and find myself on a *seppuku* platform in medieval Japan, being condemned by Vallejo (now playing the role of a *karo*, or overlord) to disembowel myself. I do so, cutting my ties to the "given life," and releasing a visionary figure of the imagination, named Yorunomado (in honor of my working place), who had until that point been chained to an altar in my solar plexus. In early 1964, the fruit of my struggle with Vallejo was not a successful linguistic translation, but an imaginative advance in which a third figure had emerged from my intercourse with the text. Yorunomado then became another guide in the ten-year process of developing a "creative life," recorded in my book-length poem, *Coils* (1973).

I was close to completing a first draft of the *Poemas humanos* in March 1963 when I had a very strange experience. After translating all afternoon in the Yorunomado coffee cafe, I motorcycled over to the pottery manufacturer where I taught English conversation once a week. Whenever I had things to carry on the cycle, I would strap them with a bungee cord to the platform behind the seat. That evening when I left the company, I strapped on the poem-filled notebook, my dictionary, and a copy of the Spanish book. It was now dark and the alley was poorly lit. I had gone a half block when I heard a voice cry in Japanese: "Hey, you dropped something!" I stopped and swerved around to find the platform empty—even the bungee cord was gone! I retraced my path on foot—nothing. I looked for the person who had called out. No one was there. While I was walking around in the dark, a large skinny dog began to follow me. I was reminded of the Mexican pariah dogs and that association gave an eerie identity to this dog. Was it Peruvian? Was it—Vallejo? I went back the next morning to search in daylight, and of course there was no trace of the notebook. So I had to start all over again.

If I had turned Vallejo into a challenging mentor from the past, I had also found a living mentor, as complicated in his own way as Vallejo himself: he was Cid Corman, a poet, editor (of *Origin* magazine and books), and translator, who had taken up residence in Kyoto. I began to visit him weekly, in the evening, at the Muse coffee shop downtown. Corman, who was eleven years my senior, seemed to like me, but he did not like the kind of self-involved poetry that I was trying to write. Since, especially in *Origin*, he presented an impressive vision of what poetry could be on an international scale, I found myself in the impossible situation of wanting to address the forces erupting in me and also wanting to write poems that might make their way into his magazine. Thus while testing myself against Vallejo's Spanish, I was also working with a Corman raven on my shoulder staring critically at what I was struggling to articulate. At times the tension between Vallejo and Corman was almost unbearable. These figures who were offering me their vision of the creative also seemed to be dragging me under. I was hearing things, having terrifying nightmares and suffering unexplainable headaches.

In the following year, I completed three more drafts of *Human Poems.* Cid went over the second and third drafts and to him I owe a special debt, not only for the time he put in on the manuscript but also for what I learned from him about the art of translation.

Before talking with Cid about translation, I thought that the goal of a translating project was to take a literal draft and interpret everything that was not acceptable English. By interpret, I mean: to monkey with words, phrases, punctuation, line breaks, even stanza breaks, turning the literal into something that was not an original poem in English but—and here is the rub—something that because of the liberties taken was also not accurate to the original itself. Ben Belitt's Neruda translations or Robert Lowell's *Imitations* come to mind as interpretative translations. Corman taught me to respect the original at every point, to check everything (including words that I thought I knew), to research arcane and archaic words, and to invent English words for coined words—in other words, to aim for a translation that was absolutely accurate and up to the performance level of the original (at times, quite incompatible goals). I learned to keep a notebook of my thoughts and variations on what I was translating, so I could keep this material separate, for every translator has impulses to fill in, pad out, and make something "strong" that in a more literal mode would fall flat—in short, to pump up or explain a word instead of translating it. By reinterpreting, the translator implies that he knows more than the original text does, that, in effect, his mind is superior to its mind. The "native text" becomes raw material for the colonizer–translator to educate and reform.

During these years of undergoing a double apprenticeship—to poetry and to translation—I was so psychically opened up by Valle-

jo that I had to find ways to keep my fantasies out of the translation. One way was to redirect them into my poetry, as I did with my
poem "The Book of Yorunomado." While in Paris in 1973, I visited Vallejo's tomb in the Montparnasse cemetery and imagined my
relationship to him and to his work in a poem, "At The Tomb of
Vallejo." Upon completing the revision of a translation of *Poemas
humanos* in 1977, I developed a culminative fantasia of my years
with this poet called "The Name Encanyoned River," a title based
on a line that Vallejo had crossed out in one of these poems. Finally, beginning with the 1977 revision, I added detailed notes to my
Vallejo collections that commented on crossed-out material as well
as arcane and coined words. Thus, I was able to excavate and
employ the psychic turmoil of my Kyoto life, all the while keeping
the translation of a body of work contoured with its own unadul-
terated chasms.

Poemas humanos is made up of poems left by Vallejo at the time of
his death, in April 1938, in a heavily hand-corrected typescript.
When his widow Georgette published them in 1939 there were
many errors and the poems were presented out of chronological
order. These errors were repeated and amplified in subsequent editions, many of which were pirated because Georgette would not
cooperate with publishers. By the spring of 1965, now back in
Bloomington, I was working from four textually differing editions
of *Poemas humanos*, having seen neither the first edition nor the
worksheets.

Instead of shaping up as I worked along, the whole project was
becoming a nightmare. Now I was having dreams in which Vallejo's corpse, wearing muddy shoes, was laid out in bed between Barbara and me. By this time I had gotten in touch with Georgette
Vallejo and explained that I did not see how I could complete the
translation effectively unless I came to Peru and examined the
worksheets. I hired a lawyer to draw up a contract and mailed it to
her along with samples from my fourth draft. I received one reply

from her in which she did not respond to any of my requests. But I was determined to go, and with Barbara several months pregnant, we left in August 1965, with just a few hundred dollars.

Once in Lima, we moved into a small apartment next to a grade school playground on Domingo Orué in Miraflores, the district where Georgette Vallejo also lived. Georgette was a small, wiry, middle-class French woman in her late fifties. Supported by the Peruvian government, she lived rather spartanly, yet not uncomfortably, in an apartment appointed with pre-Incan pottery and weavings. I was in a very delicate position with her, because I not only needed to see the first edition and the worksheets, but I also needed her permission before I could get a publishing contract. I had not been in her apartment for fifteen minutes when she told me that my translations were full of "howlers," that Vallejo was untranslatable (she was at this time working on a French translation of his poetry), and that neither the first edition nor the worksheets were available to be studied.

The months that followed were stressful and cheerless. I had been hired as editor of a new bilingual literary magazine, to be called *Quena*, at the Peruvian North American Cultural Institute. Because I was working for the Institute (which turned out to be an annex of the American Embassy in Lima), most of the Peruvian writers and critics whom I met thought I was an American spy. Only when I turned in the three hundred page manuscript for the first issue of *Quena* did I realize what the Institute represented. My boss told me that translations I had included of Javier Heraud could not be published in the magazine because, although the poems themselves were not political, their author, after visiting Cuba, had joined a guerrilla movement in the Peruvian jungle and had been killed by the army. Since his name was linked with Cuba and revolution, my boss told me, the Institute did not want to be involved. I refused to take the translations out of the manuscript and was fired.

At the end of 1965 I met Maureen Ahern, an American with a Ph.D. from San Marcos University, who was then married and living with her family on a chicken farm in Cieneguilla, about twenty miles outside Lima. Maureen agreed to read through the sixth and seventh drafts of my Vallejo manuscript with me (and she would later facilitate the manuscript's first publication after I had left Peru). Her husband, Johnny, worked in Lima, and once a week he would give me a ride to their place as he drove home from work. Maureen and I would work together all of the following day, and I would ride back to Lima with Johnny the next morning. This arrangement was ideal, but it remains indissociable in my mind from a near tragedy that marked my year in Peru. On one of the evenings that I would normally have gone to Maureen's, her husband was unavailable and I stayed home. That night—it was the week after my son Matthew was born—Barbara began to hemorrhage. After attempting to staunch the flow I realized that if I did not get her to a hospital immediately she was going to bleed to death. I raced out of our apartment and ran through the halls of the building across the street, screaming for help. A door opened, a doctor came out, we bundled her into the back of his Volkswagen and sped to the nearest clinic. We saved her life, barely—but I shudder to think what might have happened had I gone to Cieneguilla as planned.

One afternoon someone knocked on our door, and I opened it to be told by a stranger that Georgette Vallejo wanted to see me in her apartment that evening. When I arrived, I found there a small group of Peruvian writers and intellectuals, such as Javier Sologuren, Carlos Germán Belli, and Emilio Adolfo Westphalen. Georgette explained she had assembled everyone to try to determine what poems I could be given permission to translate. This turned out to be a ridiculous and impossible task, with these luminaries arguing for hours over why X poem could be translated and Y poem could not. At one point, when they all agreed that a particular poem could absolutely not be translated, Georgette cried out, "but I just translated that poem into French!" Nothing was resolved, and after the writers left, I found myself despondently sitting with Georgette. She asked me if I would like a *pisco*, and brought out a bottle. We began drinking, and I recalled that the editor of Perú Nuevo, a press that had published a pirated edition of *Poemas humanos*, had told me that Georgette and César had never been formally married, and because of this Georgette had no legal control over the estate. I think I blurted out: "Well, I really don't need your permission it turns out, as Gustavo Valcárcel told me you and Vallejo were never actually married!" At this point, she jumped up, ran to the bedroom, and began bringing out shoeboxes of memorabilia, looking for the marriage certificate. She couldn't find it. But the next morning, of course, she was furious over my confrontation. I never saw her again.

When Barbara and I returned to the States in the spring of 1966 and moved to New York City, Grove Press expressed interest in the translation. I prepared a seventh draft, and after having it checked by readers, Dick Seaver, then the senior editor at Grove, offered me a contract—contingent upon Mme. Vallejo's signature. I wrote to Maureen and asked her if there was anything she could do. She offered to go and meet Georgette. Over the next six months, Maureen must have seen Georgette almost weekly, and she did this while taking care of her kids, teaching full-time, battling illness, and trying to save a floundering marriage.

Seaver was also working on Georgette, sending letter after letter to convince her that the translation Grove wished to publish was not the one I had sent her from Bloomington in 1964. Maureen and Johnny were inviting her out to the farm for holiday weekends and sending her back home with chickens and eggs. Since Seaver was getting nowhere, Maureen eventually had to mention that she was a friend of mine and that she had worked on the translation. Georgette protested that she had been betrayed and once again it looked as if everything was off.

But Maureen kept after her and one day, Américo Ferrari, a Peruvian scholar who had written on Vallejo (and worked with Georgette on her French edition of Vallejo's poetry), appeared in the Grove offices and told Seaver that Mme. Vallejo had asked him to check the translation. Apparently he wrote her that it was publishable for a week or so later she wrote Seaver that she would sign a contract if Grove would include the following clause: when and if she found a better translation, Grove would have to destroy mine and publish the other. Seaver told me that he had had it with her.

I wrote again to Maureen, telling her that unless a signed contract were sent to Grove within a month, the whole project would be off. Maureen continued to plead with Georgette, who finally said that if Johnny would type up the contract she wanted, she would sign it. He did, she signed it, and a few weeks later Seaver called to tell me that while it was not their contract, Grove found it acceptable and their lawyer had determined it was legal. He wrote Mme. Vallejo, enclosing her part of the advance. Subsequently, Maureen wrote that Georgette had called to complain that she had never intended to sign a legal contract; she considered the contract Johnny had typed up "only a gesture," that she accepted so that Maureen would not be "upset." Grove went ahead anyway, and *Human Poems* was published in the spring of 1968.

I ended my Introduction to the Grove Edition of *Human Poems* with the words: "My work is done." I must have forgotten that I had begun several drafts of a translation of Vallejo's sheaf of poems on the Spanish Civil War, *España, aparte de mi este caliz*, with Octavio Corvalán, a Professor in the Spanish Department at Indiana University, when I was living in Bloomington in 1965. By starting this new translation project, and leaving it unfinished, I had unconsciously prolonged my relationship with Vallejo.

In 1970, I took a job at the new California Institute of the Arts outside Los Angeles, and my present wife, Caryl, and I moved to the San Fernando Valley. There I returned to *España*, made a new draft, and once again found myself looking for someone to check it. I was introduced to José Rubia Barcia, a Spanish poet and essayist in exile since the Spanish Civil War, who had been teaching at UCLA for years. While going over the draft with Barcia, I was so impressed with his honesty, scrupulosity, and literary intelligence that I suggested we work together as co-translators.

Grove Press published our completed translation of *Spain, Take This Cup from Me* in 1974. While José and I were working on the these poems I showed him the 1968 translation of *Human Poems*, which he carefully went over, penciling in the margins around two thousand queries and suggestions for changes. He felt that what I had accomplished was meaningful but that we could do a better job working together. We worked from roughly 1972 to 1977. The University of California Press brought out *César Vallejo: The Complete Posthumous Poetry* in 1978, including what had previously been called *Human Poems* along with *Spain, Take This Cup from Me*.

Over the years, initially stimulated by Vallejo, I had developed an affinity for a poetry that went for the whole, a poetry that attempted to become responsible for all the poet knows about himself and his world. I saw Vallejo, Arthur Rimbaud, Antonin Artaud, Aimé Césaire, and Vladimir Holan as examples of these poetics. All inducted and ordered materials from the subconscious as well as from those untoward regions of human experience that defy rational explanation. Instead of conducting the orchestra of the living, they were conducting the orchestra's pit.

In 1988 I arranged with Paragon House in NYC to bring out a selection of my translations and co-translations of these poets, to be called *Conductors of the Pit*. When making the Vallejo selection I got involved, once again, in revising previous versions, this time the ones that I had done with José. Some of these changes today strike me as less effective than the Eshleman/Barcia translations they were based on, and I have again, and now clearly for the last time, revised this work. But I do understand my dilemma: given the contextual density of Vallejo's European poetry, there are often multiple denotative word choices, and no matter how closely I have tried to adhere to a rendering of what I thought Vallejo had written, I have found over the years that my own imagination has played tricks on me. At the same time I have often had to invent words and phrases to attempt to match Vallejo's originality, and these back-and-forth movements, between adherence to standard Spanish and the matching of the coined and arcane, have occasionally become confused. And in continuing to read Vallejo scholarship over the years, from time to time I have picked up an interpretation of a particular word that has made me rethink my translation of it.

Up until the late 1980s all of my translational attention to Vallejo had been confined to the European poetry, written between 1923 and 1938. However, I had been circling around his second book, *Trilce* (1922), for many years, realizing in the 1960s and 70s that since it was a much more difficult book to translate than *Poemas humanos*, I should leave it alone. In 1988 I decided that if I could work with a Peruvian, a translation of *Trilce* could be attempted, so I teamed up with Julio Ortega (one of the few Peruvian writers in Lima in the 1960s who did not think I was a spy!), and we decided to do it together. We worked out a first draft of the book in the fall of 1989. Caryl and I moved to Boston for a month, and every morning I took a bus into Providence, and climbed the hill to Julio's office at Brown University where we would work for several hours. Once back in Michigan, I went over our work and realized that I often had questions about several words in a single line. While Julio would occasionally respond to my queries, it was clear by the end of 1990 that he had decided I should finish *Trilce* on my own and by then I needed his, or someone's help, even more than I had needed it in the beginning. There are still many words in this book that have gone uncommented upon in Vallejo scholarship (or have been wildly guessed at), and while critics can generalize and address Vallejo in terms of themes and preoccupations, a translator must go at him word by word, revealing all of his choices in English without being able to dodge a single one. This process is especially tricky in the case of *Trilce*, with its intentionally misspelled words (often revealing secondary puns), neologisms, and arcane and archaic words.

At this point I contacted Américo Ferrari who had inspected my manuscript at Grove Press in the late 1960s and who was now teaching translation at a university in Geneva. Ferrari had brought out an edition of Vallejo's *Obra Poética Completa* in 1988, and I figured he knew more about Vallejo's poetry than anyone. He agreed to respond to my questions; I would write in English and he in

Spanish. Ferrari was willing to go to the library and research words he thought he was familiar with but that my questions led him to doubt. We had a wonderful exchange and about two years later, after translating up to thirty versions of the most complex poems, I had something that I thought was publishable. Marsilio Publishers brought out a bilingual edition of *Trilce*, with an Introduction by Ferrari, in 1992. When it went out of print, Wesleyan University Press brought out a second edition, with around one hundred word changes, in 2000.

Once more I felt that my involvement with Vallejo had come to an end. The only poetry of his that I had not translated was *Los heraldos negros* (1918), his first book, which had always struck me as more conventional by far than *Trilce* or the European poetry. Much of it is rhymed verse which presents, in translation, its own problems: a sonnet is a little engine of sound and sense, and if you rhyme it in translation, you inevitably have to change some or so much of its meaning. If you translate it for meaning alone, there is a chance that you will end up with atonal free verse.

But as Michael Corleone says midway through *Godfather III*, "just when you think you're out, they pull you back in!" In 2003 I began to realize that all of the years I had put in on this body of work had brought me very close to a "Complete Poetry of César Vallejo," and that it would be appropriate to review all of my previous translations, and to add to them a version of *Los heraldos negros*. Once I began to work on *The Black Heralds*, I found the poems in it more interesting than I had originally thought, and since they were relatively easy to render, I took some pleasure in what could be thought of as strolling on a level playing field rather than climbing a vertical wall. When I could rhyme certain words in a sonnet and not change the meaning, I did so, and I constantly made myself aware of sound possibilities, attempting to make the translations sound as rich in English as I could without distorting Vallejo's intentions. Efrain Kristal, a Latin American scholar at UCLA who has recently edited a Spanish edition of *Los heraldos negros*, went over my third draft and made some very useful suggestions. José Cerna-Bazán, a Vallejo scholar from northern Peru now

at Carleton College in Minnesota, has inspected my *Trilce* version
word for word and proposed around a hundred changes, many of
which I have accepted. Assuming that Vallejo is not writing poems
in his Montparnasse tomb, I now should be able to make the statement that my work is done stick.

With an overview in mind, it is worth noting that Vallejo's poetic
development is quite unusual. Coming from the conventional, if
well-written and passionate, rhymed verse in *Los heraldos negros*, the
reader is completely unprepared for *Trilce*, which is still the most
dense, abstract, and transgression-driven collection of poetry in the
Spanish language. For Vallejo to have gone beyond *Trilce*, in the
experimental sense, would have involved his own version of the
made-up language one finds at the end of Huidobro's *Altazor.* On
one level, then, Vallejo took a step back from *Trilce* in his European
poetry, but not as far back as the writing of *Los heraldos negros*. In
moving from Lima to Paris, the poet hit the aesthetic honey head
of the European colonial world at the moment it was being rocked
by political revolution in Russia. Given the non-sequitur shifts in
Trilce's composition, it is possible to imagine Vallejo forming some
sort of relationship with French Surrealism (the first Manifesto
having appeared a year after he arrived). However, Vallejo had
nothing but contempt for Surrealism, which he seems to have
regarded pretty much as Artaud did: as an amusing parlor-game,
more concerned with pleasure and freedom than with suffering and
moral struggle.

Vallejo's development in his post-Peruvian poetry involves
taking on an ontological abyss which might be briefly described as
follows: Man is a sadness-exuding mammal, self-contradictory, per-
petually immature, equally deserving of hatred, affection, and
indifference, whose anger breaks any wholeness into warring fragments. This anger's only redeeming quality is that it is, paradoxi-
cally, a weapon of the poor, nearly always impotent against the military resources of the rich. Man is in flight from himself: what once

was an expulsion from paradise has become a flight from self, as the worlds of colonial culture and colonized oppressiveness intersect. At the core of life's fullness is death, the "never" we fail to penetrate, "always" and "never" being the infinite extensions of "yes" and "no." Sorrow is the defining tone of human existence. Poetry thus becomes the imaginative expression of the inability to resolve the contradictions of man as an animal, divorced from nature as well as from any sustaining faith and caught up in the trivia of socialized life.

I have thought more about poetry while translating Vallejo than while reading anyone else. Influence through translation is different from influence through reading masters in one's own tongue. I am creating an American version out of a Spanish text, and if Vallejo is to enter my own poetry he must do so via what I have already, as a translator, turned him into. This is, in the long run, very close to being influenced by myself, or better, *by a self I have created to mine.* In this way, I do not feel that my poetry reflects Vallejo's. He taught me that ambivalence and contradiction are facets of metaphoric probing, and he gave me permission to try anything in my quest for an authentic alternative world in poetry.

Human Poems redefines the "political" poem. With one or two exceptions, the poems in this collection have no political position or agenda in the traditional sense. Yet they are directly sympathetic, in a way that does not remind us of other poetries, with the human situation I have briefly described above. In fact, they are so permeated by Vallejo's own suffering as it is wedded to that of other people, that it is as if the dualisms of colonial/colonized, rich and poor, become fused at a level where the human animal, aware of his fate, is embraced in all his absurd fallibility. Whitman's adhesive bond with others comes to mind, but Whitman used his "democratic vista" to express an idealism that is foreign to the world Vallejo saw around him growing up in Peru, and to the even darker world he encountered as a poor man in Paris, where his already marginal existence imploded before the horrors of the Spanish Civil War.

I think the key lesson Vallejo holds today may be that of a poet learning how to become imprisoned, as it were, in global life as a whole, and in each moment in particular. All his poetry, including the blistering Eros that opens up a breach in the wall separating mother and lover in *Trilce*, urges the poet to confront his own destiny and to stew in what is happening to him—and to also believe that his bewildering situation is significant. To be bound to, or imprisoned in, the present, includes confronting not only life as it really is but also psyche as it really is not—weighing all affirmation against, in an American's case, our imperial obsessions and our own intrinsic dark.

Ypsilanti, March–August, 2005

NOTES:

[1] This essay appeared as an Afterword in my translation of *The Complete Poetry of César Vallejo*, University of California Press, 2007.

E I G H T   F I R E   S O U R C E S [1]

On the morning of July 20, 1965, at the University of California Poetry Conference at Berkeley, Robert Duncan introduced Charles Olson's lecture, "Causal Mythology." After mentioning several living poets that he felt compelled to study—Pound, Zukofsky, Olson, Creeley, and Levertov, Duncan remarked:

> I return to find secrets, I return to *rob* them, you know. If I had to steal fire I know where to go, and there isn't any doubt. Everywhere else I might be stealing anything. I am a jackdaw in poetry. But I know when I'm coming home with a piece of colored glass that I've found fits the design, and where to go for the fire at the center of things. For all of the poets who matter to me in my generation Charles Olson has been a Big Fire Source. One of the ones we have to study.

We are all jackdaws to varying degrees, and Duncan was one of the first to proudly acknowledge such. And the evocation of Prometheus, and the poet as thief of fire, is also accurate and timely. However, I believe that originality is still possible in art, including poetry. Those who openly admit to their plunder, as Duncan did, surely also have some tricks up their sleeves: behind such humble acknowledgments of being beholden to X or Y is a sense of poetic character convinced of the uniqueness of its expression.

Here are eight of my fire sources.[2] They focus on the formidable imaginations that I discovered soon after discovering poetry in the late 1950s at Indiana University, and my subsequent apprenticeship to the art in Kyoto, Japan, in the early 1960s. This compilation can be read as an addenda to "Novices: A Study of Poetic Apprenticeship," collected in *Companion Spider* (Wesleyan University Press, 2002).

"Tea for Two," by Bud Powell

I started glancing at *Downbeat* magazine around 1951 when I was sixteen years old. I taped two quarters to an order form and mailed it off for a 45-RPM recording with Lennie Tristano's "I Surrender Dear" on the other side.

Piano as an orchestra of sound waterfalling through "Tea for Two" changes, with the skeleton of the melody baring its trivia from moment to moment. I listened to it again and again, trying to grasp the difference between the song line and what Powell was doing to it. Melody versus improvisation; what someone else had written versus what Powell was doing to and with it. Somehow an idea vaguely made its way through: you don't have to play somebody else's melody—you can improvise (how?), make up your own tune! WOW—really? You mean I don't have to repeat my parents? I don't have to "play their melody" for the rest of my life?

The alternative—being myself—was a stupendous enigma that took me another six years to approach. I had to get completely bored with all the possibilities my given life had prepared me for before I could make a grab at something that challenged me to change my life. My mother had started me on piano lessons when I was six, and I had played fairly consistently from then on, first classical music, and then a stab at jazz. But that was part of the given life, even if it were an art form, so it had to go too.

Later I realized that Powell had taken the trivial in music (as Art Tatum often did, as in "I'll See You In My Dreams") and transformed it into an imaginative structure. William Carlos Williams I found out had done something similar in poetry.

While reading the Sunday comics on the living-room floor was my first encounter, as a boy, with imagination, Powell was my first encounter, as an adolescent, with the figure of the artist.

In *The Gull Wall* (1975), I wrote a poem that brooded about Powell's tragic life and about what he had offered me, which, in the writing of the poem, cut back to the neighborhood piano lessons my mother had started me on:

> Bud Powell
> locked in his Paris bathroom so he wouldn't wander.
> Sipping his lunch from the cat
> saucer on the floor.
> I see him curled there, nursing his litter,
> his great swollen dugs,
> his sleepy Buddha face
> looks down through the lotus pond,
> sees the damned, astral miles below,
> amongst them a little unmoving Clayton, Jr.,
> placed by his mother on a bed of keys.
> Powell compassionately extended his tongue,
> licked my laid out senses.

The Collected Poems of Hart Crane

I bought a copy of the 1933 edition in Robert Wilson's Phoenix Bookstore on Cornelia Street in NYC, 1960. On the same trip in from Indiana I also met Robert Kelly, Jerry Rothenberg, and Paul Blackburn.

Like Pablo Neruda, Crane brought home metaphor to me, but on a more complex, concentrated and challenging level than the sensuous, surreal Chilean. At first I went for the "easy" poems in *White Buildings*, like "My Grandmother's Love Letters," with its "loose girdle of soft rain," and paper "brown and soft... liable to melt as snow." I was amazed by the unexpected juxtapositions in Crane, such as one finds in the first stanza of "Praise for an Urn":

> It was a kind and northern face
> That mingled in such exile guise
> The everlasting eyes of Pierrot
> And, of Gargantua, the laughter.

The placement of "Gargantua" before "laughter" taught me something about balancing a line. And to find "the crematory lobby" in the fourth stanza suddenly contextualized "urn" and made the poem poignantly real. Small matters, perhaps, but "divine particulars," or building blocks, for a poetry in which every word must count.

Poems like "Lachrymae Christi" and "The Wine Menagerie" stopped me in my tracks in a similar way that "The Marriage of Heaven and Hell" by Blake had. I was being asked to stretch to accommodate an uncommon sense of things that I intuitively felt was not nonsense or pointless obscurity. Crane invented a term, "the logic of metaphor," to identify the way metaphor can lead to metaphor to create a narrative that is utterly imaginative. His metaphoric shifts recall improvisational moves in bebop or strokes in a de Kooning painting of the 1960s. Reading Crane is like watching colored fragments in a turned kaleidoscope slip into new symmetries, then rearrange again.

Over the years, Hart Crane has become a poet companion and from time to time I have been moved to either address him in a poem or to project his addressing me. On one hand, he is a tragic autodidact who never learned self-regulation and destroyed himself in revenge against those who would not acknowledge or support his genius. On the other hand, he is, at his best, the most charged of the major 20th-century American poets. Had he been able to sustain his relationship with Peggy Baird in Mexico in 1931, he might have been able to derail his brutal, masochistic homosexuality. In such poems, written near the end of his life, as "The Circumstance" and "Havana Rose," a voice freed of traditional verse begins to emerge.

No poet to my knowledge has ever speared memory as Crane did in "Passages":

Sulking, sanctioning the sun,
My memory I left in a ravine,—
Casual louse that tissues the buckwheat,
Aprons rocks, congregates pears
In moonlit bushels
And wakens alleys with a hidden cough.

And I have never forgotten for a moment, the last two lines of
the third section of "Voyages":

The imagination spans beyond despair,
Outpacing bargain, vocable and prayer.

The Complete Writings of William Blake

I purchased the Nonesuch Press edition in Kyoto, February 1963,
and a few months later scribbled on the title page: "*The Four Zoas*,
Milton, and *Jerusalem* in 1963 can be read as *The Bible* in 1863; *The
Bible* still makes sense but has lost energy in time." I suppose I was
attempting to say that Blake's "Prophetic Books" were, for our era,
the book of life.

In those days, when I wasn't translating César Vallejo's *Poemas
humanos* I was attempting to make my way through all of Blake. His
work hit me in gusts and putting it all together—holding *Milton: A
Poem*, say, as a single work, in mind—was impossible. So I read
Northrop Frye's *Fearful Symmetry* to discover that it was as difficult, in its own way, as Blake himself! I found a used facsimile edition of *The Book of Urizen* in a bookstore, and while reading it one
afternoon, I passed out, to wake up an hour or so later, flat on the
tatami, the book still in my hand.

Blake is the most bold of poets and possessed a confidence powerful enough to keep him at his work while facing humiliating neg-
lect. Who else might have written:

I have travel'd through Perils & Darkness not unlike a
Champion. I have conquer'd, and shall Go on Conquering.
Nothing can withstand the fury of my Course among the
Stars of God & the Abysses of the Accuser.

or:

To cleanse the Face of my Spirit by Self-examination,
To bathe in the Waters of Life, to wash off the Not Human,
I come in Self-annihilation & the grandeur of Inspiration,
To cast off Rational Demonstration by Faith in the Savior,
To cast off the rotten rags of Memory by Inspiration,
To cast off Bacon, Locke & Newton from Albion's covering,
To take off his filthy garments & clothe him with Imagination,
To cast aside from Poetry all that is not Inspiration...

Blake is also very insightful, especially as a young writer when his
thought was not entangled, as it was in his later years, with accom-
modating the Christian system. I doubt if anyone else alive in his
London of the late 18th century had the following thoughts regarding feminine sexuality and what men had made of it:

Murder is Hindering Another. Theft is Hindering Another.
Backbiting, Undermining, Circumventing, & whatever is
Negative is Vice. But the origin of this mistake in Lavater &
his cotemporaries is, They suppose that Woman's Love is
Sin; in consequence all the Loves & Graces with them are
Sins.

and:

What is it men in women do require?
The lineaments of Gratified Desire.
What is it women in men do require?
The lineaments of Gratified Desire.

Reciprocity, I discovered via Blake, is the daily, human goal.

Origin magazine, second series (1961–1964), edited by Cid Corman

In Kyoto, 1962–1964, about once a week I would walk downtown from the Japanese house my first wife and I shared with a family to The Muse coffee shop to spend the evening with Cid Corman. Since Cid lived alone in a small room, he had turned The Muse into an office of sorts, where he read, edited, and translated. Anyone who wanted to talk with him knew to find him there.

During this time, I learned the rudiments of literary magazine editing, and translating, from Cid. I waited eagerly for each issue of *Origin*, a 64-page quarterly, to appear. The magazine's motto was: "to respond, to offer, to let be" (Corman's "translation" of T.S. Eliot's "to give, to sympathize, to control"). The magazine was free—if you wrote and asked for it on a yearly basis. In Corman's words (stated on the inside back cover of each issue):

> "*ORIGIN* is not for sale; it can be had for love, as it happens, not for money. Not that anyone wanting to offer money or help, coming with love also, will be repulsed. To receive the magazine requires only writing and asking for it, one person to another. It is the minority of one to whom *ORIGIN* is addressed. I seek response; I don't demand it."

The focus of the second series was Louis Zukofsky's *A*, along with his and his wife Celia's translations of Catullus. Zukofsky was also involved in the magazine's ending after the fourteenth issue (twenty had originally been planned). My memory is that he told Cid that he would be better off just writing and translating. Cid had so much respect for Zukofsky that he ceased editing for several years.

Each issue was composed in a way that few literary magazines are. One work often sounded the one before or after it, and there was a cogent fabric of a featured writer with shorter contributions by others. Cid conceived each issue as a single, coherent work meant to be read in a single sitting. Here are some of the works

from this series that I studied carefully and took to heart as one trying to find his way in poetry:

Sections from Gary Snyder's *Mountains and Rivers Without End,*
    #2, 4, and 12
"Yashima," a Noh play by Zeami, #3
Robert Kelly's "The Exchanges," #5
Michael McClure's "The Held Back Pain," #6
Twenty-four Poems by Rocco Scotellaro, #7
"A letter, of sorts," by Gael Turnbull, #7
Giacomo Leopardi's "L'Infinito," #8
Seven Poems by Eugenio Montale, #9
Excerpts from "The Day Book," by Robert Duncan, #10
René Char's "The Lace of Montmirail," #11
Jean-Paul de Dadelsen's "Bach in Autumn," #11
Bashō's "Oku-no-hosomichi" ("Back Roads to Far Towns"), #14

All of the translations mentioned above were done by Corman
himself, or in the case of Zeami and Bashō, with a co-translator.
Watching Cid edit and translate, and then reading each issue as it
came out, was like having a seminar with these writers. This was
my introduction to what Robert Duncan would, a few years later,
identify as a "symposium of the whole." *Origin* became the model
for both of my magazines, *Caterpillar* (1967–1973) and *Sulfur*
(1981–2000). Much of what appeared in this series of *Origin* still
holds up for me as lively and vital. In the 1960s, Corman had
achieved an editorial perspective that made many of the contributions in a single issue coalesce and inter-relate.

Bashō's *Back Roads to Far Towns*

The Cid Corman/Kamaike Susuma translation of Bashō's last and
most impressive hike journal (in which poet and companion walked
some 1,500 miles) was published in *Origin #14*, second series, July
1964. It was published in handsome book format by Mushinsha-

Grossman in 1968. To the best that I can tell, it is the finest translation of haiku (and haibun, as the prose accompanying haiku is
called) that has ever been done in English.

In his Introduction, Corman writes:

> Early one spring morning in 1689 Bashō accompanied by his
> friend and disciple Sora set forth from Edo (old Tokyo) on
> the long nine-month journey that was to take them through
> the backlands and highlands north of the capital and then
> west to the Japan Sea coast and along it until they turned
> inland again towards Lake Biwa (near Kyoto). Approximately
> the first half of this journey, the most arduous part, remains
> recorded in the *Oku-no-hosomichi*.
>
> Bashō, in his 46th year and Sora in his 41st had lived qui-
> etly near each other for some time. The journey was one
> both had looked forward to and realized it would be difficult
> and even dangerous. And, indeed, one might *not* return. It
> was to be more a pilgrimage—and in the garb of pilgrims
> they went—than a case of wandering scholarship: a sight not
> uncommon even in modern Japan, visiting from temple to
> temple, seeing old acquaintances, places famed in history or
> poetry or legend, touchstones for the life lived, the dying to
> come and what life continues.

Wallace Stevens once wrote in *Adagia* that "Poetry is the scholar's art." As I read it, he means that poetry is the literary art that
should hold the greatest appeal to scholars. Poets can also be scholars without lessening the intuitive drive it takes to write substantial
poetry. Bashō is a sterling example of the spiritual poet/scholar. He
did his homework on the lore and history concerning the sites and
temples he planned to visit. The narrative drift of the haibun is like
a parachute weighted with a haiku body under it. Or to put it
another way: it is a pleasure to visit and describe precisely what one
has seen (haibun); it is more challenging after doing so to sense the
essence of the seen, to sound it in the tiny crucible of a haiku. Here
is Bashō's May 27th entry, haibun followed by haiku:

In the demesne of Yamagata the mountain temple called
Ryushakuji. Founded by Jikaku Daishi, unusually well-kept
place. "You must go and see it," people urged; from here, off
back towards Obanazawa, about seven *li*. Sun not yet down.
Reserved space at dormitory at bottom, then climbed to temple on ridge. This mountain one of rocky steeps, ancient
pines and cypresses, old earth and stone and smooth moss,
and on the rock temple-doors locked, no sound. Climbed
along edges of and crept over boulders, worshipped at temples, penetrating scene, profound quietness, heart/mind open
clear.

> quiet
> into rock absorbing
> cicada sounds

In 1991, Sam Hamill published a translation of this journal of
Bashō's, entitled *Narrow Road to the Interior* (Shambala Centaur Editions). He translated the above poem as follows:

> Lonely silence,
> a single cicada's cry
> sinking into stone

Here are three more Bashō translations by these two translators:

Corman	*Hamill*
wild seas (ya	High over wild seas,
to Sado shoring up	surrounding Sado Island:
the great star stream	the river of heaven
summer grass	Summer grasses:
warriors	all that remains of great soldiers'
dreams ruins	imperial dreams

cruel!   Ungraciously, under
under the helmet   a great soldier's empty helmet,
cricket   a cricket sings

Corman/Kamaike: language as enactment, the reader interprets. Hamill: language as interpretation, the reader abandoned. Corman/Kamaike are deft where Hamill is pleonastic and inaccurate (crickets don't sing; cicadas don't cry). In a haiku-like poem of his own, Corman writes:

> The cicada
> singing isn't;
> that sound's its life.

Chaim Soutine's Impact

I saw my first Soutine in 1963 in the Ohara Museum of Art, Kurashiki, Japan, *Hanging Duck*, painted in Paris around 1925. Seeing this painting was so riveting that I recall nothing else in the museum. It was a hybrid fusion, at once a flayed man hung from a pulpy wrist and flailing, with gorgeous white wings attached to his leg stumps—and a gem-like putrescent bird, snagged by one leg, in an underworld filled with bird-beaked monsters and zooming gushes of blood color and sky-blue paint.

In 1993 Maurice Tuchman, Esti Dunow, and Klaus Peris edited *Chaim Soutine (1893–1943), Catalogue Raisonné* (Benedikt Taschen Verlag, Cologne), a boxed two-volume collection of some 800 pages. A magnificent advance on all Soutine books up to then, it included newly discovered paintings (and rejected as fakes some mediocre pieces that had been used over the years to criticize Soutine's standing). I celebrated devouring this collection by writing a 22-page poem, "Soutine's Lapis" (collected in *From Scratch*, Black Sparrow Press, 1998).

In "Another Way of Seeing," an essay in the March 2002 issue of *Harper's Magazine*, John Berger writes: "More directly than any other art, painting is an affirmation of the existent, of the physical world into which mankind has been thrown." Later in the essay, we find the following paragraph:

> Soutine was among the great painters of the twentieth century. It has taken fifty years for this to become clear, because his art was both traditional and uncouth, and this mixture offended all fashionable tastes. It was as if his painting had a heavy broken accent and so was considered inarticulate: at best exotic and at worst barbarian. Now his devotion to the existent becomes more and more exemplary. Few other painters have revealed more graphically than he the collaboration, implicit in the act of painting, between model and painter. The poplars, the carcasses, the children's faces on Soutine's canvasses clung to his brush.

Soutine always worked from a model, whether it was a bunch of houses in a hillscape, a beef carcass, or a human being. Like Caravaggio, he never drew (with two exceptions). His "existents"—especially when he was in Céret, in southwestern France (1919–1922)—besides being his focus are also projection-spooked. Whatever Soutine looked at in Céret seems to have pulled wads of childhood nightmare out of him. These landscapes are not only in earthquake rumba mode, but are pixilated with a very personal, anthropomorphic hysteria. Houses often have grotesque expressions—something between a house and a terrified human face. Some houses even twist into humanesque shapes—they cower in clumps like frightened children or crawl up onto the backs of their neighbors.

The paintings done in Céret are Soutine's most innovative achievement (thinking of César Vallejo for a moment, they are his *Trilce*). Had he been willing to abandon his "existents," he might have gone ahead to create Abstract Expressionism (de Kooning called him his "favorite artist"). But he recoiled from his Céret canvases—later destroying a significant number of them—and his paintings from 1923 to his death in 1943, in spite of their peristaltic

agitation, are basically traditional. To put it this way is a little mis-
leading, as some of the portraits, the beef carcasses, most of the
hanging fowl, the rays, and a few of the last landscapes at Civry and
Champigny are wonderful, bold achievements—yet none are as
audacious or as intuitively fearless as the Céret work. It is as if John
Coltrane played free form jazz as a young musician and then, after
a few years, improvised off standards for the rest of his career.

In the fall of 1999, my wife Caryl and I visited Céret. We went
to the museum, had lunch, and walked around trying to get some
sense of what Céret might have been when Soutine was there
eighty years ago. Finding nothing of his presence, we got into our
car and started to drive away. Halfway out of town, I spotted an
ancient bridge and impulsively stopped the car. I asked Caryl to
wait there while I walked up onto the bridge to unexpectedly view
the aftermath of a storm the day before:

> Standing on Céret's 14th-century *Pont de diable* like a Nean-
>   derthal brow
> over muddy, cascading water spiking the shores.
> Funnel-shaped drifting smoke, plumes of mauve going
>   brown.
> At 3:00 PM, at the end of Soutine's century.
> Sky and river full of Chaim, the whole studio bobbing along,
> frames, rams, anti-ams, chicken-neck twisting river.
> As if through a beef carcass basin, the auburn water boils.
>
> Hanging on museum walls:
> his husks of chrysalis-split moments,
> his nettle shirts of transmuted hurt.
>
> Like Soutine, I inserted myself, a splinter, an anti-
>   fixation,
> churning to get loose. Today, I am still in havoc with
>   those I love,
> still at the granite dissidence that bids me to write.

Wilhelm Reich's *The Function of the Orgasm*

At the poet Joel Oppenheimer's wedding party at Max's Kansas City bar and restaurant, NYC, July 1966, I started dancing with a woman named Adrienne and by the end of the evening was wildly infatuated with her. I decided to leave my wife and infant son and to follow out wherever a relationship with Adrienne would take me. She had recently completed therapy with Alexander Lowen. During the therapy she had left Gary, her famous photographer husband, and when I met her she was hiding out on the Lower East Side, with their two children, in a steel-doored apartment. Connecting with her threw me into a black quandary: why had it taken me five years to realize that my first wife was not the person I really wanted to be with?

Impressed by the effect of therapy on Adrienne, I made an appointment with Lowen. Neither of us liked each other. So I asked her: who did Lowen study with? Who was his mentor? Before leaving for a vacation on a Greek island with her children, Adrienne handed me her copy of Wilhelm Reich's *The Function of the Orgasm*.

I sat down in the basement room on Bank Street I had cleared of trash and moved into and started reading Reich's book. Halfway through, I got up, packed a bag, made a plane reservation, flew back to Indianapolis, took a cab to my childhood home, and informed my mother that I had to talk with her. I told her that we had never had an honest conversation and that I did not love her like she thought I did. I was trying to declare independence and make a final break with Indiana. My mother, of course, was simply bewildered and hurt. After our talk, I disappeared into the basement and tried to come to terms with what I had just done. I wrote into a notebook:

> Today I have set my crowbar against all I know
> In a shower of blood and soot
> Breaking the backbone of my mother.

11 September 1966

Then, sick with remorse for having done what I had felt compelled to do, I wrote "The 1802 Blake Butts Letter Variation" in which I acknowledged that I had put knowledge over love, and had broken a heart "to save my own destruction."

In *The Function of the Orgasm*, Reich argued that the goal of individual life was self-regulation, and that the "function of the orgasm" was to enable the individual to become self-regulative and creatively responsible. For Reich there was no contradiction between sexual fulfillment and imaginative realization—they were antiphonal, mutually reinforcing. Reich's position hit me like a thunderbolt and it emboldened me to do something I had never done before: to cut through all obligation and to proclaim my right to live for myself alone, on the assumption that such was fundamental to doing anything original as a poet. The downside of this personal revolution was my guilt for what I had first put my wife through, and then my mother.

I returned to NYC, went into Reichian therapy with Dr. Sidney Handelman, and began to decompress years of stifled feelings and self-thwarted stances. My goal was to come to terms with why I had put obligation over action. Using Reich as my sounding board, I felt like, in Wallace Steven's words, "the latest freed man." I was soon to discover that abusive honesty is part of the wake of release.[3]

Rabelais and His World by **Mikhail Bakhtin**

My oldest friend, the cookbook writer, raconteur, and classics scholar, Denis Kelly, gave me Bakhtin's book the summer of 1973, not long after my book *Coils* (Black Sparrow Press) was published. In *Coils* I had attempted to excavate my Indiana background and to lay bare the stances involved with it that I felt diminished humanness. Inspired by Blake's invented mythic world, I created my own god-forms to help me free myself to explore the irrational. I revealed myself more than my rationality would accept, and when the book was published I felt that I was alone and in water over my head.

While one of the primary drives in writing poetry is toward originality, it is also gratifying to discover that one's own efforts to clear new ground have some antecedent support—that another thinker has established a background against which one's own efforts can be viewed and possibly confirmed. Bakhtin's vision of "grotesque realism," beautifully presented in the 60-page Introduction to his book on medieval folk humor as brought to fulfillment in Rabelais's writing not only back up my own grotesque fascination with the body but proposed a definition of what he called "the archaic grotesque" that helped me gain a perspective on Ice Age imagery the following year after Caryl and I visited the painted and engraved caves in southwestern France. Bakhtin's book, in effect, became a hinge for me between the deep past, the medieval past, and the present: it helped me to contextualize and understand what I had accomplished in *Coils* and it grounded the "grotesque" in the grotto, or cave, itself, helping me to make some sense out of the undifferentiated, hybrid figures to be found in Lascaux and Les Trois Frères:

> Contrary to modern canons, the grotesque body is not separated from the rest of the world. It is not a closed, completed unit; it is unfinished, outgrows itself, transgresses its own limits. The stress is laid on those parts of the body that are open to the outside world, that is, the parts through which the world enters the body or emerges from it, or through which the body itself goes out to meet the world. This means that the emphasis is on the apertures or the convexities, or on various ramifications and offshoots: the open mouth, the genital organs, the breasts, the phallus, the potbelly, the nose. The body discloses its essence as a principle of growth which exceeds its own limits only in copulation, pregnancy, childbirth, the throes of death, eating, drinking, or defecation. This is the ever unfinished, ever creating body, the link in the chain of genetic development, or more correctly speaking, two links shown at the point where they enter into each other. This especially strikes the eye in archaic grotesque.

Bakhtin's unfinished, ever-creating body—linking fecundation and death, degradation and praise—thus connects with the Upper Paleolithic vision of the human as indeterminate and initially unclosed. While Rabelais's back wall, so to speak, is the Roman baths with their interwoven forms called *grotesca*, I was able to bring to bear such forms, and such thinking about them, on an Ice Age context. If Rabelais's world represented an infringement on borders and stability, the Cro-Magnon world, I discovered, displayed itself in that abyss between no image and an image, or before there were any borders to be infringed!

Via Rabelais's book of laughter, fearlessness, and transformation, the Russian scholar Bakhtin brought across a vision of man returning unto himself, wherein destruction is but one aspect of regeneration and renewal. This is a primary gift, and it continues to inspire me even though the negations of the 20th and 21st centuries are on such a scale as to often render affirmation a Gargantuan dream.

NOTES:

[1] This piece was solicited by Peter Davis for an anthology that he edited: *Poet's Bookshelf: Contemporary Poets on Books that Shaped their Art* (The Barnwood Press, Selma, Indiana, 2005).

[2] Originally, there were ten "sources," but I have eliminated, from this version, the entries on César Vallejo and Emily Dickinson. My translational and poetic apprenticeship to Vallejo is amply documented in "A Translation Memoir." And the gist of my comments on one of Emily Dickinson's poems—not included in the Davis anthology—is in my note on the poetry of Christine Hume. This essay in its present form appeared in *Poetry Flash*.

[3] In "Interface II: 'Fracture'" (*Juniper Fuse: Upper Paleolithic Imagination & the Construction of the Underworld*, Wesleyan University Press, 2003, pp. 43–49), I recount a significant episode in my Reichian therapy with Handelman. And in *Altars* (Black Sparrow Press, 1971), there is a poem, "Ode to Reich."

SOMEBODY ELSE [1]

Arthur Rimbaud, May 1871 (he is 16 years old):

I am lousing myself up as much as I can these days. Why? I want to be a poet, and I am working to make myself a *seer*... the point is to arrive at the unknown by the disordering of *all the senses*. The sufferings are enormous, but one has to be strong to be born a poet, and I have discovered I *am* a poet. It is not my fault at all. It is a mistake to say: I think. One ought to say: I am thought.

I is somebody else. So much the worse for the wood if it finds itself a violin...

I witness the unfolding of my own thought: I watch it, I listen to it: I make a stroke of the bow: the symphony begins to stir in the depths, or springs onto the stage...

The first study for a man who wants to be a poet is the knowledge of himself, complete. He looks for his soul, inspects it, puts it to the test, learns it. As soon as he knows it, he must cultivate it!... the soul has to be made monstrous, that's the point; after the fashion of the *comprachicos*, if you like! Imagine a man planting and cultivating warts on his face!

I say that one must be a *seer*, make oneself a seer.

The poet makes himself a seer by a long, prodigious, and *rational disordering of all the senses*. Every form of love, of suffering, of madness; he searches himself, he consumes all the poisons in him, and keeps only their quintessences. This is unspeakable torture during which he needs all his faith and superhuman strength, and during which he becomes the great patient, the great criminal, the great accursed—and the great learned one!—among men for he arrives at the *unknown!* Because he has cultivated his own soul—which was rich to begin with—more than any other man! He reaches the unknown; and even if, crazed, he ends up losing the understanding of his visions, at least he has seen them! Let him die charging through those unutterable, unnameable things: other horrible workers will come; they will begin from the horizons where he has succumbed!

So, then, the poet is the thief of fire... [2]

Rimbaud is committed to self-transformation, in somewhat the same spirit that American Indian, Canadian Inuit, and Siberian shamans are, in transforming themselves from ordinary, normal people to people capable—via many means, including hallucinogenic plants, tobacco, dancing, fasting—of deep interior journeys to the land of the dead or to paradise. In these "states," shamans accompany the souls of the recent dead to paradise or to an underworld, and learn healing techniques from the spirits of shamans of the past.

But Rimbaud is not a tribal boy; he is a 19th-century French Catholic with limited means at his disposal for changing his consciousness. At the point we meet him, he tells us he is lousing himself up to get rid of his normal sensibility and to discover a new one that is deeper and more imaginative. He has discovered that he is a poet—and that he *wants to be* a poet. He compares this state to one in which a piece of wood falls asleep and awakens to find that it is a violin. Its obligation—to follow out the metaphor—would be to get itself played, or, in terms of writing poetry, which one does by oneself, generally in silence, and alone, to learn how to play itself.

He writes: *Je est un autre.* In English: "I is another, or I is somebody else." Not "I am another," which would suggest that my customary "I" is still present, and that it has something mysterious about it. "I is somebody else" is more radical: it proposes that "I" is an unidentified actor, or personality, about whom my ordinary "I" knows very little. It only knows, in fact, that there is a big difference between my ordinary "I" and a hidden, unknown "I" that seems to be inside me in some way, and that can only become known, or made manifest, through disorientation—through knocking my ordinary "I" out of the driver's seat.

The soul, he argues, has to be made monstrous. Another way of saying this would be: whoever wants to be an artist, in Rimbaud's formula, must make material in his subconscious available to his consciousness, and let the consciousness become distorted and bizarre with this new material. Most of us only experience our subconscious via fragments of dreams—some people even say they do not dream! And we know that in dreams the world is turned upside down, events both marvelous and terrible take place, and because this upside down world is threatening to our ability to keep balance in everyday survival (you don't want to start dreaming while driving on the freeway), most people keep it under lock and key, and only, when out of conscious control, in sleep, are penetrated by its phantoms.

To put it another way, Rimbaud is saying he wants to *dream awake*, to exist in a trance in which he has conscious access to his dream powers.

The formula? The poet makes himself a seer (a visionary in contact with his subconscious) by a long, prodigious, and *rational* disordering of all the senses. "Rational" is an important word here because it insists on this activity as being programmatic, that is, of taking place to make a special art possible. This is not recreational drug use.

In Greek myth, Prometheus was the thief of fire—he stole it from the gods and gave it to mankind, for which he was tortured unto eternity. If the poet is the thief of fire, he is the one who journeys into the depths of his subconscious in order to bring up the dark treasures that are concealed there. And he may pay a dear price for doing so, as the derangement process may result in addiction, dereliction, or in the kind of being out of it that makes it impossible for an individual to function in society.

❧

My first poem was called "The Outsider," and was a timid, versified re-enactment of the feelings I had picked up reading Colin Wilson's *The Outsider*, a book that introduced me to the visionary figure on the periphery of societal centers, in 1957. However, my first engagement with *poesis*, or the making of poetry, took place when I was a freshman at Indiana University, 1953, in Herbert Stern's Freshman Composition class. After having given us several assignments (which I had done poorly with), he said: write anything you want to.

I wrote a kind of prose poem, in the voice of an aging prostitute, standing by her hotel window, watching newspaper and rubbish blow down a deserted street at 4:00 a.m. Stern gave me an A- and under the grade wrote: *See me*. When I sat down in his office, he told me the piece was excellent but that I was in trouble because I had not written it. I still recall his words: "The person who wrote this did not write your other themes." I protested, and in the end he believed me, and said: "If you can write like that, there are a couple of books you should read." On a scrap of paper, which he handed me, he wrote: *The Metamorphosis*, and under it, *Portrait of the Artist as a Young Man*. To what extent Stern himself was conscious of the significance of this particular juxtaposition, I will never know—but by citing the Kafka story (which I waited two years to read), he had identified what had happened to me in my "free composition," and by citing the Joyce (which I read nine years later), had he offered me the challenge to become an artist?

In my theme I had aged myself, changed my sex, and dressed up as a parody of my mother. The figure was utterly fictional—I knew nothing about prostitutes, and that was probably part of the point too: I had entered imagination by speaking out of a place I had never personally experienced. I had left the confines of an "assignment"—my entire life up to that time and then some was framed by assignments—and wandered into a "somebody else." *Je est un autre*. I am a metaphor. Clayton is a prostitute; Clayton is not merely Clayton. Clayton does not merely live in the Phi Delta Theta fraternity and take abuse daily as a "pledge." Clayton is a 55-year-old woman looking out on a street that does not exist.

A move toward origin. Toward our so-called "face before birth." Toward that which we are but will never be. The initial fascination with writing poetry is similar to a visit to an astrologer and requesting a horoscope. My aged whore positioned me toward a past in the present, indicating (though I did not realize it then) continuity and depth. The street was empty except for blowing (unreadable) newspapers, yesterday's news. It was empty and I was to populate it with my own news—I was to learn how to read the street, and to get used to not being myself. I was, like a tree still rooted in Indiana earth, to learn how to twist within my own bark and observe "other" things around me.[3]

The DNA—double helix—of poetry is metaphor, a world that we make up, a world based on our experiences *and* our fantasies *and* our dreams. A world that has, so to speak, one foot in objective reality (roses have thorns), and one foot in subjective reality (my love is a red, red rose). A world in which the separation implied by "objective" and "subjective" are dissolved. An ideal world. A world in which the way things are is translated into *my experience of myself in the world.*

In saying that one thing is another, metaphors imply that many if not all things are connected, or correspond, in some mysterious inter-related way. Making metaphors is a way of remaking your world, a way of putting a world together as you see and feel and sense it.

To learn what metaphors are and how to use them is potentially to see through the metaphors that family, education, church, politics, and the media manipulate us with. To see through something is potentially to be free of it. We say, "I see through your lie," meaning, I know you are lying and why you are lying. One could say that liberation is to be able to create *and* to unmask, to compose things in your own fashion as you deconstruct what others would impose on you.

Creatively, metaphors suggest that the world is inter-linked, in flux, iridescent. They suggest that freedom is not only "free speech," but also *freed* speech—free associations (my love is a blue magnolia, my love is lightning and bees, my love is vermilion honey oozing from the moon), random thoughts, and crazy thoughts (my love is a horse drawn and quartered in my heart). Thus the freedom that is poetry involves taking liberties with words, breaking the rules of common speech, violating common sense not to create nonsense but to create uncommon sense.

※

The same year that Rimbaud wrote out his "Somebody else" credo, he wrote a poem called "The Drunken Boat," twenty-five rhymed quatrains in French, which I have translated, occasionally matching rhymes, but more often than not settling for a charged free verse, since I did not want to forsake meaning simply for rhyme. While translating this poem, I tacked up on a bookshelf before me a copy of Hart Crane's "The Wine Menagerie." Crane's poetry is the closest that we have to Rimbaud, so I was asking for Crane's linguistic prowess to be with me in my work.

"The Drunken Boat" is a metaphoric cornucopia, and Rimbaud's first poetic enactment of self-transformation. He likens self-release to a boat at the mercy of a phantasmagoric sea world. At one extreme, it is a poem about running away from home as a child and returning after a few nights in the woods with one's tail between one's legs, sadly eager for a hot meal and a warm bed. At another extreme, in the spirit that the teenage Rimbaud seeks to cut all background and conventional ties and to roam at large in his imagination, the boat—initially pulled down the canal by towers—discharges its directional equipment, so as to be tossed at the whims of the sea. Rimbaud had never seen the sea when he wrote the poem; so, on another level, it is an early version of a collage in which much of the fantastic imagery is lifted from picture books, like Jules Verne's *Twenty Thousand Leagues Under The Sea*.

Keeping in mind Rimbaud's revolutionary proposal, we can say that the "I" here sets up a situation in which an oceanic "somebody else" (or here "something else") can take over and manifest its wild power.

For all its fireworks, "The Drunken Boat" is very much the work of a poet who is still close to his childhood (as most artists are not at the time they really hit their stride). Two-thirds of the way through the poem, the boat begins to miss its rejected mainland and, unable to redirect itself, implicitly shatters—at which point Rimbaud recalls playing with a toy boat on a puddle as a child. In the context of the poem, such is a marvelous caricature of the "drunken" boat's visionary voyage.

The Drunken Boat

Pulled as I was down phlegmatic Rivers,
Suddenly—no longer a barge for towers!
Whooping Redskins with emptied quivers
Had nailed them naked to painted posts.

Contemptuous? Of every kind of crew:
Carriers of English cotton or Flemish wheat.
The moment my shrieking towers were subdued,
The Rivers let me plunge to open sea.

Amidst the furious slaps of racing tides,
I, last winter, blunter than children's brains,
I ran! No untied Peninsula's
Been trounced by a more triumphant din!

The tempest blessed my sea-born awakenings.
Lighter than cork, I skipped across rollers called
The eternal loop-the-loops of victims, ten nights,
Without missing the simpleton stares of lamps!

Sweeter than tart apple flesh to kids,
The green water probed my pine hull
And of the stains of blue wines and vomit
It scoured me, scattering rudder and grapnel.

From then on, I bathed in the Poem of the Sea,
Star-infused, lactescent, devouring
The verdant blue; where, ghastly and ravished
Flotsam, a rapt drowned man at times descends;

Where, tinting instantly the bluicities, deliriums
And slow rhythms under the day's rutilations,
Stronger than alcohol, vaster than our lyres,
The bitter russets of love ferment!

I know the sky split with lightning, and the undertows
And the currents and the waterspouts; I know the evening
The dawn as glorious as an entire nation of doves,
And I've seen sometimes what man thought he saw!

I've seen the sun low, spotted with mystic horrors,
Raying forth long violet coagulations,
Like actors in prehistoric plays the whitecaps
Flickering into the distance their shutter shudders!

I've dreamed of the green night with dazzled snows,
A kiss rising through the seas' eyes in slow motion,
The circulatory flow of outrageous saps,
And the bilious blue arousals of singer phosphors!

I've followed, for months on end, swells
Like exploding stables, battering the reefs,
Never dreaming that the Marys' luminescent feet
Could force a muzzle onto wheezing Oceans!

I've struck, are you aware, incredible Floridas
Comingling with flowers the eyes of panthers in the skins
Of men! Rainbows arched like bridle-reins
Below seas' horizons, taut to glaucous herds!

I've seen enormous swamps fermenting, weirs
Where in the reeds a whole Leviathan rots!
Cave-ins of water in the midst of standing calms,
The distances cataracting toward the abysses!

Glaciers, pearly waves, suns of silver, molten skies!
Hideous wrecks in the slime of fuscous gulfs
Where gigantic snakes devoured by bugs
Drop from twisted trees, squirting black perfumes!

I would've liked to show children these dorados
Of the blue wave, these gold, these singing fish.
—Flower foam cradled my berthless driftings
And at times I was winged by ineffable winds.

Sometimes, a martyr weary of poles and zones,
The very sea whose sobbing made my churning sweet
Proffered her yellow suckered shadow flowers
And I held there, like a woman on her knees

Almost an island, tossing off my wales
The squabbles and dung of gossipy blond-eyed birds.
And so I scudded, while through my frayed
Cordage drowned sailors sank sleepwards, back first!

But now, a boat lost under the hair of coves,
Flung by the hurricane into birdless ether,
I whose carcass, drunk on water, no Monitor
Or Hanseatic schooner would've fished out;

Free, fuming, risen from violet mists,
I who pierced the reddening sky like a wall
Bearing—exquisite jam for genuine poets—
Solar lichen and azure snot;

Who ran, speckled with electric lunules,
A crazy plank, by black sea horses escorted,
When the Julys with cudgel blows were crushing
The ultramarine skies into burning funnels;

I who trembled, hearing, at fifty leagues, the whimpers
Of Behemoth rutting and turgid Maelstroms,
Eternal spinner of blue immobilities,
I miss the Europe of age-worn parapets!

I've seen astral archipelagos! and isles
Whose raving skies open wide to the voyager:
—In those bottomless nights do you sleep, are you exiled,
A million golden birds, O Force of the future?—

But, truly, I've wept too much! Dawns are harrowing.
Each moon is atrocious, each sun bitter:
Acrid love has swollen me with inebriating torpors.
O let my keel burst! O let me be gone to the sea!

If there is one Europe I long for,
It's a chill, black puddle where, at the scented end of day,
A squatting child, utterly forlorn,
Releases a boat fragile as a butterfly in May.

No longer will I, bathed in your languors, O waves,
Slip into the wakes of cotton carriers,
Nor cut across the arrogance of flags and streamers,
Nor swim below the prison hulks' horrific stares.[4]

I would now like to look at some of the forms "somebody else" can take in poems by Walt Whitman, Rainer Maria Rilke, and D.H. Lawrence. Each of these poems also tells us where poems come from, as they examine the circumstances in which the voice that is deep within us is generated. I will then conclude by writing about a visionary experience I had in Kyoto, Japan, in 1962.

Walt Whitman's 1855 edition of *Leaves of Grass* presents a Whitman who claims he has realized the potentialities latent in every American. He portrays himself as a representative working man who at the same time is non-sexist, democratic, non-racist, and in amazing touch with all his senses. He writes as someone who is fully alive, intensely spiritual and sexual, with an eagle-eye for observing, in inventive detail, what is going on around him.

Given that the Whitman of the 1840s was a hack journalist and composer of sentimental short fiction, one might very well ask: what brought him to this visionary position and enabled him to make the breakthrough to a sturdy and dynamic free verse that was some fifty years ahead of its time? Some readers and scholars feel that Whitman had an ecstatic, mystical experience in the early 1850s that became the engine of *Leaves of Grass*. The closest thing to a written record of such an experience is Section 5 of "Song of Myself," the keystone poem of the 1855 edition.

Song of Myself, Section 5[5]

I believe in you my soul.... the other I am must not
    abase itself to you,
And you must not be abased to the other.

Loafe with me on the grass.... loose the stop from
    your throat,
Not words, nor music or rhyme I want.... not custom
    or lecture, not even the best,
Only the lull I like, the hum of your valved voice.

I mind how we lay in June, such a transparent
    summer morning;
You settled your head athwart my hips and gently
    turned over upon me,
And parted the shirt from my bosom-bone, and
    plunged your tongue to my bare-script heart,
And reached till you felt my beard, and reached till
    you held my feet.

Swiftly arose and spread around me the peace and joy
    and knowledge that pass all the art and argument
    of the earth;

> And I know that the hand of God is the elderhand of
> my own,
> And I know that the spirit of God is the eldest brother
> of my own,
> And that all men ever born are also my brothers...
> and the women my sisters and lovers,
> And that a kelson of the creation is love;
> And limitless are leaves stiff or drooping in the fields,
> And brown ants in the little wells beneath them,
> And mossy scabs of the wormfence, and heaped
> stones, and elder and mullen and pokeweed.

Here we might say that "soul" signfies the "somebody else," and Whitman's psychic democracy enables him to treat "I" and "the soul" in a reciprocal way. Not only are they equals but "the soul" is treated as a concrete "somebody else" with whom the poet can engage in an enraptured, sexual union. We will never know if Whitman actually had such an experience or if he merely envisioned it. If we read the third stanza as a report of an actual experience it comes off as a kind of semi-camouflaged homoerotic lovemaking. If "the soul" is holding both the poet's feet and beard in his hands, the chances are his head is not over the poet's heart but over his genitals. If this is a good possibility, then it is possible to also propose that Whitman's universal vision presented in the fourth stanza is generated by an orgasm. Whatever the triggering experience might have been, it leads Whitman to proclaim a loving brotherhood with God and all man- and woman-kind. He sees that even the most humble things—heaped stones, pokeweed—contain the infinite universe. All things are holy.

Whitman's language is ordinary speech charged with precise and arcane metaphors. Here is some brief commentary on the principal ones:

"stop from your throat": in music, the closing of an aperture in an air passage is the stop (as in organs). It is a device for modifying the power and quality of tones produced. Here Whitman seems to be saying: overcome your inhibitions to make the real sounds you are feeling—let it all come out.

"valved voice": a valve permits or checks the flow of something. Here, as an adjective, it suggests that the voice is capable of regulating its own flow.

"elderhand of my own": in card playing, the elder or eldest hand is the player on the dealer's left hand. The line thus suggests two things: God's hand is the oldest version of my own hand, and God is playing in the same game as I am and sitting to my left.

"kelson of creation": a kelson is a longitudinal structure in a ship's frame that prevents deformation, and distributes over considerable length the effect of concentrated loads. Love is thus seen as a regulating and balancing force. But it is also more: it is a kelson *of the creation*. This is close to saying that love is the regulating and balancing force in the universe, as it is known to humankind.

While living in Paris in the early years of the 20th century, the German poet, Rainer Maria Rilke, worked as the sculptor August Rodin's secretary and spent a lot of time at the city zoo as well as at the Louvre, the great museum of fine arts.

In a letter to his dear friend Lou Andreas-Salomé, Rilke described the way that ancient objects took on a strange luster once they were detached from history, and seen as things in and for themselves: "No subject matter," he wrote, "is attached to them, no irrelevant voice interrupts the silence of their concentrated reality... no history casts a shadow over their naked clarity... they *are*. That is all... one day one of them reveals itself to you, and shines like a first star."

The sonnet that we are going to look at was written off a fifth-century Greek sculpture on display in the Louvre, and was published by Rilke in 1907. On one hand, this headless marble torso is a fragment, a defaced chunk of stone, "detached from history," as Rilke said. Yet such is its perfection, its luminous sensuality, that it seems impossibly alive; an inner radiance bursts from the marble.

Our translator this time is M.D. Herter Norton, who translated a lot of Rilke's poetry, essays, and letters. She has not tried to rhyme the sonnet in translation, but like I did with the Rimbaud poem, has translated for meaning. A few of her words seem a little old-fashioned now.

Archaic Torso of Apollo[6]

We did not know his legendary head,
in which the eyeballs ripened. But
his torso still glows like a candelabrum
in which his gaze, only turned low

holds and gleams. Else could not the curve
of the breast blind you, nor in the slight turn
of the loins could a smile be running
to that middle, which carried procreation.

Else would this stone be standing maimed
    and short
under the shoulders' translucent plunge
nor flimmering like the fell of beasts of prey

nor breaking out of all its contours
like a star: for there is no place
that does not see you. You must change your
    life.

We know nothing of the archaic torso's past, only that it had originally been conceived as a vision of the Greek god of manly youth, and beauty, and the inspirer of poetry, Apollo. Rilke imagines that at one time the eyeballs were so alive in the head that they could be compared to ripening fruit. Looking at what remains in the Louvre, he feels a warm flow coming from it, and compares this to a candelabrum, an ornamental candlestick having many branches. In fact, he claims he can make contact with the sculpture's gaze, which has now descended into its chest. "only turned low" means two things: the descent of the gaze, and the lowering of its light (as one would say in turning a light down, or turning it low).

Else could not = otherwise it would not be possible for the curve of the breast to blind you, nor could a smile be running through the slight turn of the loins into that middle—the genitals—which once were its seat of procreation. The logic of metaphor in this passage is even keener than I have just stated:

It is only because the gaze has been lowered into the torso that the breast has the power to blind, as one might be blinded by light, and this lowered, and low, light also enables the viewer to notice a smile-like fold of flesh running down into what were the genitals.

Rilke of course is not speaking of literal light or literal blinding, but using these terms metaphorically to express the otherwise inexpressible. For someone who was not as imaginative as Rilke, they might stand before this torso and just exclaim how powerful or how beautiful it is.

The logic of metaphor in the sestet is a continuation of that in the octet. If there were no light, no gaze, we would just be looking at a chunk of fragmentary sculpture, something maimed, and short. Without this light, the stone would not be glimmering and flickering like wild beast fur. Without this light it could not be thought of as breaking out of all its contours, like a star, which joins the initial light in the first quatrain to a new source of light (and contextualizes Rilke's shining star comment from his letter to his friend). The torso projects magnificent energy like a star projects light. It refuses to be contained by the contours of the stone itself. It makes the viewer—Rilke, the speaker—suddenly believe that everything around him is alive—there is no place, no thing, no element that is merely object. Everything is alive and as such is turning its living power upon you. You cannot simply remain as you were before having this experience. You must take this experience as a great and next to impossible challenge: in the spirit that raw stone was transformed into a god,

you must transform your given life into a creative life.

This is what all art, at base, says to us.

Applying this to our theme: the sculpture says, in effect, make contact with the "somebody else." Of course Rilke could not have written such a piece had he not already, to a significant degree, have done so. Many authentic and powerful works of art are embodiments of "somebody else."

Both the Whitman and Rilke poems depict moments of receptive empowerment. There is another kind of poem that is written out of the poet's failure to come to terms with a particular experience. Such poems make up a significant part of the history of poetry. Here is a spectacular example of such a poem, written by the English novelist/poet D.H. Lawrence:

Snake[7]

A snake came to my water-trough
On a hot, hot day and I in pyjamas for the heat,
To drink there.

In the deep, strange-scented shade of the great dark
    carob-tree
I came down the steps with my pitcher
And must wait, must stand and wait, for there he was
    at the trough before me.

He reached down from a fissure in the earth-wall in
    the gloom
And trailed his yellow-brown slackness soft-bellied
    down, over the edge of the stone trough
And rested his throat upon the stone bottom,

And where the water had dripped from the tap, in a
    small clearness,
He sipped with his straight mouth,
Softly drank through his straight gums, into his slack
    long body,
Silently.

Someone was before me at my water-trough,
And I, like a second comer, waiting.

He lifted his head from his drinking, as cattle do,
And looked at me vaguely, as drinking cattle do,
And flickered his two-forked tongue from his lips,
    and mused a moment,
And stooped and drank a little more,
Being earth-brown, earth-golden from the burning
    bowels of the earth
On the day of Sicilian July, with Etna smoking.

The voice of my education said to me
He must be killed,
For in Sicily the black, black snakes are innocent, the
    gold are venomous.

And voices in me said, If you were a man
You would take stick and break him now, and finish
    him off.

But must I confess how I liked him,
How glad I was he had come like a guest in quiet, to
    drink at my water-trough
And depart peaceful, pacified, and thankless,
Into the burning bowels of this earth?

Was it cowardice, that I dared not kill him?
Was it perversity, that I longed to talk to him?
Was it humility, to feel so honoured?
I felt so honoured.

And yet those voices:
If you were not afraid, you would kill him!

And truly I was afraid, I was most afraid,
But even so, honoured still more
That he should seek my hospitality
From out the dark door of the secret earth.

He drank enough
And lifted his head, dreamily, as one who has drunken,
And flickered his tongue like a forked night on the
    air, so black;
Seeming to lick his lips,
And looked around like a god, unseeing, into the air,
And slowly turned his head,
And slowly, very slowly, as if thrice adream,
Proceeded to draw his slow length curving round
And climb again the broken bank of my wall-face.

And as he put his head into that dreadful hole,
And as he slowly drew up, snake-easing his shoulders,
    and entered farther,
A sort of horror, a sort of protest against his with-
    drawing into that horrid black hole,
Deliberately going into the blackness, and slowly
    drawing himself after,
Overcame me now his back was turned.

I looked round, I put down my pitcher,
I picked up a clumsy log
And threw it at the water-trough with a clatter.

I think it did not hit him,
But suddenly that part of him that was left behind
    convulsed in undignified haste,
Writhed like lightning, and was gone
Into the black hole, the earth-lipped fissure in the
    wall-front,

At which, in the intense still noon, I stared with fascination.

And immediately I regretted it.
I thought how paltry, how vulgar, what a mean act!
I despised myself and the voices of my accursed
human education.

And I thought of the albatross,
And I wished he would come back, my snake.

For he seemed to me again like a king,
Like a king in exile, uncrowned in the underworld,
Now due to be crowned again.

And so, I missed my chance with one of the lords
Of life.
And I have something to expiate:
A pettiness.

Taormina

The dramatic crux of the poem is Lawrence's argument with himself concerning the appropriate gesture toward the snake. There
are several ways to describe this inner-struggle: Pagan vs. Christian, figurative vs. literal, or receptive vs. macho. The conflict can
also be seen as one between his "I" and his "somebody else," with
the "I" insisting on egoistic self-protection and aggression as the
manly self-defining act. "Somebody else" is initially fascinated by
the snake's beauty and carefully observes its drinking. The longer
that "somebody else" looks, the more mythical and magical the
snake becomes, at one point having emerged "from out the dark
door of the secret earth." This implied mythical stature is clarified
and expanded on near the end of the poem: "For he seemed to be
again like a king / Like a king in exile, uncrowned in the underworld, / Now due to be crowned again." Barbara G. Walker writes:

Every mythology had some form of the World Serpent. Like
the Hermetic or Gnostic serpent encircling the World Egg,

he was a basic Indo-European religious symbol. Norse myth called him the Midgard-Worm, who encircled the whole round of middle-Earth (Midgard), his tail in his mouth. Russians called him Koshchei the Deathless, encircler of the underworld. This seems to have been a variation of the Japanese dragon of sea-tides, Koshi. Egyptians called him Sata (Satan), or the Tuat, on whose back the sun god rode through the underworld each night. Greeks called him Okeanos, the sea-serpent of the outermost ocean.[8]

The serpent underworld associations are complex. Not only do snakes often disappear in holes, but in a wide range of myths, the primary figure is The Great Goddess with a snake for a consort. When the serpent turned arrogant, in one Hebrew version, the Goddess banished him to the underworld. Lawrence intuits some of this, associating the serpent king with the underworld from both a mythical and personal point of view. The serpent is there, in exile, not only through mythic banishment (or simply location in some myths), but through Lawrence's own egotistic banishment, his failure to receive this "lord of life," and in his own small way, acknowledge its archetypal status.

We can imagine that after this incident, Lawrence gets his water and returns to his rented Sicilian house. What does he do then? I propose that he sits down and writes the poem you have just read. This illustrates another reason that poets write poems: art is the great second chance, offering the possibility of—having not been up to the size of an experience—returning to it, in imagination, and realizing it in a poem or in another work of art. Everyone of us can think of failed experiences in our own lives, when we were emotionally overwhelmed, when, say, at a funeral we were so filled with conflicting emotions and grief that we could not express ourselves (thus the millions of elegies, realizations of grief in poetry).

In Kyoto, October 1962, I became convinced that I needed some sign to justify attempting to turn myself into a poet. I had no sense of how this validation would take place. I had reached a point where nerve and blind desire had to be backed up by, in William Blake's words, "divine aid."

It all began with a gorgeous, red, green, and yellow spider centered in her web attached to the persimmon tree in the backyard of the Okumura house, where we had two ground floor tatami rooms. I got used to taking a chair and a little table out under the web where I read *The Masks of God* and struggled to digest and translate César Vallejo's *Poemas humanos*. After several weeks of "spider sitting," the weather turned chill, with rain, and gusting wind. When I went out one afternoon, the web was wrecked, the spider gone. Something went through me that I can only describe as the sensation of loss of one deeply loved. I cried, and for several days felt nauseous and absurd. A week later, I was picked up by some sake drinkers in our local sushi bar and spent the better part of a night drinking with them. I woke up with the kind of hangover that makes you extremely sensitive to certain mental nuances. That afternoon I motorcycled to a bar dormitory where I was to meet a male friend who managed a hostess bar. The dormitory Mama-san informed me that my friend was out, but invited me in anyway for cookies and tea. She sat me down before a TV set and left the room. There was a teenage adventure movie on in which, during a track meet, a fat boy tried to climb a pole and failed, to the glee of his peers. This made me think of the poet Robert Kelly, who in those days weighed over 400 pounds. I was once again moved to tears, this time by what I took to be Kelly's difficulties as a man. After an hour, I left the dormitory, feeling so sensitive it was as if my nerves were in the very surface of my skin.

I decided to cycle out to the poet Gary Snyder's house for an impromptu visit, and once again found that the person I had come to visit was not home—but his wife, Joanne Kyger, was, and she invited me in for tea too. I left near dusk and started home. Cycling down a wide commercial avenue I suddenly began to hallucinate: the motorcycle became an ox, the handlebars ox horns; a lumber yard turned into a manger in which I saw wise men kneeling by the infant Jesus. At first I tried to hold on and will myself home, but by the time I got to Nijo Castle, I was afraid I would have an accident, so rather automatically I decided to circumambulate the Castle and got off the motorcycle in the tourist-bus parking lot.

At the point I started around the square moated medieval structure, everything was roaring with transformation; anything I looked at instantly turned into something else. At one point I saw Kyger's eyeballs in the moat. At the far northwest corner of the Castle, I looked up into the sky and saw a human-sized bright-red spider about 30 feet away, drawing thread out of its spinnerets and weaving itself into a pulsating, quilt-like, luminous dusk sky. The appearance of the spider was the sublime moment of the experience. It signified to me (by the following day) that I was being offered my poetic totem, confirming in that way that I was a poet.

Out of my body I was to create a matrix strong enough in which to live and hunt.[9]

Since my confirmational figure is lethal as well as constructive, it supports negation as well as affirmation, releasing me from the kind of idealism that permeates so much poetry. I relate to spider, web, and prey as a complex in which building, attracting, and destroying constitute a creative maze in which the way out, or resolution, can never be seen until one is right there. Without an overview, there are bound to be lots of dead ends and wrong turns, which I accept as facets of the creative process.

I began with Rimbaud's recognition that the desire to be a poet involves the realization that I is somebody else. Such a recognition also requires an apprenticeship involving (for Rimbaud) a rational disordering of all the senses and the making of the soul monstrous. Rimbaud warns that such a course of action is Promethean, but that the suffering involved may be rewarded by reaching the unknown. Another way to put this last point is to say that such an apprenticeship may result in the clearing of new ground for art.

Rimbaud's proposals are revolutionary because they re-engage poetry with humankind's very ancient quest for visions, for the power to see through the way things are, and to thus alter the nature of reality. Rimbaud's ideas here are set against the conventional tradition, in which poetry is ordinary sentiment presented gift-wrapped—the wrapping and the ribbons proposing that the unspecial contents should be treated as special. For Rimbaud, such poetry is a mockery of the poet as seer.

I then discussed my first experience with *poesis*. Unaware of Rimbaud, I spontaneously wrote as somebody else. By doing so I entered metaphor, or saw that Clayton was part of a metaphor. I then recognized Rimbaud's realization as a metaphor. I is somebody else. This is that. I proposed that this "double helix" is the soul of poetry.

After noting Rimbaud's first enactment of his core recognition, I looked at some of the ways "I is somebody else" expresses itself in poems. Whitman implied, in Section 5 of "Song of Myself" that a union with "somebody else" is orgasmic, and filled with the mystical rapture that everyone, including God, is one's brothers and sisters. Rilke pointed out that not only is every authentic work of art an embodiment of "somebody else" but that if the viewer/reader is porous enough, such works will command him to change his life. Facing a big, venomous snake in his Sicilian water-trough, D.H. Lawrence struggled to foreground mythic reception over macho aggression, lost out, and then recovered the whole struggle by imaginatively returning to "the scene of the crime." Here we saw "somebody else" is a dual role: a power that seeks to make us open to the full dimensions of an experience as well as a power that enables us to reinvent loss as a realized work. Finally, I recounted my red spider vision in which I made contact with a "somebody else" on a monstrous level: I projected my soul in a non-human way, and by doing so, made contact with one of the creative archetypes: the web becomes labyrinth becomes creative process.

Earlier, I mentioned the ancient quest for visions. Metaphor is very, very old, and, as I understand it, occurs during the Upper Paleolithic period—the last Ice Age—as early as 32,000 years ago, when humankind began to realize its difference from animals. The first workings of Rimbaud's recognition may have been the negative realization that "I" is not an animal. Such a catastrophic negation might have jump-started the journey into history: who am I? There is an image considered to be at least 30,000 years old that I feel can be read as a proto-metaphor. It consists of a stone slab with an engraved horse head and neck across which a vulva of equal size has been incised. The implicit metaphor is horse head power = vulva power.

In the "Freedom" chapter of *Love's Body*, N.O. Brown synthesizes Rimbaud's recognition with Cro-Magnon intuition:

> Symbolism is the translation of all of our senses into one another, the interplay between the senses, the metaphor, the free association. The separation of the senses, their mutual isolation, is bondage to the tyranny of one partial impulse... All metaphors are sexual; a penis in every convex object and a vagina in every concave one... To the enlightened man, the universe becomes his body: "You will never enjoy the world aright till the Sea floweth in your veins, till you are clothed with the heavens and crowned with the stars."[10]

NOTES:

[1] This essay was originally published in *The Writer's Chronicle*. It is based on my notes for teaching Introduction to Poetry classes at Eastern Michigan University.

[2] Arthur Rimbaud / *Collected Poems* (Translated from the French by Oliver Bernard), Penguin Classics, 1986, excerpts from letters to Georges Izambard and Paul Demeny, pp. 6–12.

[3] From "Novices: A Study of Poetic Apprenticeship," in *Companion Spider*, Wesleyan University Press, 2002, pp. 19–20.

[4] This translation is reprinted from *Conductors of the Pit*, Soft Skull Press, 2005.

[5] Walt Whitman / *Leaves of Grass* (The First 1855 Edition), Penguin Classics, 1986, pp. 28–29.

[6] *Translations from the Poetry of Rainer Maria Rilke*, by M.D. Herter Norton, The Norton Library, 1962, p. 181.

[7] *The Complete Poems of D.H. Lawrence*, The Viking Press, 1964, pp. 349–351.

[8] Barbara G. Walker, *The Woman's Encyclopedia of Myths and Secrets*, Harper & Row, 1983, excerpts from the "Serpent" entry, pp. 903–909.

[9] This version of the red spider vision draws upon material in *Companion Spider*, pp. 55–57, 117–120, and 308–311.

[10] The quotation within the Brown passage is from A. Govinda's *Foundations of Tibetan Mysticism*, 1959, p. 225.

THE BACKWALL OF IMAGINATION[1]

Notes on the *Juniper Fuse* Project

Introduction

The poems in my first book, Mexico & North *(1962), on the basis of two summer trips there in 1959 and 1960, mainly respond to my excitement in discovering the indigenous sensuality of Mexico. After I settled into Kyoto, in the summer of 1962, I was hit by my Indianapolis background and came to realize that before I could inhabit the present as a poet, I would have to explore this background, much of which I had simply lived with in an unexamined way. Over the next decade, I attempted to write honestly and imaginatively about my personal life, linking it when possible to various personal mythologies I invented via William* Blake, *the* I Ching, *the Aztecs, and astrology.*

Discovering the Ice Age painted/engraved caves of the French Dordogne in 1974 confronted me with a transpersonal realm that seemed to stand in direct opposition to the personal world that I had been mining. Not only was it part of an almost unimaginable time scale, but it contained a severely fragmented depth that tested any perspective on its meaning to contemporary humanity. While all of this was overwhelming, it was also exhilarating: I had leapt into an abyss and was floating about in a mist of particulars whose roots were gone. At the same time, given the antiquity of the images, it appeared that I had made contact with the back wall of culture and possibly the earliest traces of poetry.

To begin to write into what I experienced in such caves as Lascaux, Combarelles, and Font-de-Gaume entailed mounting a research project, from scratch, and undertaking a poetic investigation—a "saturation job" as the poet Charles Olson called it—that ended up spanning twenty-five years. While I had other projects during this period—poems not associated with prehistory, a translation of César Vallejo's book, Trilce, *the essays collected in* Antiphonal Swing, *and editing* Sulfur *magazine for nineteen years—the caves were the over-arching preoccupation, and I would like to think that their imaginative breakthrough and essential unfathomability invigorated my other projects and made me increasingly humble about anything I might accomplish as well as about the cultural achievements of modern humankind.*

Ideally, every poet should undertake at least one big investigative project that brings into poetry materials that have previously not been a part of it. This is one way that we keep our art fresh, and not diluted with variations played on tried and true themes. The investigative project also makes one responsible for a huge range of materials, the assimilation of which goes way beyond the concerns of the personal lyric. Since research is ongoing in paleo-archeology, I also had to determine a cut-off point, and then invent an organizational plan for the materials I had determined were pertinent as opposed to tangential.

When Caryl and I were preparing to leave for Paris for a year in the spring of 1973, a friend in Los Angeles told us to look up the translator, Helen Lane. Our letter from Paris was forwarded to her at the Bouyssou farm in Lespinasse, a hamlet a few kilometers from Les Eyzies de Tayac, in the Dordogne, a seven-hour drive southwest from Paris. Madame Bouyssou had converted some of the space in her farm complex into furnished apartments in the 1960s when H.L. Movius Jr., then excavating the Abri Pataud in Les Eyzies, needed living quarters for his graduate student assistants from Harvard. Helen wrote back to us and suggested we meet for dinner the next time she came to Paris. Her description was so magical and enticing ("You won't really have seen France unless you visit the Dordogne!"), that we rented, sight unseen, for four months, an apartment at the Bouyssou farm, across from Helen's building.

We remember our initial drive from Périgueux to Les Eyzies, down D47. Right before we picked up the Vézère River on the left, craggy limestone cliffs appeared on the right. We seemed to be passing by, and under, tons of living rock. Signs started to appear: Laugerie Haute, Laugerie Basse, Gorge d'Enfer, Grotte du Grand Roc... the air dampened, as if we were moving through a light-mottled cavern. The rock walls took on fantastic shapes: curving cauldron sides, ribbed turret-like bulgings. The ochre, dove-gray stone was wandered by long, vertical, ragged black stains.

We drove around the Dordogne in our little white convertible, a Renault Caravelle, bought second-hand upon arrival. We were told it was the model driven by Brigitte Bardot in the 1960s. Could that explain why the car so amused the French that they would smile or laugh when they saw us in ours?

It was in our Caravelle that we first crossed the single lane bridge over the Vézère River, looking for the Bouyssou farm. The bridge was so narrow the tires squeaked against the lane edges. Looking back on that passage today, we see ourselves in slow motion, crossing a bridge between worlds. In terms of our lives for the past thirty years, we were crossing our own mythic bridge into the beyond, over a river that would appear in my dream as "Atlementheneira." At that moment, a "judgment" of sorts was taking place: henceforth, we were to try to decipher the "writing" on the walls of the oldest, yet vitally present, terribly fragmentary, paradise of all.

One day we searched for the farm woman who Madame Bouyssou told us had the key to La Grèze—a tiny cave with a single engraving of a bison. We finally found what looked to be the right farmhouse, parked, and knocked. A tall gaunt woman, who obviously worked hard on the farm, appeared. "Go back to the parking area for Cap Blanc," she said, "I will follow you in my truck." After a little walk, she unlocked the metal door to the cave. Hunching over, we crowded in. A beautiful engraving of a bison, some 20,000 years old, about two feet long, with twisted horns and stiffly fashioned legs, done with precision based on careful observation. Fifty-percent bison, fifty-percent man. "Not," as D.H. Lawrence once remarked, "ninety-nine percent man, and one percent horse, as in a Raphael horse."

Hotel people told us, "If you want to visit La Mouthe, follow the road to the left of the Rocher de la Peine until you come to a farm house. Ask the old folks there to take you into the cave." Painted animals had been discovered in the cave in 1895; in 1902 La Mouthe was one of the caves that convinced the scientific world of the genuine antiquity of Upper Paleolithic imagery. We knocked, and were reluctantly led into the cave by an elderly couple who could hardly walk. After pointing out a few difficult-to-read images in the front part of the cave, they turned around and hobbled back home. A depressing experience. We had imposed on them and seen very little. We lost La Mouthe.

It turned out that Movius's secretary (a "liberated" English woman who answered the door naked to the waist) lived on the first floor of our building. She told us she would ask Movius to arrange a visit to Lascaux (closed to the public since 1963; in 1974, groups of up to five people were allowed in the cave for forty-five minutes, four days a week). Caryl's sister, Jayne, and the painters George Herms and Margaret Nielson, joined us for our May visit. The guide, Jacques Marsal (one of the original discoverers of Lascaux in 1940) made us all wait in total darkness at the entrance to the Rotunda (having passed through three steel doors and cleansed our shoe soles in a formalin solution tray). He walked away and after a minute or so, turned on the muted lights. Four immense aurochs, at once moving swiftly yet static, appeared, occupying nearly sixty feet of a curving, crystal-white wall space. Across and below them, as if sprinkled there, moving in different directions, were small horses and deer. All of us were spellbound. I think that it was that "moment of moments" that sounded something in me that I could only respond to and realize through the writing of a book.

On occasional drives north from Saint-Cyprien down into the beginning of the Vézère Valley, I had a strong sensation of being released from all earthly constraints. The third time this happened, I tried to see what about our location might explain this extraordinary feeling. As we descended, we entered a narrow, pretty vale on the far right side of which was a limestone wall which increased in height and massiveness as we drove further into the vale. I knew that the Font-de-Gaume cave was at the far end of this rock formation and that the path leading up to the cave's entrance could be glimpsed right before our road dead-ended into a road that, were one to turn right, would pass by the trail leading to Font-de-Gaume's entrance. Was it the magic of this particular composite that made me feel that I was passing through a hallowed place? Had files of deer come down this vale to drink at the Vézère? Were they hunted here? Were the reindeer depicted in Font-de-Gaume based on such deer? I intuited that the extreme ancientness of the cave's imagery acted as a kind of roving, ensouled wiring that I had abruptly plugged into. The landscape I was passing through received and reflected its charge.

At this time, there were a half-dozen or so decorated caves in the Les Eyzies area open to the public, and I soon began to realize that each had its own personality, pressing in on me as I attempted to study the paintings and engravings. Combarelles was a three hundred yard tunnel whose walls are as furrowed as elephant hide, making it, one would think, extremely resistant to engraving. Yet Combarelles is a nearly totally engraved cave with over six hundred figures and signs. Studying the faded, polychromatic bison in Font-de-Gaume I noticed how the dorsal lines are often determined by an undulating crevice in the rock, giving one the impression that the animal was in some mysterious way already half-submerged there. The paintings in Pech Merle (near Cahors) are found in a high, vaulted hall-like space with immense and fantastic columnar formations. And Cougnac (near Gourdon) is a fairyland paradise whose ceiling bristles with tiny stalactites and whose floor erupts with knobby stalagmites. Again and again we would make our way under and around these formations to the thirty-five foot long wall with ochre megaloceroses and mammoths. Across one mammoth was painted a naked humanoid with penguin-wing-like arms twisting his snout-like head around, pierced by eight spear-like lines.

Another reason we returned so often was because there was no way to spend a lot of time in any cave. In all those open to the public, we always went in with a guide, were never allowed to linger long before a painting, and were never in total dark. While the lighting was minimal, it made such caves an extension of the daylit world. I began to realize that it would be much different experience were one able to spend a night in one of these caves, opening one's own subconscious to the cave's trickster blackness.

After we began to visit the caves, Helen Lane loaned us her collection of books on Upper Paleolithic imagery. It dawned on me that all were written by professional archeologists in scholarly, objective prose, based on fieldwork and often framed by a single theory to account for the art. It appeared that no poet, other than a poem here and there, had done a serious investigation of what, to my mind, was quickly looking like the back wall of imagination. Why did such material belong solely to archeologists and their rational classifications?

Soon after our arrival in Lespinasse, we were told that Alexander Marshack, a science writer who had discovered the Upper Paleolithic in the 1960s (and published, in 1972, *The Roots of Civilization*, an impressive study of engraved portable objects), was living nearby. So we invited him over. His first words, shouted in exasperation upon entering our kitchen, were: "What is a poet doing in the caves?" That silly defiance not only placed imagination in the caves but alerted me to the fact that the research I was contemplating would not be welcomed by archeologists (or science writers dubbing themselves archeologists). As I read and revisited caves, I determined that the roots of poetry might very well be embedded in very early image-making. At that time I had not read Henry Miller's *The Colossus of Marousi* which opens with a stirring evocation of the Dordogne. Miller writes:

> To me, this country belongs to the poet, Rainer Maria Rilke.
> It is not French, not Austrian, not European even: it is the
> country of enchantment, which the poets have staked out and
> which they alone may lay claim to. It is the nearest thing to

Paradise this side of Greece... I believe that this great peaceful region will always be a sacred spot for man and that when the cities have killed off the poets this will be the refuge and the cradle of poets to come... France may one day exist no more, but the Dordogne will live on as dreams live on and nourish the souls of men.

Once back in Los Angeles in the fall of 1974, I faced the beginning of research that I knew would take many years to work through. At the same time, I had to figure out how to get back to France, not only to re-visit caves but to extend my study to the Ariège, a department in the Pyrénées, second to the Dordogne in the number of Upper Paleolithic decorated caves, the most important of which were not open to the public. At this time around one hundred and thirty French caves were known to contain Ice Age imagery.

In 1976, we managed on our own to spend another month at the Bouyssou farm, and arranged to see areas of Font-de-Gaume and Combarelles not shown to tourists. We also revisited Lascaux, were taken to some "minor" caves near Les Eyzies (one of which had only one red dot on its rear wall), and traveled to the Ariège where we visited Niaux, Gargas, and Le Portel.

We will never forget our first visit to Niaux. We approached the cave via the one-lane, hairpin, curving road that loops up a limestone spur rising more than one thousand meters above the Vicdessos, a small river that runs along the road below. We rounded a bend to suddenly face a one hundred and fifty foot high triangular cavity seemingly clawed out of the rock. It looks like either the entrance to, or the exit from, the world. In a postcard photo of this teepee-shaped entrance, the visitor cars parked out on the porch seem to be the size of tiny bugs.

Most of the hundred or so animals depicted on the walls of Niaux are in a single large circular chamber called the Salon Noir, seven hundred meters inside. Bison and horses have been painted in black manganese over charcoal sketches. Unlike the trotting, frisking, and leaping animals of Lascaux, those in Niaux hover the walls like suspended pelts—they seem to be absolutely still. Some appear to have been rapidly sketched (I thought of Franz Klein's intersecting black strokes), while others have a lot of detail: the texture of animal coats is indicated, now heavier, now lighter. Certain hooves are beautifully handled. S. Giedion, author of *The Eternal Present: The Beginnings of Art*, compared them to sketches by Rafael.

Back in Los Angeles, I came across a book-length essay by James Hillman, "The Dream and the Underworld," which, while not concerned with the pre-Grecian past, helped release me from the traditional viewpoint that cave imagery was primarily a response to hunting anxiety, or involved "sympathetic magic" for successful hunting. Hillman proposed that dreams were not merely the reflection of daytime activities, but autonomous psychic stations, as it were, with a mythic geography that constituted what some cultures have called the underworld. Perhaps, I conjectured, cave images painted or engraved 25,000 years ago, via dreaming and imagining, transformed cave "insides" into an underworld construction.

Also in 1976, George Butterick sent me Charles Olson's lecture notes (written in 1953) on the archaic past (published in 1978 as *Olson #10:* "The Chiasma, or Lectures in the New Sciences of Man"). These notes not only offered perceptive readings of a dozen or so books (that I then read myself), but turned Olson, who died in 1970, into a companion of my own journey, reinforcing the pertinence of a poet's involvement with such materials. There followed a dream in which Olson summed up some of his life and offered me a new word—"atlementheneira"—which I subsequently turned into one of the "fathers" in the longest poem in *Juniper Fuse*, "Visions of the Fathers of Lascaux."

Gary Snyder, who it turned out had done a lot of reading on the archaic past, especially in Asia, alerted me to Weston LaBarre's "The Dancing Sorcerer" chapter in his monumental *The Ghost Dance: The Origins of Religion*, which, like Olson's notes, led me to other books.

By the late 1970s, I realized that my reading was following two dovetailing directions: the writings of French and American paleo-archeologists, *and* thinkers outside of archeology proper. What had initially appeared as a domain totally dominated by academic archeologists turned out to be, in terms of speculations that I could apply, significantly different. Anthropologists, and psychoanalytically-oriented writers in particular, made observations that, when recontextualized, shed light on the creation of the first underworld.

Weston LaBarre introduced me to shamans as the oldest soul guides of which we are aware. Such led me to the writings of Eliade, Rasmussen, Shirokogoroff, and the sighting of possible proto-shamanic activity in Upper Paleolithic hybrid images. Robert Brockway's comment on "the cosmic dive" in *Myth from the Ice Age to Mickey Mouse*, led me to Eliade's *Zalmoxis*, with its "cosmic dive" lore, which in turn enabled me to bring Heinrich Zimmer's study of the *Vishnu Puranas* to bear on this archetypal cluster.

I found materials on the basic, or uterine dream, in Geza Róheim's writings, and studied N.O. Brown's comments on it in *Love's Body* where Brown linked it to Sandor Ferenczi's theory of Thalassal regression.

While caves are surely not the only source of humanity's concept of the abyss, they are probably with their organ-like, alien, and sensory isolating atmosphere the most knowable one. For abyssal fathoming I went to Kenneth Grant, the elusive 20th-century master of this occult reservoir.

I constantly used the one-volume Index to Jung's *Collected Works* to see if he had anything to say about a particular motif, creature, or image. Again and again, it struck me as odd that Jung, Freud, Heidegger, and others with things to say about the archaic, had not visited the French caves.

Hans Peter Duerr's *Dreamtime* has a dozen or so cogent pages on "the unifying womb of things" and the culture/wilderness divide. I realized that the ancient move from no image of the world to an image was responsible for such a divide.

In terms of my own poetry, I began to nibble around the edges of the archaic as soon as we returned from France in 1974, and to put poems that seemed to work into my Black Sparrow Press collections that came out every few years (eight appeared during the composition period for *Juniper Fuse*).

In 1979, Jerry Rothenberg asked for a contribution on what he called "the new wilderness," and the prose poem "Placements I" that I wrote in response enabled me to make my first statement connecting animal extinction to the 20th-century resurfacing of Upper Paleolithic imagination:

> As species disappear, the Upper Paleolithic grows more vivid.
> As living animals disappear, the first outlines become more
> dear, not as reflections of a day world, but as the primal out-
> lines of psyche, the shaping of the underworld, the point at
> which Hades was an animal. The "new wilderness" is thus
> the spectral realm created by the going out of animal life and
> the coming in, in our time, of these primary outlines. Our
> tragedy is to search further and further back for a common
> non-racial trunk in which the animal is not separated out of
> the human, while we destroy the turf on which we actually
> stand.

During these years I was making intuitive forays into my own wilderness of materials, writing poems with no book outline or goal. Such a procedure felt right. I had decided that my imaginative response to caves would count as much as rational documentation—an approach that would differentiate my work from that of the archeologists. Since I was always working on poems, it made sense to engage archaic materials when they appeared, and to anticipate that essays would come later after I had completed my fieldwork and research. One exception to this procedure came up in 1981 when I was invited to give a paper on narrative at a USC conference. I used the occasion to approach the narrative "scene" in Lascaux's Shaft. Under the pressure of the irresolvable complexity of this "scene," the prose at one point gave way to poetry.

In 1978, a Guggenheim Fellowship enabled Caryl and I to spend several months in southwestern France. We had dinner in Tarascon with Jean Clottes, then in charge of prehistoric sites in the Ariège. Clottes arranged for us to visit the most significant of the state- or privately-owned caves in his region, expanding my vista considerably. In the fall of 1980, he set up a visit to Le Tuc d'Audoubert, a very important cave outside of St. Girons, entered by the owner leading small groups only once a year. Caryl and I rented a stone cottage in the woods outside of Les Eyzies for two months, during which time we planned to drive down for the Tuc d'Audoubert visit.

As readers of *Juniper Fuse* will know, I had a bizarre car accident that fall near our cottage, was hospitalized for a week in Sarlat, and had to cancel the trip to Le Tuc d'Audoubert. What I did not discuss in my book was the effect of the accident on Caryl. After finding me and getting me to the hospital, she found out our rented car was totaled and that she had to take the train to Paris to pick up another car. A man came into her sleeping car in the middle of the seven-hour trip, and this disturbed her so much that she arrived in Paris without having slept. After being hassled by the car rental people, she got stuck behind a garbage truck for a long time and finally drove back to the Dordogne with the help of every ounce of adrenal she could muster. She realized that she had to find a new ground floor place for us to stay because it turned out I not only had a broken ankle but broken ribs, and could not climb stairs. Hotel Centenaire offered us a first floor room in their Annex outside of Les Eyzies. Driving to it, because a truck was blocking a sign, she took the wrong fork and ended up stuck in the town dump. Beside herself, she started crying and screaming. A sweet, older woman living nearby, hearing her, took her into the house and made her some tea. When the woman's sons came home, they picked the car up, turned it around, and put her on the right road. We then moved into the Annex for a couple of weeks before heading off for Germany, Caryl driving, me in a cast, for a set of readings that had been arranged by the American Consulate in Bonn.

Before the accident, while eating at Hotel Centenaire, we would often talk with the owner, Alain Scholly, about how to finance future trips to the region. Alain suggested that we propose an article on some of the best young chefs in France, and supplied us with names to contact. We sold the story idea to *Frequent Flyer* magazine, but the fee offered was not nearly enough to cover such a trip. By 1981, we figured we knew enough about the caves and the regions to lead a tour. We got together a group of seven people who would connect with us at various stages of our chef-oriented work, and then let us be their guides to the caves and inns in the Ariège and the Dordogne. We ended up taping and transcribing interviews with chefs who have since become famous: Maximin at Hotel Negresco in Nice; the late Loiseau at the Côte d'Or in Saulieu; Gardillou at the Moulin du Roc outside Champagnac-de-Belair; Chabran at Pont de l'Isère, and Mazère at Hotel Centenaire. With no explanation, *Frequent Flyer* paid us a kill fee.

After saying goodbye to our tour group, we drove back to the Ariège, and while spending an evening in Foix, called up Clottes to say hello. He told us that the following evening, he and Robert Bégouën (the current owner of the land containing the cave) would be taking some students, who had spent the summer excavating a midden outside of Le Tuc d'Audoubert, into the cave, and that there were two places left. What serendipity! We entered the cave at around 6:00 PM and emerged around midnight, covered with mud, bruised, dead tired, but, in my case, completely exhilarated. Given the amount of crawling involved, Caryl was less exhilarated. Early the next morning I wrote the first draft of "Notes on a Visit to Le Tuc d'Audoubert," which as an "anatomy" became the nuclear form for *Juniper Fuse*. Throughout the 1980s, the book project continued to put out podia in many directions, like a kind of centerless organism.

We took a second group to the caves in 1982 and went back yearly through 1985, mainly on the basis of travel article assignments from *Destinations, Diversions, The Chicago Tribune, Frequent Flyer*, and, in 1984, *Pan Am Clipper*, which featured our article on Les Eyzies on the cover and brought hundreds of clients to Hotels Cro-Magnon and Centenaire, both of which were heralded in our article. The Hotel Cro-Magnon owners responded by never letting us pay again for room, food, and wine. With the Centenaire, it was, sadly, another story. We were not in control of the photos in our article, and upon seeing the published piece were shocked to notice that the owners of the Cro-Magnon were featured, smiling, before the ivy-covered front of the hotel, in a full-page color photo, while the chef of the Centenaire was shown, in a postage stamp-sized photo, standing before a shack that looked like something animals would be kept in. Alain Scholly and his staff were incensed and while we explained what had happened, he treated us coldly, terminating what we had taken to be a solid friendship.

Partially because of our *carte blanche* at Hotel Cro-Magnon, we visited in 1987 and 1989 and developed a true affection for the owners, Jacques and Christiane Leyssales, and for their hotel—its old-fashioned, rural woodwork, their Upper Paleolithic flint and tool collection, and the terrace where under linden and chestnut trees we had many enchanted dinners (at the beginning of one we discovered a signed copy of the Abbé Breuil's *Four Hundred Centuries of Cave Art* placed on our table). The hotel's back wall was the limestone embedded in the hill up against which the hotel had been built. Around in back was the rock shelter where in 1868 the first skeletons of Cro-Magnon people were discovered. I wrote a lot in notebooks during these two visits and discovered a bonus: I felt that I had come home. I was at home in a way I had never been at home in Indianapolis where I was raised. Home on the back wall of imagination! Not only was the hotel aptly named, it was located in a vibrational field of such prehistoric resonance that "home" was leavened and emptied, at the same time, by a terrible absence and a transcendental presence.

In 1989 I also began my translation of César Vallejo's book, *Trilce*, the most demanding translation project I had taken on, and this work took up most of my creative time until the fall of 1992 when it was published. With the support of a research leave from Eastern Michigan University, Caryl and I rented a house owned by the Leyssales south of Les Eyzies on the Dordogne River. There, for the first time, I began to sketch out an outline for a book on "Upper Paleolithic Imagination & the Construction of the Underworld."

At this time I also discovered some writing that Barbara MacLeod had done based on long sits in caves in Guatemala and Belize. Her strange experiences stimulated not only by the sensory isolation experienced in forty-eight hour sits, but by "entities," according to Barbara, in the caves themselves, made me review all that I had hypothesized about Cro-Magnon mental activity in caves. No archeologist had brought up the matter of sensory isolation and how it might affect painting and engraving. I was now more than ever aware that because of the time limitations imposed on my own visits that I was not going to penetrate the mental realm opened up via darkness and sensory isolation. It now seemed that there was a link between bizarre hybrid images (bison-headed men, bird-headed women, schematic hominid figures), synesthetic experience during sensory isolation, and proto-shamanism itself. Hybrid images, combining the human and the animal, might be, I figured, attempts to rebind (or tie back, as in *religare*, from whence "religion") with the animal that was otherwise being separated out of the newly discovered Cro-Magnon imagination. This became the basis for my two part thesis on why imagery occurred where and when it did. Such images strongly evoked the kind of inner journeys reported by historic shamans: adventures, conversations, and mergers with animals and birds. Mental travel. The roots of poetry. Yet there were also many cave images that could not be proposed as shamanic.

Most of the last half of *Juniper Fuse*, about half of which is prose, was written during the 1990s. In 1995, working with Caryl, I started assembling the Notes and Commentary section, which at one point was over two hundred pages long (unlike many poets, I like footnotes and commentary, and have included such at the end of my own poetry collections). A number of the commentaries were long enough to be expanded as texts. But the text at this point was so complex and long that it did not seem right to make it even longer. At this point, I had an outline of the manuscript's contents and sections, based on chronological progression. While the completed book is essentially chronological, several pieces written in the mid-nineties were fitted into already shaped sections.

In 1997, I was finally, after numerous requests, given permission to descend into Lascaux's Shaft. Caryl was given permission too, but when she saw that she would have to swing across the Shaft's opening onto a narrow and vertical iron ladder for the eighteen-foot descent, she decided it was too dangerous, and stood in the semi-dark under the Apse while I studied, for roughly a half hour, this stupendous "scene." Standing before the painting, I remembered that my project had caught fire with our first visit to Lascaux in 1974. Here I was, in 1997, in the terminal depths of the cave, studying its most esoteric image. I knew it was time to start wrapping things up. End of research. Time to face closure.

In 1998, I had breakfast in Berkeley with the paleo-archeologist Meg Conkey, to whom I had shown around one hundred pages of my manuscript. At this point I was facing what to keep and what to take out. Meg urged me to not turn the book into a single thesis work, throwing out everything that did not fit the thesis. She said, "give them the kitchen sink!"

At this point I had an eight hundred page manuscript, with some early writings that now seemed dated, plus writing that in one way or another was repetitive. I realized that Meg's admonition was based on reading only a small portion of what I had written and that no publisher was going to accept an eight hundred page manuscript for publication. So Caryl and I cut out two hundred pages, and I began to send a description of the book out to agents and publishers.

All turned the project down without asking to see the manuscript. Typical responses: "It sounds rich and fascinating, but it'd be costly and heterogeneous in nature—two big no-nos." "Your thesis is brilliant but you need to approach it in a much more rigorous and disciplined manner." "When it comes to titles dealing with ancient history, we are seen as an academic house and a book that is as literary in tone and flavor as yours simply wouldn't flourish under our imprint." A friend suggested that I contact David Stanford at Viking Penguin, who was the Kerouac and Burroughs editor. David asked to read the manuscript and wrote me that he loved it. We arranged to meet for lunch in NYC. A week before our meeting, he called and informed me that he had just been, after eighteen years there, fired. We had lunch anyway, and David said that had he not been let go he would have done the book. He passed it on to the managing editor with a strong recommendation to publish. Paul Slovac then held the manuscript for sixteen months without reading it. I had to contact his boss to get him to make Slovac mail it back.

While the manuscript was collecting dust at Viking Penguin, I decided that I would also show it to Allan Kornblum at Coffee House Press, who had expressed interest in reading it. After six months, he wrote and said that if I would cut it in half, chances are that Coffee House would publish it. Of course he gave no indication as to which three hundred pages should go. I thought about this for a week, and rather than turning him down, I decided that I would see how much I could cut without damaging the manuscript's integrity. Caryl and I found that on re-reading it, certain poems that were good in themselves bore only a tangential relationship to the book's focus. For example, here is "Fracture," the title poem for *Fracture*, 1983:

The crutch you hand to another
is a furious indescribable beast,
tectiform of your own shape as Eve staggers

out of Eden, the vile legacy in hand,
wandering the dust, offering to whoever
passes by a rotting piece of it, one peso,

by a Mexican roadside, her palm outstretched—
an open heart ceremony announcing
that all dark, all light, is the sawing

of being on being, a circular coring,
a ceremony lit by tapers made of entire
kingdoms. Earth, pieta. And as the dark

is serrated by light you will start to hear,
as if at Gargas, the chalky cries of
hands, mutilated negatives, clouds of mouths

rising up the walls, virgin moths
mourning over caterpillars they have gathered
into their wings, crying the oldest cry,

that earth is responsible for our deaths,
that if we die collectively
we will take the earth with us *if we can*—

who does not hear our cries
seeks to contain us in that American cottage
where a nameless stand-in coils about

the solitary fang of Snow White dead at 27.
Please let our howls, elastic with water,
become that still lake most men abhor,

out of which Excalibur rises in the grip of
a drowned living Harlow whose wavering
stench of generation is holocaust to

all who seek to destroy their need
for that gleaming nipple below whose face
enwound with coral snakes is a squid haze of stars.

The several lines on the mutilated "hand negatives" in the Gargas cave did not seem to us to justify including "Fracture." We also decided that a seventy-page set of lectures on caves visited by our tour groups (which I read on each tour before a cave was visited) could be dropped as too introductory relative to the purpose of the manuscript. We ended up cutting it to four hundred and twenty pages and presented this version to Kornblum. I heard nothing more from Coffee House Press for another six months (surely, I thought, someone there would have something to say about what we took out versus what we left in). Then an email one morning: "Book is too expensive for us to produce; we are $200,000 in debt." I had the strong impression that no one at Coffee House had read either all of the original manuscript or any of the revised one.

[In mentioning our cave tours above, I should bring that *Juniper Fuse*-related activity up to date: after our second tour in 1982, Caryl and I decided that it was too much work to handle such a tour completely on our own. For years we did nothing more about it. Then in 1995 the School of Continuing Education at Eastern Michigan University offered to sponsor us, and we went in 1996 with Gary Snyder coming along as guest lecturer. In 1999, Continuing Studies and Special Programs at the Ringling School of Art and Design in Sarasota took on our tour and have sponsored trips from 2000 to the present; Robert Creeley, Dale Pendell, and Wade Davis have joined us as guest lecturers].

After the depressing experiences with Viking Penguin and Coffee House Press, I sent the edited-down version of the manuscript to Wesleyan University Press, which had already published collections of my Vallejo and Césaire translations, and had under contract a collection of my essays. Wesleyan accepted the manuscript, and *Juniper Fuse* was published in a handsome format in October, 2003.

Caryl and I initially went to France at the point when I had worked through my apprenticeship to poetry—in *Indiana* (1969), *Altars* (1971), and *Coils* (1973)—years of self-confrontation involving an excavation, at times ruthless, of my Indiana background, in effect, my given life, including its racist, Christian, and sexist values. In 1973, I was hungry for an alternative to myself. Going to the Dordogne the following spring was utter serendipity. I was suddenly faced with an ancient transpersonal world, one that is still, decade after decade (starting for the most part at the turn of the 20th century), revealing the shards, as it were, of its once magnificent vessel. Involving a 25,000-year continuum, caves and objects were decorated by groups that had no knowledge of each other. Yet there are continuities, filled with variations, spanning thousands of years. The Venus statuettes, occurring from southwestern France to northeastern Siberia, appear to have been carved for over 23,000 years. While they vary considerably, they appear to share an archetypal design. While numbers and kinds of depicted animals vary from cave to cave, the frequency of horse and bison images suggest that these animals appealed to many groups of the Cro-Magnon people. Middens reveal that such people for the most part did not depict on cave walls what they ate. Decorated caves were not lived in nor were they used as burial sites. There are no hunting scenes per se, only a few sketchy indications of intercourse, no birth scenes, no images of babies, and only a few scenes that could be interpreted as depicting violence. There is no evidence in these caves of what we would call war.

Have I, through these crawls and research, reached the back wall of imagination? Yes and no. New caves are discovered almost yearly, and the discovery of Chauvet in 1994, with one 32,000 year old painting—nearly twice as old as those in Lascaux—indicates that image-making as we understand it today is much older than previously thought. Gouged patterns on stone, crude human figurines, and apparent ritual use of red ochre have been found in South Africa and Australia at dates before the Upper Paleolithic. While on one hand, there appears to be a dynamic "coming into image" at the beginning of the Upper Paleolithic, it now seems clear that imaginative vectors were shifting about and assembling in visual patterns thousands of years earlier. At this time, the earliest points in which metaphor appears certain include a Chauvet painting in which a "minotaur" bends over a Venus figure with a huge black vulva, and:

> At Abri Cellier: the neck and head of a blowing
>   horse
> crudely engraved in a stone block.

Across the neck, a vulva a bit bigger than the horse
    head has been gouged.
"The original sentence, the original metaphor: *Tat
    Tvam Asi*. Thou art that."
Blowing horse head = vulva,
thus: a blowing horse head vulva,
"Convulsive beauty will be veiled-erotic, fixed-
    exploding,
magic-circumstantial or it will not be."
The *exploding* and the *fixed* at 30,000 B.P.,
the Aurignacian "hydrogen jukebox."

NOTES:

[1]This essay appeared in *American Poetry Review*. The quotations from
the poem "Matrix, Blower" (from *Juniper Fuse: Upper Paleolithic Imagination & the Construction of the Underworld*), which ends this essay, are from
N.O. Brown's *Love's Body*, André Breton's *Mad Love*, and Allen Ginsberg's
Howl, respectively.

II

LENINGRAD JOURNAL

Leaving creates an undertow
resplendent with abyss.
The Bashō thrill of setting forth:
possible illumination, possible demise.

Caryl will stay home.
As I fly off, the ants of the abyss
will centripetally draw my tears into
a tiny wreath which, at 36,000 feet,
I will place on her head.

Dear things
because of dearest you.

Each coupling enNoahs a wake
in which the dreamer and the dead are dipped
flamehood. For each, a single face
more potent than light.

Caryl, swirl of leaves settling on
prow of the ark I can be.

Wedges of ice-wigged khaki firs.
  Villages enclayed with snow.

Jung's gibbon to be reconstructed in the square—
the garroted center to be
reconstructed from a circumference
where ego is satellite to a body growing downward into ice.

               I too am frozen,
a gnat on the edge of the grindstone of desire.

Dinner: December 9, 1989. Meatballs, pot-stickers, sweetened
curdy cheese, Georgian brandy.

Smoke-filled bus ride to the Repin House, now a museum.
Given foot slats to tie on before entering.

Sense of Repin's house: an attempt to hold a vision in place—veg-
etarian dinners—no servants—"do it yourself" protocol at dinner
table. On each Wednesday a flag was raised: visitors were welcome.
Repin called wine "sun energy."
  Round dining room table with Chinese lazy susan. Drawers for
guests to put dirty dishes into. If you failed to follow dining protocol, the "general" would order you to climb a small stairway up into
the corner of the room and make a witty speech.

Back at our living quarters, "Repino." Big boring official welcome.
Speeches. Red chairs and curtain turning the sun into a glassy glare
behind the speakers' heads.

     Sun over
       ice over
     unregenerate gulf.

Most Russians seem to smoke incessantly.

Bureaucratic stiffness. No "perestroika" in action yet. Churls run things. Artists struggle on a periphery. Eighty percent of their energy goes into survival.

We Americans took a walk in solid zero cold. Tried to figure how to alter the five-day program.

Film: *Fountain* by Yuzy Mamin.
      Sterotypical satire on housing.
   Entropy defeats hysteria—
      or: Soviet life,
a carnival of hysteria and entropy.

❦

8 p.m., December 10. This trip is a mistake. At least the so-called "Seminar" is. Perhaps the last five days with Arkadii Dragomoshchenko will be more engaging. No way to talk with the Russians. The "Seminar" consists of formal, poorly translated special presentations. Cross-purposes galore. Unless real Russian interest in my work is demonstrated, in the future stay home.

Dinner: cheese-egg curd, cold perogi (I gave mine to Arkadii), small fish fried with carrot strips, mashed potatoes. Then to the bar where a bottle of brandy was placed on each table.

Russian language sounds: consonant corduroy and slush.

❦

6 a.m., December 11

Jackie Och's noble film, *Agent Orange.*

> Your photo over my head
> by what would be the bedstead—
> your intense all-piercing gaze.
> I live by it, under it, ashamed and moral.
> I've entered, via a baffle gate,
> the mortal difficulties of a man.

By bus into Leningrad to a tourist hotel to change money. Heavy, salty, fleshy-tasting mineral water. Before the hotel: bus tour of Leningrad. Italianate building colors (pink, rose, light blue, green, yellowish gold). Immensely spacious city, enrivered. Forty-one islands. In the beginning (1703), there were over one hundred (the city being built on coastal swamps). Rarely any lightness, frill, arabesque. Ships in ice. Nuclear ice-cutter. Occasionally an art-deco-like store (the one we visited, beautiful! with people buying sweets, canned goods, no charm to the produce).

Then walk six hours. To Pan American Airlines to see if my suit-case has arrived. No luck. Then to a kind of bar/café. No tea. Fresh very sour cranberries in goblets stuccoed with sugar. Sweet Turkish coffee. Well-dressed young people ("black market" involved, our poor student guide, Vasily, guessed).

I turned into a scream and locked on the sound.
In hollow majesty: the frozen canals of Leningrad.

Russian person dwarfed by vast avenues, giganticized in tiny rooms.

On the street: exploding, fur-capped zigzag. Queued clumps along a wall for gray bricks of ice cream (handed out of a crate like mili-tary supplies).

I tread behind Vasily's army-overcoated back—
sensation of following an endless domino train.
We are up to our neck in backs,
and very old...
                    will we reach a door
where Nausicaä will be rubbing the grayness out of newborn
    babies?

A door through which is a green meadow, friendly dogs?

Or is each door the side of a large garbage container on which
the poet Dragomoshchenko, a fifteen-pound raven, is beating his
    wings,
king of frozen green orange rinds?

                    Russian Communism forces
                        the individual to reinvent capitalism daily.
        The work of Communism:
        to scotimize.

The soul of Russia is ice,
Germany fire,
America money.

A twelve-foot bronze Vladimir Mayakofsky (in rivet-studded vest),
proclaiming a metro stop.

"I want to show you something very, very special,"
Vasily's mother said, leading me into a five-year-old apartment
    complex,
already a crumbling labyrinth.

People, tiny ships, oceanic immensity.
"Hey Jude" with mushy strings.
A pepper so void of pungency it brought tears to my eyes.

In public: no laughter, *no noise.*

Back to Repino for dinner: kasha and stewed beef. Double sauna one hundred feet from the lodge (afterwards, tea with Abigail Childs, the two of us wrapped up in huge towels). Finnish (dry), Russian (wet). Ex-sailor-cook runs it—very obliging—I thought I was to pay him, but he refused to take any payment. Walked me back to the lodge back door and said good night, after brushing my back and stomach with odiferous branches.

Child's video *Mayhem* of some interest. Saw several by other women. All of some interest: portmanteau piggyback dismantling of the archetypal text in narrative media material. Goofy 1940s skin flick "resolved" in *Mayhem.*

Now bed. Midnight.

[Go back to "A Cross Section of the Incarnation" as possible title poem for book; check worksheets. Perhaps add an "Argument" before the poem, as Blake did. Something like: the discovery of the generate power of semen was the beginning of the discovery of the monotheistic god. Suddenly, in the parthenogenetic dark of wo-man, a white star glowed, turning the womb into a stage, conduct-ed by God's wand...]

"Eliot's Drawers"   THE WASTELAND
                        THEA TSE LAND
collage/cut up of poem   revealing the subtext,
i.e., destroy it.

Tom's Drawers

April and Cruelest are breeding,
mixing waste, race, and mind.
April's furrow is called Rat's Alley.
Cruelest's harrow, the Dead Man Bone, or
        Boner, if you prefer to be vulgar,
Loner, if you think of the world as a womb.
"I, April, in the cloak of Vivian,
rattle my epigram again, I, in my bottle,
forever awaiting carbuncular Cruelest, or
        Tom, if you prefer to confess,
TSE, if your criterion is indifference.

Supine on the floor of Possum's canoe
bleeding bleeding bleeding—
Was she Graves' great white bitch,
and did Tom bleed her, as one milks a ewe?
Behind her did heretic Eve
entwine grail castle?
Cruelest still creeps April's vegetation,
Cruelest still fishes haha hehheh hoho in her dull canal,
for the sink below mind has yet to be surveyed,
its phallic plumbing, packed with wands and bones,
broken plungers, has yet to be flushed.

So I have hung Tom's drawers from the spike of the poem
in honor of his human scale
—not that all men must be virile—
        but that it is time to notice
what is behind the objective correlative,
in poetry to lift the Tiresias helmet mask from Vivian
and to hand her what her soul in eternity requires:
the dull roots of modernism on the confessional pyre

Hermitage Noon–4:20 PM

> Rembrandts (twenty-six or twenty-seven, some falling out
>   of their frames)
> · Velázquez!
> da Vinci
> one of the Zubarán *Crucifixions*

  We started out in the late-19th collection,
 then taken to "the gold room"

Scythian mythology (4–600 BC)
    vs.
the Tsar's jewels   like stallion testicles.

If you peer into the diamond spermwork, you can see peasant arms
disappearing.

"We met in a town about 4 hours from Leningrad—
everyone there is either an alcoholic, in prison, or insane."

Candles wrapped like flowers in cellophane against the wind,
hundreds clustered about an angel with a cross
        for Sakharov
"he had a message to deliver
but since he was surrounded by goons
he couldn't get it through…
        I sat by him… his hands trembled,
    his face was blotched."

Dinner at Writers Club restaurant:
    fish plate   salmon roe
meat (?) and wild mushrooms
  mineral water
    brandy.

The opera *Khoranshchina*
    Romantic Russian 19th-century view of the 17th century—
    like our "wild west"
        melodramatic, turgid, some sets striking.
Sense of massive, clumsy power overgilding. Doing everything
to excess, or *badly*. Curious filigree—lightness—tiny women,
frail delicate people every so often.

Feels like a medieval world
    draped Revolution,
then almost immediately sealed over.

      When a Russian stands up for himself:
crazy major chord: an army of accordions
                  masticating "Giant Steps."

                        ❦

Repino, 13 December

Almost dawn, and it will stay this way
all morning long. A solitary figure
trudging through snowy woods recalls Stevens'
"dark shape moving in a shapeless incessance,"
near never-light, the condition north of Leningrad…

Mind, windhover, would brood itself,
draw off its impulse accumulatives…
a specific marrow inside of what can be imagined—

I look up—   tall branchless birch at break sway.
There is a false sense of poetry in saying
    the "truth" is in the break, as if
in the white splintered stump
the birch's meaning is discovered.

Yet one does want one's heart to emerge
followed by all the ark organs, led by heart,
to create the vessel of the poem…
this too is momentary. Cauldron, keep fuming,
scent this troubling period. Aging, low testosterone.
How ashamed I am to not fulfill you so that parental death,
Sam and Irene, in one year, does not clog
    your own heart's vibrancy.

    The sky tightens—the snowfall ceases—
birches, ghostly priors, are manganese in black bark welts.

Being stands forth, most dreaded absence.

Am I not now, at 54, an active hospice, filled to capacity?

Minutes, lace on pins. At no moment will I be free, transparent.
At no moment will life difficulties lift.
Something in childhood said they might.
It is mother again, the cradle archetype entering midnight's room.
A good, one might say,   eternity pulsing
    below the awareness of mortality.

A loose mucous stains my sense of powerful self.
I'm a male in my cage in outer dark,
rattling the heart bars, testing the "why" a woman
    complexly curls about.

Diane Hall and Doug Hall slides.

Visits to four Leningrad artist studios:
- #1: pathetic "how to draw" painter
- #2: artist not home
- #3: Arkadii's son (20, with some talent)
- #4: the painter "Africa," who had no paintings
  in his studio!

time to go home   Dinner was to be served.
                         It was not.

*

14 December, Thursday

Appears that my suitcase is irretrievably lost. I am entitled to $250 "inconvenience money" on the 19th. *Ariadne, wish me luck!*

Victoria Vartan, Russian-Armenian widow tells me over porridge and coffee I make for both of us: she sold one million copies of her last book. The government took all but 5500 rubles [Interruption: thirty seconds after calling out to Ariadne, a call from Pan Am: my suitcase is in Kennedy! Never left—will be flown in this evening!]

When I returned from the phone, Victoria presented me with a colorful soup spoon (she also wants my help in finding an apartment exchange in Washington DC or NYC, so she can complete a novel there, but she has no dollars, so unless someone offers her complete expenses there is no way to pull it off). A small brunette, black-eyed woman in her mid-fifties. Her husband died of cancer a year ago. She offered to loan me some of his shirts.

Excellent film, *Day of Eclipse* (reminded me of a Russian version of *The Passenger*) by Andrei Sokurov, this afternoon. I was the only American who stayed through its 2½ hours.

❧

15 December

This morning I read "Placements I" and "The Death of Bill Evans" at The Writers Union. Small ornate table. A dozen deep ornate chairs. We rode there in zero weather in our *air-conditioned* bus. Got my suitcase, minus one wheel—but I almost did not get it.

After lunch at The Writers Union we were told a better bus would pick us up and pass by Pan Am on the way back to Repino. We waited. Then we were told: *bus is here, but no driver.* Then: *bus is here, driver is inside The Writers Union.* More waiting. After twenty minutes I pestered Arkadii: if the driver is here, why can't we find him?

That is a good question, and it is soon discovered that the driver is somewhere in The Writers Union café. So I then said: why don't you go get him? Others were enlisted in our cause. Then we were informed: *driver has been standing on the far side of the bus all this time.* So we all got onto the old bus. Driver got in too. Nothing happened. Driver got out. WHY? We were then told: *Arkadii is not a member of The Writers Union, and the Director said that since Arkadii also has another publisher (?), he, the Director, is not concerned about us.*

I watch time melt. Maybe you could take me to Pan Am in a taxi, I ask our guide, Tatania. She finds a car (in front of the bus) with a man sitting in it. He agrees (she pays him) and we arrive at 4:30 p.m. (all of this having taken two hours). Now, with baggage, we wait (outside, as Pan Am closes early) forty-five minutes for the "new bus," with our group, to come and pick us up. Finally the bus comes, but it is the old one we had gotten back into before, with the driver who would not take us. Because Arkadii criticized rhymed verse in a discussion in Russian after my reading, I am told, we were not told that *the driver could be hired!* Hired? Yes, they found out, after a one-hour wait, for fifteen rubles (= $2), he would drive us back to Repino (one hour). So, we're off. This time there is no air-conditioning but the heater and the windshield de-icer do not work. He stops every few minutes and with a salty rag tries to clear the huge windshield.

I gave some presents away. Ate a typical dinner. Now it is 8:30 a.m. Absolutely dark out. No, not quite—traces of snow can be seen on trunks and branches.

"I want to know where my first loved one is buried"—Arkadii's "dad," year after year, filling out government forms.

"One of the advantages in having used the Cinema Club Lodge at Repino," Arkadii also said, "is to have provided left-over food for the employees to take home."

‌‌‌
‌

17 December. Sunday.

Dinner Saturday night at Arkadii's. Rice and squid.

Met Dimitri Spivak, who writes books on altered consciousness, and Mikhail Khazin, who has translated Rothenberg, Creeley, and Hejinian. I proposed to try to raise $50 a month, for a year, for four Russian translators to work full-time on the American poetry of their choice. Also met the poet Parschchikov's ex-wife, Olga, who proposed several essays on Russian art for *Sulfur.*

We have now moved from Repino to an outlying district of Leningrad. I am in a tiny apartment of the Kan family. Endless seeming proliferation of rectangular five- to nine-story buildings.

No interior décor. Arkadii lives five minutes from the Kans. Supposedly very dangerous to walk this neighborhood at night. I walk home around midnight. No problems.

This afternoon I am picked up by Olga—who talks without pause and whose English is about forty percent comprehensible. We visit the Leningrad painter Timor Novikov. Walk through the apartment to a small room where four men are watching TV. Novikov is not friendly. Reminds me of "cool" jazz musician stance of the 1950s. He had told Olga he had some paintings to show us. Once we arrive, he says he has no paintings in the apartment. Instead, we are handed his publicity pack and a stack of snapshots of paintings. We stayed only half an hour.

Bus to Dimitri Spivak's lovely old apartment. He and his wife live with his parents; father a retired army psychiatrist, mother an ex-ballet dancer. Warm sophisticated people. The apartment is large, well-furnished, comfortable. They put out a simple but tasty dinner: crab salad, warm quiche, white wine, tea. Then Dimitri's father invites me to the circus.

A fast half-hour walk through the park and wide desolate avenues. His friend manages the circus and gets us front row seats. One ring, with flag-draped entrance. 7:30 to 10 p.m., one intermission. More like old-fashioned vaudeville than our three-ring circuses. Lots of clown skits. Suddenly I was picked out of the audience by the young woman ringmaster and asked to spin a large ball on upraised forefinger, which I was unable to do. I suspect my invitation was secretly arranged by Mr. Spivak. Lots of animal acts. Dogs, pelicans, horses, elephants, two monkeys, one cat.

Joke: in Capitalist hell, they pound a nail into your butt every day. In Communist Hell? Well, there the Devil is drunk most of the time (the newly-arrived brightens at this news to then be told: except near the end of each month when quotas must be met—then you get five nails in your butt every day).

◖

Monday, 18 December

No public aesthetic here. No walls with posters, not even a simple white Spanish wall, with some flowers, or craft. It seems to be planned, as if beauty is evil, or capitalistic. I will never forget those people shivering in the cold, standing in line, waiting for bricks of ice cream. In Novikov's room (where we were told he paints), the most prominent thing was the TV. Nothing to look toward, or up to? Through? At the circus: the grim expression on the faces of the women selling buttons and programs. Again and again, the unending correspondence between wide avenue, pushed-back architecture—everything falling back and into stolidity—and the lack of color, of contour, *immediate presence*. One is a dwarf outside, a giant inside. Does this tell us something about Russian psychological make-up?

> The Spivaks own a 1765 grandfather clock.
> It rang while I was in the study,
> non-vibrational, friendly, hollow
> > purring gears.
> I ran my fingers down its side, sort of petting it.

> Out of the roasted goose cavity
> the eyes of those with frost for eyebrows stare.

Large Santa Claus figures in the streets, like homecoming parade constructions. Father Frost, the New Year ceremony, the only ones, they say, that survived Stalinism.

◖

20 December
10:15 a.m.

Ride through nearly dark Leningrad one hour on the way to the airport. Headlight dots, lion pupils, ambering through dense non-light. Thoughts of Jack Spicer, of Humbaba, the god whose face is composed of entrails, enemy of Gilgamesh, a labyrinth figure of at least Neolithic antiquity. So I composed the following:

The man whose face is composed of entrails
is honest about the labyrinth—
its spill and its anti-spill are hydrant in his gaze
—if it is a gaze (the pinhole eyes of Jack Spicer,
dawn headlights in Leningrad ambering through).
Humbaba wears his dilemma as his puss,
he has a puss, not just a face, but the pus
under, the pile-driven confusion under mask.
No emergence can occur other than through his pores.
All seek Humbaba in any met face—
all seek a labyrinth man to lead through
what for the baby croc is more and more mother,
recombining shells.
                    Humbaba wears a fortress
in his brow, he is a weight-lifter
whose power is concentrated facial timber
(Should we surround Schwarzenegger with praise?
                    Or with dynamite?)
Humbaba has charisma, charisma is a labyrinthine
block.
          Your need for affirmation pulls you in.
Humbaba is the resistance to getting out.
Humbaba lies in wait as the encirclement's core.
Humbaba cannot be taken by storm.
          Humbaba is the middle wall.

Russian pop rock: an undulating, heavy, dirty velvet curtain.

Yesterday, Dimitri Spivak arranged a meeting for me with ethnol-
ogists at the Kunstkamera. I was taken to meet *the* Russian special-
ist in Upper Paleolithic image-making. He delayed his class for fifteen minutes to talk with me, very enthusiastically, at breakneck
speed, explaining his theories (via Vasily's poor English—Spivak
had to leave after introducing us—the one time I really needed a
bilingual interpreter!). Then he gave me a signed copy of his book,
saying, I think, that he recognized me when I walked into his office
as one of those who love the long story of mankind. He and the
Spivaks were jovial sparks in the unending night of this place.

Then walked with Vasily for a couple of hours. Ate lunch in a
mournful hall that used to be a bank. Consume; plate of potatoes;
part of a pepper. Coffee-flavored water. Bill for the two of us:
$1.50.

Then out into the slush looking for gifts. Walked an hour to a place
closed for inventory. Then to another place half-open, with a rope
closing off the section with nice gifts. In a third place I found a little handmade box for Caryl, dolls for nieces, and four funny pink
cherub candles.

Then by metro to Mikhail's where I was to have my last supper in
Leningrad. He is one of the four translators I have promised to try
to raise support money for. He and his wife and four-month old
baby live in his deceased father's flat. It is bearable. Sweet, friendly
people. She speaks French and at considerable cost and effort had
made a tasty meal: pickled tomatoes, eggs, cheese curd, sauerkraut,
chopped apples, followed by stewed beef and boiled potatoes. I
brought a bottle of Chianti. Mikhail had stood in line, outdoors, for
several hours in order to purchase a small bottle of vodka. After
dinner a friend of theirs showed up, with Zeena, Arkadii's wife. He
is a small, intense man, with sparkling eyes and a bushy beard from
Siberia. He and his family—including two young children—live in

a communal apartment with "a demented homosexual." Nearly everyone here has a story that breaks your heart.

My feet feel pounded. No memory of dreams.

[1989]

BACON STUDIES (III)

"Bacon at Pompidou"[1]

Bacon's studio: volcanic midden.

1935: an animal pawing up into a garden—sensation probing interior decoration.

...*at the Base of a Crucifixion*—the crucifixion itself: Europe, 1944.

Figures like larvae spawned in concentration camps.

The inhuman as the exhaust of the grotesque.

Bacon's roller rink starts up in the 1945 *Figure in a Landscape*—the orange ground in the '40s (rust–fire–blood exotica) essentially his studio. The world put into a stained box. An ex-interior decorator working in a slaughterhouse.

Bacon's flesh: plaster-tarred, cream-tinted, pink smoke bodies. Black ham snowing through debris-littered skin.

Evoking T.S. Eliot's:
"Withered root of knots of hair
Slitted below and gashed with eyes,
This oval O cropped out with teeth:
The sickle motion from the thighs."

Bed as crib sweating with primal abuse.

White bandage-like arrows, cupidic caricature.

Head II (1949): lower teeth become a tiny white hand attempting to reach palate.

Bacon's screaming mouths are mute, frozen, open manholes. They appear almost without heads, as if the body's toothed sewer can manifest in any of its members.

"The street caved in like a syphilitic's nose"
                              —Mayakofsky

Executives in tub-like cribs with apple-shaped open mouths. Eden-inverts. As if one could sink one's teeth into the Pope's solid, apple-shaped scream.

Eisenstein at Nuremberg.

But Popes do not scream or suffer Jewish genocide. These Popes are Bacon-projected, holy sadism pinned to a throne, or immersed in a uterine bath.

Painting as snail trail, a painter's mental excrement.

The painter as nebbish in tennis shoes, a chump, a comma parked without sentence.

The limits of Bacon's commitment to his own experience: no scenes of flagellation, cocksucking.

Muted buggery, naked lunch *sur l'herbe*.

Man in Blue (1952): corporational hives as imperial saloons.

Bacon's bravura: unceasing deconstruction/titillation of calligraphic grace.

Dog about to vomit into a gutter grate: Hecate before her mirror.

Van Gogh holds his blackened cock, pissing an aster into the bloody surf of a Bacon basin.

Bacon's titles rhyme his figural ambiguity.

Muriel Belcher, battered Medusa with red bulb clown nose.

Human baboon taffy barber pole.

Looks like mastodon bones form the Bacon roller rink around the base of the right-hand panel of *Crucifixion* (1962).

The strife in de-elegantizing.

The lure of beauty in remembered sadism.

Deft Pope crinoline meringue under a blood-stucco shawl, 1965. I sense the horrors of Vietnam in the Pope's exploded face.

Legless Pope on a motorized throne navigating the floor of a closed department store.

Henrietta Morae's flaccid, swollen, wild-boar visage.

Can anyone look hard at this century for a minute without turning away?

Overheard on the Bacon phone: the ongoing party on the *Lusitania*.

Does Bacon study police photos? He never fully renounces decorative elegance. Example: the man chewing into another man (in the 1967 *Sweeney Agonistes*) has vanilla ice cream buttocks.

Bacon's males, penile heads plastered-down with black hair, often excrete deformed shadows.

No end to the pulling down of the hunting blind of history.

Man as a Dionysian junk bond.

Polypus of two men mirrored with an arched forearm jamming in the anvil.

George Dyer as a Hitlerian triskelion boxer revolving along a scarlet beam.

The more coherent the more unstable.

Swastika of male flesh opening a black umbrella.

Figure in Motion (1976): thigh-arm, peeled to the rose of its violet bone, jutting out and out, charred. Not even death will stop it. An eye opening in the stump.

Realism in underwear at the end.

NOTES:

[1] Based on notebook entries made at the 2000 Bacon Retrospective at Pompidou, Paris. This piece has appeared in *House Organ*, *T-L-E* (Paris), and *Everwhat* (Zasterle Press, La Laguna—Tenerife, Canary Islands, 2003).

BACON STUDIES (IV)

"Bacon the Headhunter"[1]

Bacon's portraits (heads) are made of semen, blood, and soot.

George Dyer's head—hunted relentlessly in the 1960s—is composed of battered irregular bolts, chunks of semen-smeared rock, soot-packed sockets, the head as a sooty body sock of blood and sperm.

Faces in which a dog jerks against the leash while attempting to bound from its head kennel.

Heads lathered with white as if the brain were semen, as if the extension of the locus of life was the marrow in male bones.

George Dyer with no knowledge of who he is,
scored metal, punished ore,
asnore in shock, in mufflered stress,
cold meat blue, an anal rose rolled nose,
no knowledge of who is,
poop dribble chin,
no who ledge, no is.

Isabel Rawsthorne's face, sibyl and alley cat.

Rawsthorne as a head hide or hair-hived head on a tiny hair body, flesh torqued as if by a rotary blade.

There is a police museum in Henrietta Moraes' gore–magenta–black hair wound about and twisted through her skull.

Well, is it cruel or not to see an "elephant man" in a beloved face? Or is it to accept the chance and fate that clambered aboard the sitter's fetal raft?

Does one dishonor sexuality by viewing the head as genital tripe? Is Bacon in effect sticking voodoo pins into his portraits? Is his swirling bravura designed to eliminate the pain from these trophy heads?

In thatches of blood, semen, and soot, being stands forth over the depth charge of absolute absence.

Ah, the seltzer of self, the carbonated, carboniferous antiquity of the ever-evaporating self!

NOTES:

[1] This piece was published in *Hunger* magazine, *Everwhat* (Zasterle Press, La Laguna—Tenerife, Canary Islands, 2003), and the online *Double Room #7*. The imagery at the beginning of this piece draws upon Weston LaBarre's *Muelos: A Stone Age Superstition about Sexuality* (Columbia University Press, 1984). According to LaBarre, participants in ancient as well as modern skull cults believed that the semen-like marrow in the bones was the source of semen, and that the skull, "as the bone enclosing the most plentiful *muelos*–marrow in the body (the brain) is therefore the major repository of the generative life-stuff or semen." This superstition would appear to account for aspects of human behavior that would otherwise remain mysterious or misinterpreted. It not only, in part, explains cannibalism and head-hunting, but adolescent fellation, sodomy, and superstitions concerning ejaculation and women.

Bacon's heads often appear to be sites of violence, grotesque distortion, and psychological tumult, slashed and contoured with swirls of black, red, and especially white paint, evoking a fantasmagoric vision of the brain that is discussed by LaBarre in his book.

P L A N E T   T R I L C E [1]

The temperature is a constant 33,000,000,000,000,333 calories.

A feminine planet, immortally dead, garbed in tenacious carbon attire, *Trilce* gave birth to her husband as her first child.

Her equator is nickel-plated with a single stripe.

Eternally drizzleshined, she has ciliate reefs. Because of a great collapse, the highest points are craterized, leaving Sunday bigmouthed and dumb with sepulcher.

Mountainous minutes ceaselessly midwife and date the atmosphere's insurgent niches.

Her mountains are mis-asphalted oxidants of Hindu furniture.

Guano, that simple treasurreal ponk, is toasted by brackish pelicans.

Rain rises from below—her people rise downward.

The Mondays of reason are incised with muck.

Waves, fanged with transfixed chelonian ls, unfold on labiate tungsten platters.

All births take place at 1 p.m.

The elderly spend their days unplugging the tap of dusk.

Souls using white crowns saw through the hearts of the living.

Dead exist who have never lived.

No two days ever touch each other.

Orgasm's mute thunder sounds Rednuhtetum!

Shops are plated with carnivores in rut.

News item: Saintgabriel has just penetrated ecumenical mary.

Suffering from myth to myth, messengers arrive chewing ice.

When that which cannot burn does burn, pain doubles up its
   peak in laughter.

While fodder is always in leaf, only absurdity is pure.

Substantives, in honeyed crystalline molds, adjectivize in self-
   offerings.

All retreats are made across exploded bridges.

Each coin urinates natural grandeur.

Nuance is prepared with a strong stock of wings, mashed causes,
   and fried boundaries.

In the hospital, Wednesday peels back its camphor nails while
   Death solders limits to strands of lost hair.

On *Trilce*, there is more than enough sweetness for the whole
shroud.

On *Trilce*, there is still hope of finding, for the saltatory power,
eternal entrance.

NOTES:

[1] This piece appeared in *Verse* magazine and *Everwhat*. While translating César Vallejo's book *Trilce* (1922) in the late 1980s, I became aware
that he was assembling in a kind of jump-cut cubistic way a world that
operated with much different laws than we think ours does. It seemed as
if he was envisioning a new planet. My piece is thus a collage of some of
the elements that to my mind make up "Planet Trilce."

THE   SURREALIST   REVOLUTION [1]

Pompidou, Paris, 2002

Picasso's *Le Basier*—eyes, mouths, cogs turning in a tar of penetrating heads.

A cavity tolling like a bell in what is called the occult.

As a fish undresses a man emerges, molten steel, the hallucination
of a man, the true untouchable: lava language.

Icarus disappearing into the Breughel pond now plunges as an
Ernst angel behind a steel partition.

Unregistered powers, unloosened chthonics, are to be inducted
through the practice of art.

A Man and A Woman Absolutely White   [by André Breton]

In the depths of the parasol I see the marvelous prostitutes
Their dresses faded beside the streetlamp the color of the woods
They take a big piece of wallpaper out with them for a walk

One you cannot look at without heartache over the demolition
  of ancient floors
Or else a white marble shell fallen from a mantel
Or else a filament of their necklaces that blur in the mirrors
  behind them
A powerful instinct for combustion seizes the streets where
  they wait
Like singed flowers
Their eyes raising in the distance a wind of stone
While they remain engulfed and motionless at the whirlpool's
  center
For me nothing can equal the significance of their careless
  thoughts
The fresh gutter water in which their little boots steep the shadows
  of their beaks
The reality of those fistfuls of cut hay into which they disappear
I see their breasts put a dot of sun into the deep night
And the time these take to fall and to rise is the only exact
  measure of life
I see their breasts which are stars over the waves
Their breasts in which the invisible blue milk sobs forever.

Maya glyphs scoured of animals revisioned by Dali as pebbles crawling with keys.

The Idi Amin bird, flayed with its Charon cap, the holding pattern in Blake's "Glad Day."

"For each man to refuse to consider anything beyond his own deepest sensibility, beyond his inmost self—this for me is the point of view of the complete revolution."
    —Antonin Artaud, 1927

Mother just passed gas in Miró's blond smile.

Cockroaches turning into hog crock corn, Ghana rococo mercs, Charon crammed geckos.

I just watched a bird-headed man pass his sleeping excrement into the mouth of a man-headed falcon. Extraordinary exchange. Time to stop digesting, to imaginalize everything.

As for my guardian avatar, my cobra-spread umbrella, I made it out of split umbilicus.

Surrealists siphoning oil from Mozart's burial sack to set moving the static midnight of the poet's floor.

Bosch's magical berries become the vermilion ball held as Ernst's limpid-fingered word.

The air itself   radication of infinity.

Mother just passed gas again, this time in a clothes closet where my two-year-old head grapples with her molting expressions establishing my subconscious swamp.

Or was that gas Magritte's? whose enigmatic signifying women rummage my background, or what is left of it, turning over toy blocks, each a landing deck for the Zeros of infancy.

Here to recall Wilhelm Reich's compassion for he who cannot revolt because he has strangled himself with his own body.

In Matta's *L'Année 1944* (*La mise à mort des pères*), painted in 1942, I make out a cosmic scape with kidney pulp in red rain, whirring swastikaed blurs, horse skulls, bodily inlets, propellers behind drifting sheets of glass, a pink tit, figures and trees in black crimson smoke. What to bring to bear on the year of D-Day, Omaha Beach, Kamikazied aircraft carriers, The Warsaw Uprising, Dresden firebombed—WAR WAR WAR. Surrealism's "total emancipation of man" renders abstract such horror and suffering. Facing world catastrophe (the death of 50 million), the creative act is blown through itself.

NOTES:
[1] This piece appeared in *Verse* magazine and *Everwhat* and is assembled from notes taken while walking around in the huge Surrealist retrospective at the Pompidou Museum in Paris, summer, 2002. The Breton translation appeared in *Conductors of the Pit*, Soft Skull Press, 2005.

B A N D S   O F   B L A C K N E S S [1]

"Black leads back to the foundation,
to the origin."
—Henri Michaux

A sly filament of light sags, winks, ascends to rejoin the granite-like blackness that produced it.

The painter as a man-shaped shadow in common shadow clothes. He stands in front of a target of which only a smear of upper arc, a ruined halo, remains.

A bulb of light, pale apricot, hangs within blackness girdled by an apricot serpent, tail in mouth. Or is this a gonad in a solution of masculine self-enclosure?

I am thinking of blackness spun upon itself, black hives of black bees producing scarlet honey. Color as rupture. Blackness as an earlier rapture.

Within a black sphere, an anatomical purse rests, gleaming, an amputation, a potential. Is this the closed vulva of the black goddess which, when spread, reveals the aged face of blackness, the infant crone, black tongue balled in wizard lips?

I was black and blue for you, a confused mass turning toward the light. So I sang the blues, or tapped them out on my bones. I was a nigredo beginning to break up, blue glints, melancholy undermined. Blues are the transition from slavery to song in whose registers the "middle passage" repeats, blue sea, black hold.

Am I free in this blackness to dissolve daytime generalities and to determine the particularities of the mauve zone? I have placed my genitals out in front of my thighs so as to press their tallow into dreams. Have arranged both arms under the side of my head, a Jolly Roger nest, good for all recumbents, alabaster queens as well as those still gazing at their grain.

What does a black circle mean? Flow with it, mind, draw out its orchids, especially the prostitute orchid whose curves, spots, and hairiness convince certain insects that it is a female viewed from behind. Draw out the drive-in diner trays of the dead heaped with hollow caviar, as well as the swatted flies that reincarnate as maggots in flux on garbage-filled black bags. The Milky Way? The "starry vast" as worm organic turf. Flow with it, mind, do not be stopped by the positive, the given. It is the negative that is to be struck here, the *bindu* which girders conception.

Conception a drop, a slow vertical ooze into the pit of many colors.

Splintering self-obliterating spheres. Hoops with charred Ojibway feathers. Spheres working against their own circumference: the artist's daily return to his starting blocks. The blockage that startles, cold ignition to dig in, dent the matrix. The artist in cask to himself, staved about with the oily blood of Dionysus.

Again the subliminal uroboros looms, my blood circulation and yours, an ancient idea: Okeanos is the serpent girding the world as a solid belt. "If each event does not itself unfold its meaning then there is no meaning at all."

O murdered circle! My larval ghost encoils, unable to get its end into its beginning…

No-gate where the two blind mammoths of generation meet, seem to kiss, fuse, push into the magnificent poverty of blackness, logic stripped of its mirrors. I face germination as the antennae-driven word, the word with its feelers probing its torn, denotational circumference. More light? No—more bands.

No. And in that word a masked dancer emerges—from eternity? No. From the riverbank where she was murdered? No is the gate of sagging breasts the pilgrim must part. With whose permission? Only thy own, O law unto thyself. Finger the hard nodule of a nipple on the wall in that cave where you see nothing. You will be breathed into manifestation by the blackness's plasma. The blackness is within you, and it is the blackness that draws.

NOTES:

[1] This piece appeared in *Verse* magazine, *Everwhat*, *Double Room*, and with an engraving by the Japanese painter Matsutani as *Bands of Blackness* (coordinated by Kate Van Houten), 2002, in a signed and numbered boxed edition, including translations of the piece into Japanese by Eda Takaomi and into French by Jean-Jacques Viton. My piece was stimulated by pondering certain paintings of Matsutani dominated by the color black.

THE AUTOBIOGRAPHY OF UNICA ZÜRN [1]

The expanse against which I swarm is packed with bubbles, dead plant stems, milling like I mill, a baggy buoy bulging in and out, serpentine, intestinal compression. This will be my modus operandi: a nomadic map of sacred Zürn mirages, wells that turn into camels in heat.

A single face is working its way through, pronouncing its feline/human apparitions. On its forehead I place a rosette, dotted with coital traps. Face plowed and planted, composed of furrowed and stone-covered fields. Mouthless scape, eyes narrow with the non-expressed.

Some days I am bushy, plumed, orchestral, a patchwork creature in draft. An ocular vagina, vertical between hind legs. The living muff into which you've thrust your hands.

The slate sky hung with eye islands, jester bells, drifting chalk-white roots. Is forever coming undone? Every act tugs at greased strings, mind loops slipping mind mass. To populate one's options, to proliferate the fray...

Martian, then, four-armed, with a girdle of red-nippled breasts, knock-kneed tumors, wired to echo only what curls in the wombs of stars.

Projection of my refusal to project woman. That I am combines sensations from rootlets, gourds, strangled peacocks, cut-open fruit. A pale lavender goiter, million-pored, at the crown of which a legless grasshopper is embedded.

As if windshield spattered, a purple bat-insectile shroud. Out of the impact, to hold all here, to replace the lie of Unica with hovering as the refraction of fear.

I have this fear of being a diaphanous lion clown, a complicated clawed bubble with pus peaks, a jouncing lion, watery amber, dissolving as it jells, a folly, a fabulous split-level joke, ha ROARED, HA snored...

Now that I'm asleep inside a cinder, white spider-thread buildings gleam. Orbs come undone, skeins of fraying cocoons. A star, a minaret... Evocation of the street I've dreamed, width-long, tao-deep, mazed with outer dark...

Near dawn, an upturned top hat out of which a tentacled pink fish form jumps. The party ends as a star lowers on a spider thread and holds, as if regarding me, a fabulous machine made up of dials, clocks, and accordion-like pleated planes.

All my ghouls, at this deathday party, hailing me as they dribble and melt. The Black Root That Walks. Gray Hannah With Expanding Glands. Bramble-Haired Eleanor. Hands, without musculature, pointy-fingered, glove-like gas...

I rub my knuckles against closed eyelids and the circus kicks in. Pepper-grindered bits of light, ladders, wheels. On a tightrope, a goose-stepping doll. Under an opened umbrella, a tiny cage on one wheel. Structures so frail they blur, upon knuckle release, into a donut of light...

The eyes in the tits hanging from the underside of the tan hill...

Or the pink-lavender, undulating goddess, mouth clamped by a gray hand, whose four-fingered mons veneris has a vulva like a slit wrist...

Now I have two kissing heads, and a third of an amphibian whose leg turns into a serpent swallowing whole a ball of sprouting hair. This dissolving lavender, ivory body... These huge needle bones of a prehistoric hand, my looking glass, my bloated waver...

A coiling, red, bird-headed serpent is all that is left from a fight between four red-eyed wounds... Lots of dots and crinkles, a roast-cold rash...

For you did I become a pink broth of writhing lime, gold and lavender eye-embedded snakes. With my iguana hands I dove, through your rainbow gale, to arrive knotted at the double helices.

For you did I throw this whole shadow depth into an astral mucus of salamanders strolling on a liquid unlit moor of no Unica, no Hans, just our two hundred selves, pustular in grievous adhesion.

Once I splinter, I recombine in apish, self-raping, sprig alerts. Funny? Try to draw your state of mind as it sucks all potential into hamsters that collapse like litanies of lead.

The sky-blue cosmic diver, white-beaded spine, seeking below, that's me, a fish in a secobarbital haze. I've put on big eyes for this one; I've jettisoned all my flesh.

I am the spider they drugged and told: weave! As I ravel-flipped, I never ceased to spur on what kicked into me. Drawings like somersaults knotted with flies.

A medieval armored head with wiry tufts... Why do my bottom sprouts flail about in what has died?

Down a musical chart, a head with eyes and bulbous forehead plunges. Stasis. The forebulb musical with held-back semen.

Over my headless, bristle-bladed, bi-abdomened body, a cute black toy. He looks out from the *Norma* score, tapping what remains of my shoulders.

I'm starting to get the gist of what I'm not. The thought that anything can occur is curbed by the abyss-leash directing transgression.

Two-headed snail pointing down. The main head a penis, loaded with feline smile. The other head beaks back into the shell body, where it is pinched by black tweezer-like feelers.

Still alive in the nursery of the children's hour: nourished by spectral rhymes, the tatters of comfy toys.

Come into this nest that's weaving itself, piercing its inhabitants with a shrubbery of eyes. Music leaking through the heartbeats of avian particles. A central fang-fenced mouth.

I am a proliferating hive of mauve breasts, a bubble lava sustained by the frailest of webs. An affectionate ram holds vigil over my churn. Paralyzed Ares stares out of my lower hatch.

You, coelacanth body, with your hundreds of colored dots, like pins in a map turning nebula. Stars and gas, with dorsal fin and vestigial lung. The near-amphibian Unica, really out there, with no way back.

Charred spatter gas. Clumps sprouting gray ferns. Sallow blood-colored smoke. All of it rushing out of the unseen as if the unseen were unity, and its progeny this pyrotechnical fade...

Meeting. Giving the devil head. Not swallowing, forcing the red semen back in and up those empty bone tunnels, into the deserted marrow palace, into his blackened hands.

Contact. Semen become red thread through me, entering me where once I sucked, bypassing the head I hold in my arms, exiting my fontanel. Behold my new background: a protozoa-grid of red nines.

Caught, through a shard-shaped peephole, lip to lip. We share a tongue in common that smiles as it reddens and blackens with coral snake bands.

Cartoon of the Beast and Whore of Babylon. He is three-legged, wearing lipstick, with a stethoscope attached to his anus. As for me, well, I am sort of there, forever, a head on a body of finger-nail-webbed wings.

Can a life be fully displayed in imaginative release? 1960. I gave off bodies, a creatrix issuing serpents who begged to return, bursting into black-striped baby magicians. I carried within me Hans, my Ethiopian homunculus. I farted pinions, blossoming plumage, out-raking quills.

To be, in profile, gorgeous. To ride whatever Beast I choose. To be attended by a flying centipede whose breasts anoint my proffered hand.

On it goes, heads producing heads kissing heads turning away. Terror sweetens, prances about with little stag feet. By a tattooed Nausicaa-wave am I kissed!

To live in a parrot's puffed-up ass, a double-faced Madonna, breasts packed in, no feet, no arms, just rippling checkeredness, finned with scarves!

With Henri Michaux: cornucopias of nimble lace proliferating through asunder attraction. We met to palpitate the blind from which we were shooting. You can see our finger wraiths oinking and drooping. I in my aviatrix-brain-cap, with Cerberean Michaux guarding the entrance to the rat-tracked palimpsest of madness.

Fizzlings attempting to fire, scotched. Out of nowhere: red smut. Crushed butt ash as desperate semaphore. Who across the leonine vast will titillate my loneliness?

Black-thorned bulbs, patches of them, under which, as if attempting to ignite, I scrawl in a vermilion trance. Hold what is left of me. Tie me to my flare!

Rash-prickled heartfire, blood rips tendriling. Like the burning bush, I fail at self-consumption.

Outfall, in self-recognition falling even further away—from what? Failure to scale the Eden wall. The horror of being cored.

On the night side of the fallen tree, I am that tree, rampant. Inside the pencil foliage, a penile blow out.

You wonder why. I do too. As a tacky flapper, my belly pulsing with moronic lighthouse eyes, I twist about.

Furl into self tighter. Compress to the first spindle, the Lady whose swerves led to the lathe.

In exchange for my face, the gods granted me horns, a hump-breasted back, a severed hand to hang from my navel. Then they inserted my sweet profile into my butt.

Let me kneel on my neck fingers to kiss your death ring with its stone of a petrified lotus. Bury me with your doll.

Peaceful schematic kin. Butt to butt the alpha lopes, sharing omega space, anal ties.

To drain the dregs from the Homer bowl, to smell the blood in Tiresias's trench. To be so blocked no line connects, even the one you passed down to me, far below, in the angler mud.

Exploded maternal shrubbery still adrift in outer space...

Strong down draft. Out of foaming cinders a glove flaps toodle-oo.

Look, schools of leaves and fish are crossing the paper void... I have connected your eye phones to my breasts...

A vertical shark in a robe, ecstatically sniffing the fetid air. As if he were Rodin's *Balzac.* An excited grasshopper is about to bugger this make-believe.

Working the bellows of Bellmer's organ, I emerged, armored, a prehistoric sculpin, priceless, worthless.

A veiled viper in mourning over her venom loss. Her scribble sister draws near. Detonation. I always draw the afterclap.

The bouquet of sparking tinder I pulled out of your armpit. Now, as if on top of a tombstone, it has been tossed on me. Rest in havoc.

The gold, goggle-eyed salamander whose limbs are fjords seen from a plane. The fat red and brown woolly worm with long crinkly hairs. The broken-backed mosquito, the pink dragonfly whose wings are now shredding plumes... They amble about on the thread lines of my mind, the opening act for "The Spider Queen's Lunch."

Out of Unica Zürn Hans Bellmer suffocation, to pull the anagram-matic, magical command: *Alchemize! Unsnarl! Burn!*

The anguish of being a head on a body of brown smoke. Of being squiggles, filler. Only a gaping, rueful mouth to organize pathos.

I laid a mass of eye eggs, bird parts, and flounders. Out of this marsh, a bird with a twisted beak, in a metallic halter bra (with eyes for nipples) stares. Quagmire of the mind where the never seen gnaws on the seen too often.

To be dyadic, double to myself, a clown fish pressed to its clone, Unica against Zürn, attended by a winged jester worm, antennae-bound to our tail fins. Until we are rigorously one, a terrible wed-ding awaits us.

A hopeful spirit with eel ears, scaled body ending in a fin. Each fig-ure represents the blank of my destiny. No description is true? Agi-tated sea urchin at 4 o'clock.

Limp-billed soul bird, all its energy discharging out the rear of its head (a feathery tumor), its back (a tubular wing-work), and the back of one leg (a monstrous spur). Excremental wind. Crux of someone with only exit confronting entrance.

Heads like self-hoods emerging from a divine vacuity. They are the result of the disaster right behind my eyes, where a hierarchy-bereft totem loses its vertical head-to-head adherence.

You were two, Robert Schumann. Chain-mailed faces arrested your music. Beast arabesques entangled your struggle toward the ulti-mate altar. What did you find there? Chicken feet? Clara wearing a necklace of slugs?

My knitted kitten-masked hierophant, uncrowned. An egg-shaped human face blooms in your esophagus. Trolleys of black ball lightning race through your skull.

No goal, no afterbirth. Fleck-knotted flight as the only righteous stride. She with an Ice Age spring in her steps. He, mammoth-trunked, with muffler worm, linked to her plight.

Over the soul bird's crest, the Hitlerian moon doubled and held. In the pale salmon night, I was without refuge and so I invented: two-headed, ferned sea worms, pre-Permian conscience-free sprites.

Inky splotches of crinoline-nested air deliveries. Mine by the right of the black election! Mine by the sign in the scarlet abyss! Only lines reveal!

Like clouds growling from their moldy undersides, the anti-forms arrive: the tyrannosaur-headed cobra, out of which an alarmed bear head pops. The cycloptic beaver. I pluck at our partition, as if at some harp from Hell.

In the milk of dream, an undulating, noctilucous manta, gentle messenger from the ocean now reaching to my mouth.

In a mantle of leaping fish and twisting lips, I appear, part of God's annihilative profile, rich with macerated creatures, dinosaur-gradient with life's first eyes.

To draw the beginning of the visible, as absence curdles: bacterial apocalypse.

Poppy ghosts, in gust with rained-on bloodstained window drift…

Plesiosaur in free fall, through fathoms of shale, to alight here, decomposition's deity.

[May—June, 2005, Ypsilanti]

NOTES:

[1] The German artist Unica Zürn (1916–1970) appears to have begun to draw after becoming the companion of Hans Bellmer (1902–1975) in Paris in 1953, undoubtedly stimulated by Bellmer's darkly erotic and meticulous art. While in Paris she had some contact with some of the Surrealists, like Breton and Matta, and is said to have been introduced to mescaline by Henri Michaux (who she referred to as "The Jasmine Man" in one of her several books). In *Sulfer #29* (1991) Renée Riese Hubert edited a forty-page section of Zürn's texts and drawings. She committed suicide in 1970, via defenestration, from the couple's Paris apartment.

In the spring of 2004, I visited a show of some seventy of her drawings at the Ubu Gallery in New York City. Up to that point, I had a hazy image of her as a drawer, and mainly thought of her as Bellmer's disturbed companion. But this show revealed that her art belongs with the best that Surrealism has to offer. She is, in my opinion, the peer of Matta, Michaux, Ernst, Varo, Hoch, and Kahlo. I brought home a catalog from this show, *Unica Zürn: Bilder 1953–1970* (Verlag Brinkman und Bose / Neue Gesellschaft für Bildende Kunst / Berlin 1998), with reproductions of over two hundred drawings. I wrote two pieces off these drawings. The first and shorter of the two pieces, "Unica Zürn," is a lyrical attempt to register in several pages the impact of Zürn's work, based on images that she evoked in me. "The Autobiography of Unica Zürn," the second and longer piece, is an attempt to articulate many of the first sixty or so drawings in the catalog.

This piece appeared in Germany, translated by Andrew Niedermeiser in *Aksente* (Munich) and online in *Double Room*.

THE ASSAULT

Introduction

*My initial response to the 9/11 assaults, as a citizen reader/investigator,
was to start making myself more aware of what we might have done to
others, beyond our borders, to instigate such an action. I read William
Blum's* Killing Hope, *and then his* Rogue State. *Learning of Bush's
bizarre immediate response to the attacks on the World Trade Center, I
also began to learn more about him by reading Mark Crispin Miller's*
The Bush Dyslexicon. *Then Gore Vidal in an* Observer *article alerted me to the possibility that the official version of what happened on 9/11
was bogus. I read Nafeeze Mosaddeq Ahmed's* The War on Freedom
and checked his information against Paul Thompson's The Complete
9/11 Time Line. *I have not found any official response that contradicts
Ahmed or Thompson. The compressed time line data in the first part of
my piece is mainly taken from Ahmed's book. The lyric outrage in part
two is all my own (other than when factual), and participates in the tradition of the sirventes; Robert Duncan's poem, "Uprising," which con-
demns President Johnson for the carpet-bombing of Vietnam, hovers over
"The Assault," a predecessor ghost.*

I sent my piece to The Nation, *a weekly whose politics I respect. I sent
it to the editor, Katrina Vanden Heuvel; she wrote back that* The Nation
had covered all the points my poem raised. Since I read The Nation
weekly, I knew this was not true. In fact, The Nation, *to my knowledge,
had not published a single article disputing the official version of 9/11. So
I wrote Vanden Heuvel back, asking her to point out to me where my
information had been discussed. Her response was to ask me not to write
to her anymore. So I sent "The Assault" to Lewis Lapham at* Harper's
Magazine. *Lapham wrote me that it was an interesting imitation of*

Archibald MacLeish and e.e. cummings but not for them. The poem was ultimately published on the Possum Pouch *website, in* Hambone *magazine, and in French translation by Auxeméry in* Momentum *(Paris).*

In the past several years, additional information contesting the "official" story about 9/11 has come to light. Much of this information is summed up by David Ray Griffin in The New Pearl Harbor *and by Eric Hufschmid in* Painful Questions: An Analysis of the September 11th Attack. *The most pertinent new information discussed in both of these books concerns the sudden, rapid, and total collapse of the towers (and Building 7), and the nature of the penetration of the Pentagon. Cobbled together roughly a year after 9/11, my poem will no longer be news to those readers who have reflected on any of the materials I mention above. However, especially in light of the 9/11 Commission's failure to thoroughly investigate the disaster, I have decided to let this piece stand as it is, as the testimony of a poet's immediate investigation of and response to the event that remains the basis for the invasions of Afghanistan and Iraq.*

I

Mid-July 2001: The U.S. government—having decided that the Taliban regime was too unstable and too hostile to serve as a vehicle for U.S. entry into Central Asia—had planned on an Afghanistan invasion for October.

National support for such an invasion depended upon a widely perceived direct threat. Now known "enemy attacks" used to whip up and mobilize people for war include the *US Battleship Maine*, the *Lusitania*, Pearl Harbor, Tonkin Bay. Our atomic bombing of Hiroshima and Nagasaki: the beginning of the Cold War.

September 10: Bin Laden was in Rawalpindi, Pakistan, courtesy of the ISI, for kidney dialysis (in July he met with the local CIA agent in Dubai; no attempt was made to arrest him).

September 6–10: United and American Airlines stock shares were massively sold short, as were shares at Morgan Stanley Dean Witter (occupying twenty-two World Trade Center floors) and Merrill Lynch (headquarters near the WTC). Insiders with advance knowledge of an approaching national catastrophe are believed to have made over fifteen million dollars. If they knew, would you tell me that Bush, the Secret Service, the Air Force, and the Pentagon did not know?

(The alleged lead hijacker Mohammed Atta, with an expired 2000 tourist visa, re-entered the United States three times in 2001 for flying lessons—for which he lacked the required M-1 work visa—while under FBI surveillance for stockpiling bomb making materials.)

August 2001: The FBI was informed that Zacarias Moussaoui was linked by French intelligence to Bin Laden (top FBI officials blocked field agents' requests to search Zacarias's computer).

August 2001: Attorney David Schippers was approached by FBI agents and given the names of the hijackers, their targets, proposed dates, and the sources of their funding. He tried to contact John Ashcroft who did not return his calls. Schippers' informants were pulled off their investigation and threatened with prosecution if they went public (Schippers is now representing one FBI agent in a suit against the U.S. government in an attempt to subpoena its testimony, so he can legally speak about the blocked investigation on public record).

Standard Operating Procedures (SOP) requires fighter jets to scramble and intercept under emergency conditions. No approval from the White House was ever required (when Payne Stuart's Learjet pilot failed to respond to the air controller at 9:33, twenty-one minutes later an F-16 traveling at 1500 mph reached the Learjet at 46,000 feet).

On September 11, Flight #11 was clearly way off course by 8:20 a.m. SOP calls for immediate notification and response.

North American Aerospace Defense Command (NORAD) was not informed of an emergency by Boston air traffic control until 8:38.

Initially, according to former NORAD Commander, General Richard Meyers, no jets were scrambled until after Flight #77 struck the Pentagon at 9:40 (one hour and twenty minutes after Flight #77 was suspected of being hijacked).

Within days, this story changed: at 8:44, we were told, two F-15s were scrambled at Otis (Cape Cod), 190 miles from Manhattan. If these jets flew at top speed (1850 mph) they would have reached the towers in six minutes. But at 9:03, when Flight #175 struck the South Tower, the Otis jets were unexplainably still seventy miles from Manhattan (and why sent from Otis? McGuire, a major, active facility in New Jersey, is seventy-one miles from the WTC. Arrival time: three minutes. No planes were scrambled from McGuire).

The apparent shut down of SOP on Flight #77 is even more sinister: known to be hijacked by 8:50 (at which time it was also known that #11 and #175 were hijacked, *meaning a national emergency was at hand*) NORAD was not notified until 9:24—and after NORAD was notified, jets were scrambled from Langley (130 miles from Washington, DC) instead of from Andrews (ten miles away), with two combat-ready squadrons (the Langley jets arrived fifteen minutes after the Pentagon was plowed into).

9:16 a.m.: NORAD was informed that Flight #93 had been hijacked (at which time it was known that three other flights had been hijacked and that two had already blown up their targets). *No jets were scrambled to intercept #93.*

No one has been charged with incompetence.

After both towers had been struck, President Bush, in Sarasota, visiting a grade school, was informed. He continued to listen to
children read to him for seven minutes before informing Americans of what they already knew.

Myers, at the Capitol, was chatting (about "terrorism") with Sena-
tor Max Cleland. They saw a TV report that a plane had hit the
WTC. "We thought it was a small plane or something like that,"
Myers said. So the two men went ahead with the office call.
Meanwhile, the second tower was hit. "Nobody informed us of
that," Myers said. After the Pentagon was struck (seventy-five
percent of the assault now successfully completed), a cell phone
was handed to him; finally the Chairman of the Joint Chief of
Staffs is informed!

According to Assistant Secretary of Defense Victoria Clarke:
"Donald Rumsfeld stayed in his office until the Pentagon was
hit, with the excuse that he had some phone calls to make."

II

A composite vision: our callow, illiterate, Supreme Court-
appointed Fool, drifting in photo-op with school children,
Myers discussing "terrorism" with Cleland,
Rumsfeld, in effect, hiding in his office,
                                    while flames
drink debris-blocked staircased bodies.

    My head shudders with
    the mortification of sensing Bush in my own eyes.
Yes, for I do not see myself outside of the male coagulate.
Part of me is a lazar born of mass guilt,
funhouse horticulture, where the decency facets
    I've struggled to file ripple with
        "Full Spectrum Dominance"

Out the window, in weak autumnal green:
tent caterpillar encampments, opaque, milky, creating,
as if under camouflage, deadly screens—I envision elected American presidents in the democracy-subverted host tree:
                                        Bush, Jr. entangled with pa
crawling Nixon's raging animus,   Nobel Carter
    mottled with Khmer Rouge horror,   Johnson cloaked in
"We seek no wider war," whipping out his dick to reporters, declaring, "This is why we're in Vietnam!"
Reagan as a goggle-wearing grub, chirping:
"Contras are the moral equivalent of our Founding Fathers."
Nest camps where baby Pinochets bud   (Nobel Kissinger
on his knees gripping the altar-bowl, vomiting up a stomach hash
    of millions—
    suddenly his ghost stands up through him,
    called to lead the 9/11 investigation!)

The nests enweb electronically through the American mind.
Whitman's visionary "eternal present" has become the language of
    TV, transfixing the audience in a memory-less now.
I'm taken in, as are you, fellow citizens, failing instantly to recall
    background particularities.
A week later, I come to, recalling, while reading, details I should
    have brought to bear.
The mainstream media cartel beams its needles out of the screens,
who is not injected, anesthetized by conversion-spiked patriotic
    aura?

Like a depth charge dropped into 9/11: Fifty years of Cold War
    mobilization against the Soviet Union has left the country with
    "a boiling residue of paranoid anxiety."

Greed become a crazed intoxication to re-determine history.
If the Bush family become trillionaires, might they, led by angels,
    slip into eternity, skipping over death?

Jackknifed bodies plummeting against the photo-serenity of a
    tower.
Not Crane's bedlamite,   but a secretary
                                exploding
                        in blue September sky.

Living in America right now is like being on a revised Flight #11.
The nave of this self-righteous citadel extends for miles—
in section after section: our cluster-bombed Yugoslavians, jerking
    nerve-gassed Laotians, napalmed Vietnamese girls, our chop-
    ped-apart Guatemalans, mowed-down East Timorese
and there's Sharon, in high heels, tightening the thumb-screws on
    Palestinian immiseration—and below? Right here?
Bush is in my gas,   Cheney's in my steering wheel,   Ashcroft
                                under our bed!

Should 9/11 be seen as a 3000 body count down payment on a
    Turkmenistan–Afghanistan–Pakistani UNOCAL oil pipeline?

3000 dead? More like 8000—
for this figure must include the Afghanistan dead bombed in retri-
    bution for what? Nothing they did but inhabit land we
—and here "we" partitions my heart—seek to exploit.
The unutterable humiliation of 9/11!
Holocaust of firemen to make millionaires billionaires!
Workers, executives, of the capitalist epicenter—
but much more importantly: beloved citizens who went to work
    that day
(overhearing me, bored Bush turns aside:
"Adolf, let's go fishin.")

            In our hearts we know
            In our hearts we do not know

Baby Bush now spectre-entangled in the entrails of the nation.

                                [November–December, 2002]

FACING INVASION[1]

Standing with Caryl by curb in Ann Arbor last evening,
candles flickering within our cup shields—
so something up there could see that we are here?

An officer's report from the "demolished" village of Gusukuma,
Okinawa, June 1945 (from George Feifer's *The Battle of Okinawa*):

> I was surprised to feel that the ground was soft and soggy
> under my feet. I looked down to see the knee of a dead
> Japanese soldier protruding from the dirt. The stench was
> terrible... green flies were everywhere, blowing the bloated
> bodies. I stepped into the entrance of a large cave and saw
> the half-clothed body of a Japanese soldier. A rat scurried
> away to hide beneath a pile of rubbish. I noticed the body
> had a ghastly hole in the stomach where the rat had bur-
> rowed, feeding on the dead flesh. The soldier had been dead
> for several days and had swollen to abnormal size. His legs
> burst his leg wrappings and a bulge protruded over his shoe
> tops where the shoe would not permit it to swell further...
> his eyes were bulging from his head and his close-cropped
> black hair seemed ready to pop from his head.

Every American teenager, before graduating from high school,
should be required to read Feifer's 65-page chapter, "Close Combat," a masterly description of the hell that war is.

"War's horror exists partly because outsiders can't know it. 'If people really knew, the war would be stopped tomorrow,' said Prime Minister David Lloyd George in 1916, when trench warfare oddly similar to the Okinawan fighting was bleeding his British white."

18 March 2003: I told my three classes today that one civil disobedience option, once invasion took place, was to boycott classes, and that I had decided not to do this. Instead, I read each class William Rivers Pitt's "Into the Darkness" article, from the "truthout.org" website. Pitt is a high school teacher in Boston. His summation included the following:

> The Bush administration's reaction to 9/11—placing blame on "evildoers" instead of starting an honest dialogue, blocking an independent investigation of the attack for over a year, nominating master secret-keeper Henry Kissinger to chair that investigative panel in what was perhaps the most disgusting insult possible to the families of the lost, ignoring the real terrorist threats in order to focus on the politically expedient annihilating of Iraq, instituting the most ham-fisted diplomatic push ever seen in the history of this nation by utterly ignoring the eleven Security Council members who said no to this war, disrupting international relations vital to the pursuit of true terrorist threats, and all the while under funding the homeland defenses necessary to protect the American people—has led us to this dismal place.

Stunned silence in each class. I think the information was so overwhelming they did not know how to respond. At the end of two of the classes, several students came up and thanked me for reading the article.

Walked out onto our front porch with the last of the dinner wine. Blowing spring rain. Across the street, in the lit-up First Methodist Church basement, a group of people clapping. As I watched, I heard a scream—maybe a block away—with a melodic waver at the end like an Arabic woman's ululation. Then: *total light*. I took a step back—tremendous thunder, bomb-like, overhead.

Did we call The World Trade Center site "Ground Zero" out of hyperbolic identification with "our" Hiroshima?

I stand in the stale safety of my armored nation's out-pronging surge.

[19 March 2003]

NOTES:

[1] This piece appeared in *Unarmed Chapbook* and *Call* magazines.

WORKROOM [1]

What a writer surrounds himself with, or places before him, while he works, are companions as well as watermarks, examples of the rigor and imagination he hopes his own efforts will be up to. Somewhere I recall reading that, while in Paris in the 1930s, Henry Miller wrote in a nearly unadorned room, and on a desk that held only his writing materials. My guess is that by the time he got to Big Sur, and was seriously doing watercolors, the context in which he worked took on more image life.

Visitors to the Pompidou Art Museum in that same city can now view "Breton's Wall," the wall behind the poet's desk at 42 rue Fontaine for many years, with its shelves full of found objects, pictures, and photographs. I saw it at the 2000 surrealist retrospective there; it was one of the most striking "works" in the exhibition. In fact, I wondered how André Breton could function imaginatively facing this tidal wall of primitive and modernist psyche. It made me think again of Miller's unadorned room (against the lushness of *Tropic of Cancer*)—no distraction, no presence of the great dead or one's own contemporaries. Workroom as Zen temple. Outward ceremony removed to encourage the priest or artist to bend all efforts toward an interior world.

Writing about Sigmund Freud's antiquities collection, Lynn Gamwell states:

> Throughout many years of collecting, Freud frequently
> rearranged his antiquities, but they were always located only
> within his study and consultation rooms, never in his living

quarters. These hundreds of human and animal figures all faced him like a huge audience—from his desk, from cabinets, from across the room. Freud chose in particular to confront many figures of scholars, wise men, and scribes; some were always on his desk. He wrote thousands of manuscript pages facing Imhotep, the Egyptian architect who, in late antiquity, was revered as a healer. Freud's desk was also the home of the baboon of Thoth, the Egyptian god of the moon, wisdom, and learning, and of a Chinese sage. He was in the habit of stroking the marble baboon, as he did his pet chow, and of greeting the Chinese sage every morning.[2]

These "hundreds of human and animal figures" facing Freud "like a huge audience" make me think of a shaman's paradise, or a range of differing orders in attendance as Freud excavated legendary reality. On the basis of the photographs in *Sigmund Freud and Art*, it would appear that Freud owned, and worked before, at least twenty-six Egyptian artifacts. One tie in between such artifacts and his thinking is hieroglyphics. He wrote:

> "If we reflect that the means of representation in dreams are principally visual images and not words, we shall see that it is ever more appropriate to compare dreams with a system of writing than with a language. In fact the interpretation of dreams is completely analogous to the decipherment of an ancient pictographic script such as Egyptian hieroglyphs."[3]

Freud was also possessed by the way the dead live on intrapsychically and work on the living mind. I imagine that under Harold Bloom's "anxiety of influence" is Freud's preoccupation with the commands, prohibitions, and fears of the deceased on the living. However, I believe that the poets I have spent the most time with— Blake, Crane, Olson, Vallejo, Césaire, and Artaud—have not carried a restrictive charge. Primarily, they have given me permission to say anything that would spur on my quest for authenticity and for constructing a unique alternative world in language.

In an unplanned, chancy way, the objects I have chosen to surround myself with in my Ypsilanti workroom (since 1986) are not only watermarks or rigor to emulate but things to be around and to enjoy, presences that give me heart, as well as odds and ends that have just appeared and asked to be included.

❦

Directly over my head as I sit and write (now on a computer; until 2003, I used a 1984 Swintec electric typewriter) is a wasp nest in pristine condition retrieved from a neighborhood tree branch:

> I write below
> a wasp nest
> strung to the ceiling,
> immense weightless grenade of masticated fiber,
> inner walls honeycombed with tiny samurai
> frozen this past October—
>
> my work here is to bury
> and keep alive
> a fertile queen.[4]

My workroom is on the northeast corner of the second floor of our 1919 craftsman's bungalow, which we think originally might have been purchased (as a house kit) from Sears Roebuck. In contrast to Freud's placement of his collection, much of our art collection is distributed throughout the house, especially in the dining and living rooms.

On the part of the north wall directly in front of me is a framed torn dust jacket, found on the basement steps of the Gotham Book Mart in NYC in the late 1960s, with a black and faded-rose Plate 70 from Blake's *Jerusalem*. Under a massive dolmen framing an occulted sun are three tiny figures, one of whom is holding what looks like a Druid harp. When I remember to, I look up and read, in Blake's hand:

> Imputing Sin & Righteousness to Individuals: Rahab
> sat deep within him hid: his Feminine Power unrevealed.

For Blake, Rahab signified, I think, among other things, the
Whore of Babylon, the false church of this world, the opponent of
Jerusalem, and the crucifier of Jesus. Such lines goad me to exca-
vate the hidden, to confront my own spectre. They also reflect
Blake's dark division, as he aged, concerning woman.

Over the Blake are two small drawings of me reading at UCLA
in 1971 by R.B. Kitaj. Above them is a multi-colored pencil drawing by Robert Duncan (a wiry-haired mandrill head, bust of a
Poundian-looking man, and a large, long-necked headless bird).
Stuck with scotch tape to the bottom of the Blake frame is a snapshot of the Dun Bhaloir area of Tory Island off the northwest
Donegal coast of Ireland. We took a boat out to the island while
visiting in the summer of 2003. The photo was taken by one of my
students at the Donegal Poets House who accompanied us. Dun
Bhaloir, in the photo, looks like a lizard of craggy rock, settled into
the water, its head turned toward open sea.

Headland

> Risen like a sewer of precognition,
> of lacertilian biotite
> folds, cerebral
> lobes, anacoluthic
> evocations of Coatlicue,
> risen directly from Tory Island's ocean floor,
> cankered into
> its own principle of petri-growth,
> with heather, like rooted nightcrawlers,
> swarming between
> the bony plates extending
> along its crest, Dun Bhaloir
> turns its headless
> head to eyelessly

stare into the Atlantic's horizontal
dark blue depth-
flat shades,
                which are a
banished Adam to
this apple-tree abyss of erective crag.[4]

The east wall, to my right, and the south one, behind me, are mainly covered with bookshelves holding single author volumes (A through S) of American poetry (P through Z have extended into the guest room). Two shelves are book free. I used the lower one on the east wall for manuscripts, postcards, and three framed photos of my wife Caryl. On the wall behind this shelf are two more Blake reproductions ("The Arlington Court Regeneration"—part of which was used on the cover of *My Devotion*, Black Sparrow Books, 2004—and "The Great Red Dragon and the Woman Clothed with the Sun"). There is also a piece of calligraphy by Ohno Hidetaka (a Kyoto painter friend of Cid Corman's) that was commissioned for another book, *The House of Ibuki*, Sumac Press, 1969. The calligraphy reads: "ibukinouchi." Next to the Ohno is a framed snapshot of a charging wolf spider. Rudy Novak, my first wife's father, spotted the spider on the dining-room table, dropped down to table-level with his camera and snapped the spider as it ran toward him.

There is a second spider in the workroom, a large rainbow-colored, wood Mexican one with a baby on its back, perched on a stake in the philodendron by the west window.

On the end of the east wall bookcase is a straggly collage of images tacked up over the years. Under a photo of a box jellyfish (that looks like an extra-terrestrial skull) is a postcard reproduction of "The Arlington Court Regeneration," and under it a postage stamp of Dagwood Bumstead serving himself one of his towering midnight-snack sandwiches. Under Dagwood is a frazzled (from being carried around in my billfold for years) *National Geographic* photo of four New Guinea headhunters sitting on a log. One of them is the living simulacrum for my mythic headhunter, Yorunomado. Under the headhunters is a glossy black and white reproduction of a painting by Francis Bacon: a naked man writing at a desk, his back reflected in an adjacent mirror. Sticking out from the side of the Bacon is a picture of Bugs Bunny. Attached to the bottom of the Bacon is a "Gusano Rojo" Mescal label, with a cute cartoon worm in a diaper trudging along, winking at the viewer, a jug of mescal in his shoulder sack.

Like the poet Ron Padgett, my introduction to the world of imagination was through newspaper comics. There were no paintings or books (other than *The Bible*) in the house where I was brought up in Indianapolis. As a kid, I would sprawl over the Sunday comic strips on the living-room rug, daydreaming with Dagwood and Blondie, Jiggs and Maggie, Moon Mullins, The Katzenjammer Kids, and Smoky Stover.

The north wall to the left of the window is filled with two large framed reproductions of Hieronymus Bosch triptychs: the Lisbon *Temptation of Saint Anthony* and *The Garden of Earthly Delights*. They have been there for fifteen years, and I have found them very difficult to "read" and assimilate. Then several years ago I found John Rowland's edition of *The Garden of Earthly Delights* reproduced complete, in color, in the original size. This book enabled me to study the triptych area by area. Last year I applied to the Rockefeller Study Center at Bellagio on Lake Como, Italy, for a one-month residency to write about this triptych. Armed with a rolled-up reproduction in a tube, and Rowland's book, Caryl and I left for Bellagio in mid-October. Now I have a sixty-page work, in poetry and prose, called "Tavern of the Scarlet Bagpipe."

The last painting reproduction in my workroom that I will mention is Caravaggio's *The Beheading of Saint John the Baptist*. This is his largest painting (12x17 feet), painted on the island of Malta in 1608 when a price was on his head for a murder committed in Rome (apparently accidentally in self-defense). My reproduction is so dark that it would not be possible to use it to write about. In 2002, Caryl and I spent a week in Valletta, Malta, where the painting is to be found in the Co-Cathedral. The guards in charge turned off the double alarm system and let us get up close. I was standing with my nose inches away from Caravaggio's sole signature on any of his paintings, scrawled in the blood oozing from the neck of the just-decapitated Baptist. Later, I wrote an eight-page poem on Caravaggio called "The Beheading."

I have two old Japanese *tansus* (wood chests) in my workroom, a small one on my desk, and a larger one under the Bosch triptychs. On this latter *tansu* is a chunk of granite holding pieces of a dried pomegranate. In front of it is a bird nest holding an egg-shaped stone. Between nest and rock is a 19th-century stereograph of a Lapp shaman in ceremonial dress standing in the doorway of his log teepee.

My desk is a wood-stained door. On top of it, by the wall, are three large chunks of jasper, and two photos of painters: my dear deceased friend, Nora Jaffe, and the painter whose work means the most to me: Chaim Soutine.

🍃

Having described my workroom "arsenal," I now have to acknowledge that all of it vanishes when I get involved with a poem. Time also disappears. But this is not exactly a trance. I have taught myself to critically see through what I am writing, to assay its implications. I am also able to move back and forth to my *Webster's International Dictionary* on a little table by the typewriter. Suddenly a question of factuality arises: in what year did Caravaggio complete such and such a painting? Break my concentration or bury the question? Both options are problematic. I don't Google much.

The antiphonal process of spontaneity and self-critical blowback is seldom perfect. In a first draft, there are bound to be some clichés, obscurities, and irrelevancies. For over thirty years, Caryl has been a wonderful sounding board, reading and commenting on just about everything I have written or translated, usually sending me back to the workroom to rewrite—which I am happy to do. Allen Ginsberg's "First thought, best thought" motto presumes that a spontaneous phrase is a thought. I have found that the thought in a poem often takes months, sometimes years, to fully flex its articulation.

About a decade ago, I realized that if I attempted to revise a poem immediately after completing a draft or two, the self-critical faculty that was useful during composition would take over and grind the poem down to nothing, turning me into an animal eating its cub. So I started turning over first drafts, setting them aside for up to a year before investigating them. I have felt that this works. What is most distinctive about a draft often looks stupid to the critical inspector. By delaying a year, I re-approach the poem as if somebody else had written it and learn to respect its oddness.

For the past nine years, Adrienne Rich and I have sent poems, often in drafts, to each other as part of our correspondence. From Adrienne I have learned something about self-restraint: where it does and does not strengthen a piece. How much elaboration one needs to give any nodal point is a dilemma that must be confronted poem by poem.

My workroom vanishing during composition makes me wonder: exactly what am I improvising upon? It would have been interesting to ask Willem de Kooning that question in the 1970s when he appeared to be traveling upon improvisation alone. When Bud Powell or Charlie Parker improvised, they were working off a chord structure that provided them with patterns on which to choose their notes. Even though Bud Powell's version of "Tea for Two" is outrageously original (it feels like an all-out attack on the triviality of the song), the listener can detect the ghost of "Tea for Two" via his improvised lines and clusters. In this respect, the poet improvising has nothing immediately feeding him a base on which to direct his moves.

Or does he? I suppose the subconscious should be brought in here, but it would not make sense to simply substitute it for musical chord changes, which are from a previous score. The base, if it can be called that, I experience when improvising is a complex of spontaneous words increasingly channeled into a focus (a word I prefer over "subject"). At the same time, unless spontaneous input persists, the poem can easily settle into a repetitive pattern, signaling the reader that he can shift into cruise mode and cease to be actively engaged as a reader. If, while I am in the middle of something, a particular word or phrase announces itself as closure, I do not set it aside and direct the poem toward it. I pitchfork it into the next line then see what's around that corner.

The material that the subconscious provides (spontaneous words and phrases that do not make common sense, but may be of symbolic significance) recalls dreaming.[5] Perhaps improvisation in poetry, moving at the urgency of image propulsion, can be thought of as dreaming awake, which would be another way to state the antiphonal process I mentioned earlier. Still, I am not happy with the word "dreaming" here. Conscious input during composition involves more modeling than it does reception. Most of us experience dreaming as something happening to us. Writing poetry can be the most intensely active mental performance possible, with the subconscious induction speeding through a labyrinth of conscious filters, hitting dead-ends, entangling with more subconscious material. Perhaps "envisioning" would be more accurate than "dreaming awake," as long as one can embed the word in the compositional process and not let it stray into the realm of traditional prophecy. I would also want to qualify it, in terms of my own writing, as containing not only the irreal ("existing in imagination only"), but language shadows of the all too real. And I would also want to acknowledge that spontaneity while writing, in my case, often is partially contingent upon months of research and thinking into an area beforehand.

While cooking dinner, I sometimes wander out of the kitchen and into the living room where Caryl often sits, watching the evening news on TV. One evening I caught a glimpse of Dick Cheney speaking, noted his unusual mouth, and then returned to the kitchen. For the next couple of hours, that mouth floated in and out of my awareness; attached to "it," like fishing lines heading out into the invisible, were swarming sensations about our theocratic junta and its dreadful invasion of Iraq. Then I went up to my workroom and sat down.

Dick Cheney's mouth
slides on circular-saw teeth, with rakers,
to rip out the throats of words,
to drape their worm-casts,
scare-nets, over brains hypnotized by
the blind light of innocence,
that tunnel of camouflaged history called
"it's a free country."

[2005]

NOTES:

[1] This essay was written, at the request of editor Steve Berg, for *American Poetry Review.*

[2] "The Origin of Freud's Antiquities Collection" by Lynn Gamwell, in *Sigmund Freud and Art*, SUNY Freud Museum, Binghamton, NY, 1989, p. 27.

[3] Sigmund Freud and Art, p. 75.

[4] From "Erratics," in *My Devotion*, Black Sparrow Books, Boston, 2004, pp. 95–96.

[5] Dreams, reported, generally do not make for very interesting poems. The remembered dream is just another kind of description, out of step with the immediacy of being in the poem, here and now. My experience recalling dreams is that the recollection is always partial, making me add conscious material as the telling proceeds. Thus I find it much more exciting to begin a poem with a dream fragment and then to begin improvising, not worrying about describing the dream accurately. Since dreams are mainly visual, putting them into words usually only skims off material that is immediately transferable to a verbal equivalent.

SPECTATOR, SPECTRE, SITTER

Antonin Artaud's final period (1945–1948), which involved a complex interpenetration of drawing and writing, may be viewed as the successful culmination of his 1930s concept of a Theater of Cruelty. This evolution had three stages. The first project failed to materialize because Artaud was dependent upon the financial support of others for a spectacle that remained sketchy even for him. In the second state, this theater abandoned its projected space in outer ceremony and took up residence in Artaud's own mind and body, becoming a psychotic shadow drama he could neither control nor share. The third and final stage began in the Rodez asylum in 1945 when, after more than a year and a half of electro-shock sessions, Artaud began to draw in a way that completely engaged him—which probably saved him from future shock treatments. His Theater of Cruelty was then realized in the one-on-one exchanges between Artaud and his sitters for the post-Rodez portraits. Artaud's commentary and incantations often scattered through such portraits link them to the daily notebook entries in which writing and drawing vie for space, and to those texts with incantational nonsense syllables unpredictably inserted in veering, witty tirades.[1]

Eliminating playwright and script, the original Theatre of Cruelty was to be directed by "a kind of unique Creator to whom will fall the double responsibility of the spectacle and the action." It was to be immediate (no spectacle was to be staged twice), gestural (physically articulated signs; actors as hieroglyphs), and dangerous—threatening the identities and bodies of both participants and spectators. Defining cruelty as a kind of charged rigor ("Everything arranged to a hair in a fulminating order"), Artaud proposed that the barrier between stage and performer should be obliterated, with the spectators placed at the center in a bare, undecorated building. Language, including screams, was to be used as percussive marking. This Theater of Cruelty was to evoke the plague, and be up to the forces of life at large, with the actor "an inspired ghost radiating affective powers."

Sources for this theatrical vision included Balinese dance, Marx Brothers films, Lucas van Leyden's painting *The Daughters of Lot*, the Conquest of Mexico, and Artaud's psychic dead-end, exacerbated by drug addiction, which he described throughout the 1920s and early-to-mid-1930s as one of total exhaustion, "acidic burning in the limbs, muscles twisted and as cut through to ribbons," an inability to think, and a paralyzing sense of non-existence. As an organism in a constant state of self-destruction and self-reconstruction, the Theater of Cruelty was a phantasmagoric elaboration of Artaud's own life. In spite of being, as he put it, "not dead, but separated," he produced during this period nearly two dozen film scenarios and books which masterfully charted his predicament.[2]

Artaud completely cracked in the fall of 1937, becoming his own deliriously paranoid double, Antonéo Arlaud. He spent the next eight years and eight months in five insane asylums. At Ville Evrard, the interns recorded their amazement at the ferocious energy with which he would fight the demons he claimed surrounded him day and night. He believed that the interns as well as his friends in Paris were infested with Doubles, who were Initiates. They invaded him at night attempting to steal his semen and excrement, dictated letters in his hand, and spied on him, stealing and possessing his thoughts before he could make them conscious.

This last dilemma evokes Artaud's 1923 correspondence with Jacques Riviére in which he protested against someone or some thing intercepting his thoughts. What had been invisible forces in 1923 had, by 1939, taken on identities in a Theater of Cruelty conceived and performed by and in the body and mind of Artaud/Arlaud. The beginning of Artaud's regeneration seemed to take place at this time. Although he still believed that his thoughts were being robbed, he was identifying the robbers as fantasy formations and assigning them names: Astral, Flat-nosed Pliers, Those Born of Sweat, and Cigul the Incarnation of Evil. At this time, Artaud was a savage parody of a creator/director/dancer, a one-man gestural theater, whirling about his intern-spectators, screaming, indeed a true "inspired ghost radiating affective powers."

After Artaud's 1943 transfer to the asylum at Rodez, much of his demon-fighting energy was channeled into sound experiments: condensing syllables, grunting, humming, praying out loud while eating, and declaiming in a range of sonorous, monotonous, and full tones. In hindsight, one can see that these eruptions were leading to the vocal writing of 1946–47. However, Gaston Ferdière, the doctor in charge of Artaud at Rodez, detested his patient's "happenings" and, in a cruel attempt to redirect Artaud's energy, put him through fifty-one electroshock sessions.

In January 1945, Artaud began to draw on large sheets of paper, using pencils, crayons, and colored chalks. He also funneled his Ville Evrard cast of Doubles into a multi-prismed Catholic drama in the notebooks he began keeping. Near the end of 1945, he began to draw as well as to write in the notebooks, initially depicting bulbous, rigid, naked human figures tattooed with spots.[3]

The drawings on large sheets done between January and September in 1945 are tentative and tensionless, with human bodies, protozoa, and tubular sponges putting forth pseudopods, adrift like loose molecules in an unstable, psychic fluid. The first of the hermaphroditic totem poles and wheeled cannons appear, along with thin columns of syllables.

Over the next several months, Artaud experimented with various layouts and ways of constructing figures. The drawings are playful at times, and include tiny figures strapped to tables, wheeled penis-cannons, cartoonish women holding huge scythes whose handles are penises, free-floating spread-eagled imps, envelopes turning into torso-like machines, and tubes, cylinders, and bubbles. Artaud's first fully articulated drawing, "The Totem" (December 1945), is an assertively-reworked, smudged, mutilated, faceless, spindle-shaped female who will reappear in later writings as "the strangled totem," and "the innate totem."

From February 1946 on, until his release from Rodez the following May, Artaud's drawings become increasingly bold and slashing. His first self-portrait (the last drawing to be completed before his release) scathingly captures the asylum's assault in a face cut through with sores and scars, and measled with black spots. One eye is glazed, dead, the other starkly watchful, and aware. This is probably the drawing that Artaud's one doctor friend, Jean Dequeker, watched him rework for several days, "shattering pencil after pencil, suffering the internal throes of his own exorcism."

Once free of Rodez, and based in a clinic outside of Paris, Artaud turned a derelict pavilion into his workshop. By the end of his life (less than two years later), he had intestinal cancer, but his actual death may have been brought about by an overdose of chloral hydrate); the damp, dirty walls of this last "theater" were smeared with blood; his worktable, his pounding stump, and the head of his bed were gouged with knife holes.[4]

Artaud would draw standing before a table, making noises, and often pressing his pencil point into the part of his head that corresponded to the part of the sitter's head that he was depicting. The sitter was forbidden to move, but allowed to talk. Artaud made dots by crushing his pencil lead into the paper; his strokes were so violent that he sometimes tore the paper, at others so insistent that the drawing took on an anthracitic gleam. Paul Thévenin—Artaud's dearest friend, sitter, and editor—told Stephen Barber that sitting for Artaud was like being flayed alive.

Glancing back to the original Theater of Cruelty, we can see how faithful Artaud was to his all-embracing project. He compressed its grandiosity into a one-on-one face-to-face combat: the creator–director became a creator–drawer, the spectators a single, targeted sitter. Identities and bodies were still threatened; no performance was restaged; doubles were everywhere—in Artaud's sense of himself as a demonized, electro-shock punctured body and its idealized opposite, a virginal, organless body always in the process of being achieved. The paper on which he drew was at once a receptive support and a betraying subjectile that he was forever harrowing. The completed portraits—dappled with moldy and vital flesh, crawling with wiry agitations on the verge of becoming writing, and animated with inner forces that appeared to be redefining the skull—were the sitters' doubles. Or if, as Artaud believed, his friends had been replaced by Doubles, these portraits could be thought of as Artaud's capturing of the sitters' real faces marked by the counterfeiting phantoms. If portrait drawing enabled him to engage the spectator in a full nelson of psychic impingement, his texts and the thousands of notebook pages served to redouble the sitter/spectator into an audience of reader/viewers.

In Artaud's last period, every position taken to attack its opposite must, in turn, be rejected and attacked. Writing at once protects yet attacks the drawing, as drawing attacks yet protects the writing. In the texts the same ambivalence occurs between the incantations and the tirades. Based on nothing, a vertiginous, revolving movement cuts like a band-saw through the paper as well as through Artaud's maternal language. The containing wall for these antipositions is that they are at the mercy of a no longer repressed but still infantile consciousness. At the same time that Artaud sends out volleys of sparks, he regrinds his obsessions.

It had taken nearly two decades of rejection, abuse, and internal mayhem for Artaud to grasp that the only site at which he could exercise his faculties at large was one where he could completely control the unfolding of an event.[5] His Stations of the Cross, as it were, now look satanically and meaningfully planned. He had tried to project an unrealizable Theater of Cruelty onto a new kind of stage, but it boomeranged at him and imploded. Rather than silencing or totally destroying him, the implosion populated his inner wasteland with saint-quality demons and willy-nilly placed him in the hands of that doctor who fried him alive for twenty months. Artaud's terrible saga evokes the poet Kenneth Rexroth's stanza about the knob cone pine, "whose cones / Endure unopened on the branches, at last / To grow embedded in the wood, waiting for fire / To open them and reseed the burned forest." Opened by fire, Artaud revealed "being's disease, the syphilis of its infinity."

NOTES:

[1] For the portraits, see *Antonin Artaud: Dessins et portraits*, with essays by Paule Thévenin and Jacques Derrida, Gallimard, Paris, 1986. More available in the USA is *Antonin Artaud: Words on Paper*, edited by Margit Rowell, The Museum of Modern Art, NYC, 1996, with useful supplementary material on the drawings. Some of the notebook pages with drawings are reproduced in *Dessins et portraits*; there are eight pages from such notebooks reproduced in *Sulfur #9* (1984). Selections from Artaud's writing from 1945 until his death in 1948 may be found in *Watchfiends & Rack Screams*, translated by Clayton Eshleman, with Bernard Bador, Exact Change, Boston, 1995. This paper was originally presented as part of a panel discussion on Artaud's writing and drawing at the Drawing Center in NYC, October 11, 1996, in conjunction with the exhibition of Artaud's drawings at MOMA. Organized by Sylvère Lotringer, the panel also included Jacques Derrida, Margit Rowell, Nancy Spero, and Gayatri Spivak. A slightly edited version of the paper first appeared in *Grand Street* magazine; a full version appeared in *Rain Taxi*.

[2] For Artaud's writings from the 1920s and '30s, see *Antonin Artaud: Selected Writings*, translated by Helen Weaver, with a substantial introduction by Susan Sontag, FSG, NYC, 1976 (now a University of California Press paperback). For some of Artaud's film scenarios in English, see *Tulane Drama Review (TDR) #33*. Another scenario, "The Spurt of Blood," appeared in *TDR #22*. "The Philospher's Stone, a mime play," is presented in *TDR #27*.

[3] Previous to the 1945 Rodez drawings, Artaud produced two series of *sorts* ("spells") in 1937 and 1939. The first ones, sent from Dublin, retain the appearance of letters, with diagrams, marks, and holes burned through the paper, transforming the message—usally a curse on the recipient—into a visual hex. The second series, sent from the Ville Evrard asylum, is more elaborate: torn into burned, shield-like shapes, the sheets are heavily marked with crayons and colored inks, clearly visual works rather than decorated messages. Paul Thévenin has catalogued seven, but there were undoubtedly more. These "spells" were Artaud's first attempts to antiphonally charge writing visually. In a 1947 text, "Ten years that the language is gone" (my English version to be found in *Conductors of the Pit*, Soft Skull, Brooklyn, 2005), he states that since 1939 he has not written

without drawing, indicating that the second series of "spells" marks the beginning of his extraordinary final period.

[4] For Artaud's life in and outside of Paris after his release from Rodez, see Paul Thévenin's "Letter on Artaud," *TDR #27*, and three recent books by Stephen Barber, *Antonin Artaud: Blows and Bombs*, 1993, *Weapons of Liberation*, 1996 (both published by Faber and Faber in London), and *The Screaming Body* (Creation Books, 1999, London).

[5] Artaud also gave three public performances in Paris in 1947. On January 13, at the Vieux-Columbier, as a declaration to Paris that he, as "Artaud le mômo," had indeed returned, the poet faced a packed audience of some 900 people, some of whom were audibly hostile. During the first part of his program, Artaud's voice repeatedly broke, and he kept misplacing his papers. Unnerved by the antagonistic atmosphere, he then abandoned his prepared text, and for the next two hours, between screams and gaps of silence, dramatically described his asylum incarceration and electro-shock torture (the closest thing in American letters to Artaud's Vieux-Colombier performance is probably Charles Olson's four-hour improvised reading at Berkeley in 1965). Artaud considered the evening a failure, and in a heated exchange with André Breton stated that for the kind of language he was trying to create, a theatrical medium was inadequate.

When the Galerie Pierre offered to exhibit his drawings in July of the same year, Artaud seized upon the occasion to do two performances over which he could exert a directorial degree of control. The events would be by invitation only, and to avoid the physical pressure he experienced at Vieux-Colombier, he invited two young friends (who had assisted in his release from Rodez) to read texts he would select for them. The opening event was marred by nervousness on the part of the readers, so Artaud aimed at even greater control over the closing event. He chose to read one text himself, and exhaustively rehearsed Roger Blin and Colette Thomas who read with him. Surrounded by Artaud's drawings and a small, enthusiastic audience, it was by far the most successful of these Paris performances. Yet Artaud left the Gallery Pierre that night exasperated, and told his friend Jacques Prevel: "For me, it was a disappointment. To have made all those people understand what I was doing, I would have had to have killed them."

In effect, any audience beyond a single, accepted individual was impossible for Artaud, in part because of his fury over his nearly nine year incarceration (behind which was the total rejection of his Theater of Cruelty project in Paris in the 1930s), and in part because verbal manifestation per se had become suspect. Anything short of a transcendental physical manifestation in which, as he put it, would "shit blood through my navel," was hopelessly inadequate. It is under these circumstances that I have proposed that the only realization of the Theater of Cruelty project was in the one-on-one portrait drawing context, where Artaud was able to "perform" in a way that made him eager to invite new sitters for sessions up to the end of 1947 (after which he was too weak to take on any artwork other than a few drawings which did not involve sitters).

JUDITH SCOTT'S FIBER ART

Scott's work process may symbolize her "abduction" at seven years old from home to state institutions (where she spent thirty-five years), and to her release, engineered by her normal twin sister in 1987, to a care facility with daily visits to the Creative Growth Art Center in Oakland. A woman with Down's Syndrome, who cannot hear, speak, or read, Judith steals things that she finds around the Center—sticks, branches, pieces of cut rugs, parts of a broken electric fan, conical cardboard spools, parts of a rolling pin—to begin a fiber structure. Might not these thefts represent Judith's "theft" at seven? Such would make the object she secretes in her work bag the seven-year-old Judith, then taken to her work table, wrapped and concealed as Judith was "concealed" from her family (and the family concealed from Judith). The repeated wrapping (string, yarn, towels) with no apparent end-form in mind evokes the monotonous "overlays" of institutional life—its isolation, its repetitional emptiness. However, the buried "thing inside" is also being protected, cocooned, for Judith knows, I think, that as she was put away she was also taken out, and is here, as a wrapper-concealer-protector, to testify.

Scott appears to not complete her structures, but at a certain point, losing interest in them, abandons them. Again, her own "abandonment" in institutional limbo seems pertinent.

            Like a spider cocooning its
prey in thread—   it hangs in the web, an

artifact—   to be imbibed later.
                        Abandoned now.
              "now" as that to be abandoned.

I first saw her work displayed at La Musée d'Art Moderne (Villeneuve d'Ascq, outside Lille, France), June 2002. I jotted in my notebook: "unevolved toys, lost chords, pieces of no whole, gateless gates, everwhats."

A few of her pieces evoke Upper Paleolithic faceless, armless, footless "Venus" statuettes, with fronts and backs. One of them looks like a crib with a head, with a long, wrapped object inside." "Venus as a Cradle for a Sleeping Erection." Such forms suggest that Scott's inner lake is fed by very ancient sources...

In fact, it is truly amazing that one of humankind's first forms, created some 35,000 years ago, appears to be still latent in mind and accessible to one who is, for the most part, dependent upon her inner world as her only world.

Such forms tell us that our "are" is deeper than our "we," that the capsized Upper Paleolithic still sings.

Scott navigates, I would propose, interior being without the distraction/attraction of sound, language, or text. Charles Olson's articulation of his own interiority, two years before he died, might apply:

> Wholly absorbed
> into my own conduits to
> an inner nature or subterranean lake
> the depths or bound of which I more and more
> explore and know more
> of, in that sense that other than that all else
> closes out and I tend further to fall into
> the Beloved Lake...[1]

John M. MacGregor tells us that Scott rocked her first structures, calling them "baba." The inner lake is "Beloved" because it is the source of psychic life. Such structures—all of which attest to the unknown having been possessed and bound—are less "babies" than they are "Judith's Story," parthenogenetically rehearsed again and again. But there is no opening night. MacGregor writes: "All her work seems to involve an ongoing preparation for an event that has not yet occurred." One scenario for such an event might be: Holding up any one of her fiber pieces, eyes blazing, speaking clearly, Scott declares: "This is the story of my life."

To entomb something can be to protect it from life's assaults. Desperate, deranged mothers sometimes are said to have killed their infants in order to protect them. A few of Scott's structures look like contorted, tied-up "bodies." One has yarn-wrapped curved branches arching out of it and re-piercing it. Simultaneously, it is self-feeding and self-torturing. Protection bristles with its own nightside: hurting.

Foetal erratics. Stillborn rhapsodies. Shackle strains. Scott's "blues."

Judith the stolen stick girl, a mongoloid with a boner, trussed in the doldrums of thirty-five institutionalized years to re-emerge so as to symbolically return as a realization. Dead pupa in dead cocoon with its yarned legs jutting. Via bondage, she bonds with the rejected and the stolen. She is detached from and adhesive to a work table altar penal colony fiber script.

You are separated. Conceive now.

I am notherally moved by what she has made of nothing. By her ability to have dislodged her remoteness from simply being on remote. By her oflessness that in its own way *is* with of.

NOTES:

[1] The Olson quotation is from *The Maximus Poems* (University of California Press, Berkeley, 1983), p. 585. The MacGregor material is taken from his book, *Metamorphosis: The Fiber Art of Judith Scott* (Creative Growth Art Center, Oakland, 1999). This piece appeared in *Hambone* magazine.

FOUR INTRODUCTIONS[1]

A Note on the Introductions

When I began to teach in the English Department at Eastern Michigan University, the fall of 1986, there was no visiting writer program. I decided to try to raise some money that would enable us to bring in a few writers each year, and began by going to the text bookstores that sold books to our students. I suggested to the managers that since our students regularly bought books from them, that it would make sense for such stores to contribute to honorariums for visiting poets and prose writers. While the Shaman Drum Bookstore in Ann Arbor did not do business with our students in Ypsilanti, the owner Karl Pohrt liked the idea of more writers coming into the area (some of whom he would go ahead to invite to do programs in his store), and he offered us $1,000. I raised another thousand from local Ypsilanti stores, and with my $2,000 went back to EMU, saying, in effect, to the department head, and other possible donors, if the book stores are willing to contribute, don't you think the university should contribute too? Colleagues Janet Kauffman and Larry Smith contributed to this work as well, and we ended up with around $3,000 for the first year.

Ever since, the English Department has been sponsoring several readings per year. Our visiting authors have included Gary Snyder, Jerry Rothenberg, Amiri Baraka, Jayne Cortez, Bei Dao, Eliot Weinberger, Ron Padgett, Nathaniel Mackey, Pierre Joris, Forest Gander, Carol Maso, Rickki Ducornet, CD Wright, Keith and Rosmarie Waldrop, Adrienne Rich, David Matlin, Amy Gerstler, Diane Wakoski, Sherman Alexie, Diane Glancy, Mary Caponegro, Will Alexander, Michael

Palmer, Michael Davidson, Christine Hume, Anne Waldman, Kenward Elmslie, Michael Harper, Jeff Clark, and Andrew Joron.

Besides sharing the fund raising, Janet and Larry and I, in the late 1980s and throughout most of the 1990s, shared the introductions as well. I used the preparation time for mine to read or reread several of an author's books and to go beyond the generic introduction that mainly lists books and awards. I sought to quickly identify what was special about a particular author's body of work. In Companion Spider *(Wesleyan University Press, 2002), I included my introductions to readings by Gary Snyder and Michael Palmer. Here are four more, for Will Alexander (February 4, 2001), Christine Hume (February 4, 2002), and Jeff Clark and Andrew Joron who read together on October 12, 2005.*

WILL ALEXANDER

Born in 1948, Will Alexander has lived all his life in Los Angeles. While he attended UCLA (and earned a B.A. in English and creative writing), he is artistically self-educated and until fairly recently wrote and painted in almost total isolation. I met him in 1981 at a political discussion about the American military involvement in El Salvador, and soon after discovered the strange uniqueness of his writing. Will's appearance in *Sulfur #2* (1981) may have been his first national literary publication.

Until the mid-1990s, Alexander lived off low-paying jobs in Los Angeles (for example: the ticketing department of the Los Angeles Lakers basketball team). In recent years, he has done writer-in-residence stints at UCSD, the New College in San Francisco, and Hofstra University. His first book, *Vertical Rainbow Climber* (Jazz Press, Los Angeles), appeared in 1987, but it has never been distributed. More recently, four short and one full-length collections have appeared:

Arcane Lavender Morals (Leave Books, 1994)
Asia & Haiti (Sun & Moon Press, 1995)

The Stratospheric Canticles (Pantograph Press, 1995)
Toward the Primeval Lightning Field (O Books, 1998)
Above the Human Nerve Domain (Pavement Saw Press, 1998)

To this list can be added a 25 page section of and on Alexander in *Sulfur #32*, edited by Eliot Weinberger, a 60-page section on the poet in *Callaloo* (Vol. 22, #2), edited by Harryette Mullen, and Alexander's 60-page poem, "The Brimstone Boat / for Philip Lamantia," in Jeff Clark's magazine *Faucheuse* (unnumbered issue). In conversation with Mullen, Alexander addressed his sense of poetry:

> I find words every day that I've never used before. I might use words that I create, words that didn't exist in the language... I feel foreign language rhythms while writing in English. Writing a foreign language within your own language creates another language... I'm what you could call a *maroon* (in the West Indies, a fugitive slave); I'm a psychic *maroon*... The poet has to be infused with the plasma, the river of poetry, so that the river sweeps through, and takes everything in its path... Surrealism is perfectly conjunctive with my understanding of an African worldview. It deals with the visible and the invisible. For me the invisible is something that not only takes place in a subconscious realm, but also in a supraconscious realm as well as a conscious realm. It's back to that river again. You're dealing with a triple mind instead of a single mind, which is part of the scape of the mind, but definitely not the end of the mind... I have no problem with my identity. You can get to a certain level of consciousness, which is available to all races. In every race you want to work at the higher level... I carry a central fascination with the scorching connective between meaning and sound, as if I were that first genetic connection, magically naming stones from primeval eras... "

In an essay printed along with her conversation with the poet in *Callaloo*, Mullen writes:

> "Alexander's poems are unpunctuated, their expanding struc-
> tures suggesting that each might be read as a very long, very
> complex sentence. Readers might apprehend each poem as
> one sentence or many, or perhaps as a potentially unbounded
> structure of dependent and independent clauses... Each poem
> is a complex sentence machine turning out elaborate gram-
> matical parallelisms, extensive series of epic catalogues, and
> open-ended syntax of discordant clauses and appended
> prepositional phrases."

While Alexander has clear affinities with certain surrealists (Aimé Césaire above all), if he is a surrealist, he is a transcendental one, apparently able to access a 250,000-word English vocabulary while in a state of trance. His verbal flights strike me as more shamanistic than free-associational or automatic. His evocation of upper and lower worlds and his vocabulary, which bridges poetry, philosophy, myth, and science, gives his verbal fulgurations a sense of linguistic seed that suddenly sprouts, then resprouts, in accelerating exfoliations of triadic units (which evoke the three levels of consciousness he speaks about). On one level, he is like watching a plant grow in a speeded-up film, in which all shoots, however obscure, appear to contribute to a veering and uncanny structure. On another level, he is an outsider artist whose self-propelled soarings call to mind Simon Rodia's "Watts Towers" as well as Siberian ecstatics.

CHRISTINE HUME

Christine Hume completed her Ph.D. at the University of Denver in 2000, her dissertation being *Musca Domestica*, a collection of poems with a critical preface investigating literary hybridity. That spring, the collection, with a preface by Heather McHugh, was published by Beacon Press as the winner of the Barnard New Women Poets Prize. To date, Hume's poems have appeared in over thirty journals. She has published articles on Ann Lauterbach, Ben

Marcus, Rosmarie Waldrop, Anne Carson, and Susan Howe, and has received grants from The Fund for Poetry, Illinois Wesleyan University (where she taught in 2000 and 2001), and the Colorado Arts Council. She joined the Eastern Michigan University English Department as an assistant professor in 2001. Those of us in the English Department are pleased to have her as a colleague.

The title *Musca Domestica* (Latin for "common housefly") evokes the words "muse," "music," "musing," and "a muse meant" (a pun worked by Robert Duncan in his 1956 book, *Letters*), as well as ancient fly lore. Because flies were thought to be the common forms taken by souls in search of rebirth, they took on the stature of Baal-Zebub, Lord of Flies, an alternative name for Satan in medieval Christianity. In Emily Dickinson's poem #465, the dying speaker and her attenders prepare for "that last Onset—when the King / Be witnessed—in the Room." The fly that then appears may be taken as a caricature of God or Death; it may also evoke this ancient fly lore: the fly as psychopomp, or Lord of Souls, appearing as a nick in time to accompany the departing soul to the afterlife location from which she addresses us at the beginning of the poem: "I heard a Fly buzz—when I died—."

Flies are for Hume what grass was for Whitman: common, tenacious, ubiquitous, and, from a non-scientific viewpoint, magical: maggots appear on garbage as if by spontaneous generation. They may also be thought of as the spirit of incongruity in Hume's phrase and line fusions, or her compositional flightiness, her associational flits, in which traditional narrative direction is scattered laterally. As a Hume poem works its way down the page, it associationally splices in curves to its story, cubistically redesigning the "floating world" of the subject. These are poems that run a mental gauntlet, losing pieces of what they start out with as they pick up the flashes and gaps of irrational incursions. Increasingly riddled, they become a riddle, the answer to which may be partially composed by the poem at hand and partially by the reader, who must become a very active one or be lost—though perhaps dazzled while lost by Hume's verbal dexterity. These poems perspire potential meaning through what often seems to be chance pores.

The reader thus learns more and less at the same time. The more may be thought of as the wilderness of folds and facets Hume's shifts create. The less might be identified as over-acculturated thematic repetitions; the story lines of traditional verse now become clichés. To put it this way approaches one sense of the hybrid, which is at the base of Hume's compositional method: the wilderness and cultural boundary-crossing by shamans and witches that is underscored by exchanges between the feral and the tame ("hybrid," from the Latin *hybrida*, is defined as "the piglet resulting from the union of a wild boar with a tame sow"). Another way to contextualize the hybrid in Hume's poetry is to think of a wildness offsetting the presumed, or the unknown interfusing the known. As if a chasmal backdrop to Hume's enterprise, Baudelaire's words of one hundred and fifty years ago, from "Le voyage," still ring true (in Richard Howard's translation):

> Once we have burned our brains out, we can
>   plunge
> to Hell or Heaven—any abyss will do—
> deep in the Unknown to find the new!

JEFF CLARK

Jeff Clark was born in southern California in 1971. Of his two trade books to date, the first, *The Little Door Slides Back* (1997), was chosen by Ray DiPalma for The National Poetry Series and published by Sun & Moon Press. It was reprinted in 2004 by Farrar Straus & Giroux at the same time this press published Clark's second collection, *Music & Suicide*, which received the Jay Laughlin Award from the Academy of American Poets. Since late 2003, Clark has lived in Ann Arbor, where his book design studio, Quemadura, is also based.

Very few poets display the charged turbulence that fills Clark's apprentice volume. Its soul-searching, stimulating negations bode for great potential development as a poet in somewhat the same spirit that a rich neurosis at the beginning of psychotherapy is of tremendous value for a patient and can lead to a powerful resolution. The title, *The Little Door Slides Back*, refers on one hand to the shock of womb exit, and, on the other hand, to Clark's subsequent realization, at twenty-three, that without "personal logorhythms" he had slid the door back a second time, enclosing himself in what he calls "the terror in the Hangar." Here, with his coined word "logorhythm" (based on the mathematical term, "logarithm," and suggesting the rhythm of the Logos, or wordrhythm), it is appropriate to comment on Clark's language: charged with neologisms, arcane words, and syntactic break-offs, it veers in an exhilarating way between speech and sound-tuned alignments. One prose poem, "Marie-Pristine," an imagined letter by a young French woman to the man who has abandoned her, written in English-as-a-second-language mode, plays with the fascinating blur between the awkward and the inventive.

The action in *The Little Door Slides Back* is controlled by a doppelganger, or double, identified only as "he." Percolating through what Clark refers to as "the blue byways of my interior," this figure, often erotically entangled with the speaker, goes through chameleon-like changes. He is variously identified as a jeweler, a palmist, an assassin, a nympholept, a horse, the wicked technician, Larousse, a nighttime turd in Desert diaper, and Lord. This early David Lynch-like, tenebrous atmosphere, dominated by sadomasochistic vignettes, evokes the alchemical *nigredo*, in which patterns of self-recognition are formed by means of horror and obscenity. Three-quarters of the way through this collection, the speaker states that he wants to "waylay and molest the beast that has imagined and pent me here." At this point, the doppelganger turns into a spectral companion who helps the poet "dismantle the nest."

The opening poem of Clark's second book, *Music and Suicide*, places the speaker as "an ailing fallen jester" in the grass of a "ribboned maze." Mazes, unlike labyrinths, have no center, but, unlike the grinning cul-de-sacs that characterize the first book, they do allow interior circulation, a kind of errancy that enables Clark to create some terrific narratives stitched with jump-cuts and switch-backs, re-emergences, creature contacts, and cunnilingus. Again, in contrast to the fragmentary, muffled violence in the first book, in "Farewell Antithesis," we find an exacting vision of a goat being torn apart by a pack of dogs. The book's final poem, "Entrance," situates the poet with "an ally in a maze / that will stay exitless each lane / more alive than the last." Clark now also writes: "We are not looking for a crystalline being, but for something in the process of melting. Allowing each of us to move within the otherness of the other."

Having cracked his subconscious strong room and kissed what crawled and flitted from it, Clark has capably laid the groundwork for a reversal of his *Little Door* complaint: "Never was I able to say a man long enough to remain him."

ANDREW JORON

Andrew Joron graduated from the University of California at Berkeley with a B.A. in "History and Philosophy of Science," and spent the early part of his writing career infusing poetic avant-garde techniques with science fiction. Most of his poems in the 1980s were published in science-fiction magazines and anthologies. With the 1992 collection, *Science Fiction*, published by the surreal-ist Pantograph Press, he signaled his leave taking from science fic-tion. His first mature book, *The Removes* (Hard Press, 1999) syn-thesized surrealism and language poetry. This collection was followed in 2003 by *Fathom* (Black Square Editions, and beautiful-ly designed by Jeff Clark at Quemadura), which was well received and widely reviewed (it was selected by the *Village Voice* as one of the "Top 25 Books of 2003"). From 1982 to 1988, Joron published and edited *Velocities: A Magazine of Speculative Poetry*. Brought up in a German-speaking household in Stuttgart, he has also translated the German Utopian Marxist philosopher Ernst Bloch's *Literary Essays* (Stanford University Press, 1998).

In Joron's poetry, words appear to carry, as if cargo, half-stowed, half-visible, sister and brother words. Discovering such cargo and setting it forth can determine the direction, or spread, of a poem. For example (from *The Removes*):

> Enter *here*
> Inter *here*
>   —turn among
>   the torn, the Entire.

Or this longer passage from *Fathom:*

> Now, *cloak*
> Approaches *clock* like a prayer.
>
> Hued, as in air; hewed, as in stone.
>
> Where bells of
>   *dissonance* are still
> Half-submerged in *distance.*
>
> Where the quickening of *eyes* equals *ice.*

As one who has spent many years studying the earliest art of mankind, in particular the Ice Age cave art in southwestern France, I find that Joron's method here evokes one way in which Cro-Magnon hand lamps, some 20,000 years ago, appear to have made aspects of wall contours suggest animal and human anatomy. A significant number of engravings, paintings, and wall sculptures employ natural formations. In the way that Joron discovers words possessing word shadows, it may have seemed to these early explorers that animals (and, less often, humans) were partially embedded in, or emerging through, such walls, and that such presences only needed the assistance of some man-made lines to be completely present. If a wall was "with animal," then some Cro-Magnon mid-wifery could help it give birth.

In a way that beautifully parallels the ancient emergence of something from nothing, or an image from no image at all, Joron defines the first mark as "an arc sinking upward, crowded with sen-sations," and stone as "curv[ing] thought toward the drinking of its shadow." His poem "Mazed Interior" in *Fathom* is, in part, an orig-inal meditation on what might be called "the construction of the underworld."

I also want to point out the way that Joron's constantly interrupt-ed syntax, and fragmentary clauses, break off where the imaginal density quits. No explanations here, and no narrative in a conven-tional sense. Rather, reading a Joron poem is like watching an orb-weaving spider weave a web, a labyrinthine process, as he says, "imprisoned in liberties." His tense and flexible line breaks and positionings recall the taut yet airy stanzas of the late Gustaf Sobin. In a recent meditation entitled "Language as a Ghost Condensate," Joron sets forth the idea of a poetics poised between order and chaos, a position that for a change seems really cutting edge. He writes: "Poetic 'lines of force' point toward uninhabited wilder-nesses within language, toward removes of irreducible meaning—so that a poetic impulse will cause the system of language to exceed its own boundary conditions, and to undergo a phase transition toward the Unsayable."

NOTES:
[1]This piece appeared in *American Poetry Review*.

STEPHEN BERG'S
"THE ELEGY ON HATS"[1]

Sheep Meadow Press, 2005

According to Stephen Berg, Charles Baudelaire planned to write an elegy based on his fascination with hats, on what he referred to as their frivolity, uselessness, elegance, and evocation of guillotined heads. He wrote out a few pages of notes, and then never wrote the elegy. Drawing upon what he tells us was his own mother's huge collection of closeted hats (which he writes that she collected to "allay the boiling anxiety / that scarred her mind"), Berg has, in his own fashion, written the poem Baudelaire never penned.

Berg's *Elegy* is eighty-two pages long, in fourteen sections, written entirely in couplets, with meager and erratic capitalization and punctuation. Words and phrases jam up against each other in a charged, choppy way, with much paratactic tension (I often thought of Allen Ginsberg's "boxcars boxcars boxcars" while voicing the poem; Thomas Meyer employs a similar couplet structure in his *diode jing*, published by Flood, 2005). Berg states in section 13 that his method here is based on a description of writing by Soren Kierkegaard:

"desultory"

meaning for him leaping from one point to
another to illuminate the subject

> from all sides or in order that the un-
> intelligibility might be broken
>
> down into its several parts...

On one level, Berg's *Elegy* is an existential dialectic in sympathy with Baudelaire's probing of his own suffering. Supported by Baudelaire's professed self-judgment, soul openness, and lack of sentimentality, Berg's own writing is comradely, metaphysical, funny, and vulgar, as he feeds into his saltatory patterns bits of Freud, Frost, Aristotle, Conrad, Weil, and Stevens, among others. His poem is also scholarly, the result of a wide range of reading.

The Berg Baudelaire entanglement is more complex than I have so far suggested. Along with one poem by Vallejo and Saint John of the Cross at least a half-dozen Baudelaire poems are presented in Berg's translations, most of which are actually Berg's own poems. In this respect, *The Elegy on Hats* reminds me of Jack Spicer's *After Lorca* (1957), a mixture of Spicer's translations of Lorca's poems and original poems by Spicer himself (presented as Lorca translations). Thirty-four poems are interspersed with six "letters" that discuss Spicer's evolving sense of poetry. Berg's fake Baudelaire poems are recognizable, to some extent, by the fact that they are more openly bawdy or coarse than Baudelaire's poetry. A quick example: here is my literal rendering of a tercet from "La Gouffre," followed by Berg's handling of it in his *Elegy*:

> I am afraid of sleep as one fears a deep pit,
> Filled with nebulous horror, leading who knows where;
> I see nothing but infinity through every window,

> Sleep's dim cruddy pit swallows me—
> flesh, mud, shit: I'm not sure what or where—
>
> infinity feeds infinity outside my windows...

Both the Spicer and the Berg texts raise interesting questions about author identity and appropriation. Not only do their "loose" translations pull the original authors into their own language terrains, trimming them to fit, as it were, their own styles, but their own poems in Lorca's and Baudelaire's names employ a reconstruction of the original authors' psyches; Aztec priests dancing in the skins of the sacrificed comes to mind.

In Berg's case, a more appropriate metaphor might relate to hats themselves, of putting on a Baudelaire hat so that the poet's words "enter / the mind by osmosis creating a new / holy text a new source matrix for prayer." Berg also writes that he wants to make contact with the ghost of himself, with his unrealized self. The implication of such a projection, in the context of this poem, is that one way he can do so is by writing as if he were Baudelaire. Yet, unlike Rimbaud, he is horrified that his "I" is "somebody else." He laments that his "wild fate has been to act as if I were somebody else."

Again, in contrast to Spicer's *After Lorca*, which heralds Spicer's most significant work, Berg's *Elegy on Hats* is a summational work, probably written in the poet's late 60s. There is a very accomplished interplay in this poem, between Berg's singed fluttering about the flame of the self, and his speculations about the mysterious roles hats play in peoples' lives:

> why this is an elegy I can see now
> obviously hats wait longer than other clothes
>
> to be worn compared to shoes eyeglasses
> underpants socks shirts belts trousers so
>
> in my mother's closets and in my own
> I can hear hats weeping for themselves
>
> whispering *useless useless* to each other
> one or two fall to the floor others

lost out of style crushed unseasonal it's
tragic the way hats essential as they are

continue to be treated as outcasts
just as the unquoteable impossible-

to-arrange posthumous shattered elegy
on hats by *mon semblable* must

always remain unknown like the sky he
tried to punch a hole through to touch God.

NOTES:

[1] This review appeared in *Rain Taxi*. My essay on Jack Spicer's *After Lorca*, "The Lorca Working," appeared in *Companion Spider*.

TELLURIC CLOCKWORK [1]

Horst Haack's *Chronographie Terreste* is a labyrinth whose right angles forward our centripetal unfinishable journey. Verticality of the 20th century. Screens as reversible monuments. Prehistorically, image was first, alphabet second. In the panels of these screens, images appear on blank ground that is then filled trilingually: a centripetal train of uroboric sentences, the tail of one disappearing into the mouth of another.

Figures full of blocks and convulsive bubbles, dread of the red rock-knobbed earth, the beauty of yellow light falling through raspberry-stained bodies, microscopic explosions, balloons and swipes, a slug poised vertically over mugs with spoons.

Chronographie Terrestre: the Cretan labyrinth screened, updated. "The bitter combat at the center" now the silent visitor's mental drift.

Caucasian man, disoriented, muscle-eternal, roaming Dogon alleys.

Chronographie Terrestre: the broken telluric zodiac of the fallen mansions of the sky. The Snail crushed. The Chariot toppled. Sequence unsprung. Coded is decoded is recoded revenant. Metaphor is chowder, and the chowder is in millrace. Where are the Voguls, Siryenians, Ostyaks of yesteryear? We have forgotten who we were, but have not yet forgotten that we were.

Looking at Haack's piles of dead animals and severed women's heads, I see the Great Harlot on her Scarlet-colored Camel making their way down a Paris fashion show walkway. They then turn into a Global Hawk. In my mind's cog-like movement, they become limbically entwined coils of DNA.

Chronographie Terrestre: imaginal bodies eaten into by a textual "solution." Text as the figure's aura, or panels as fields with furrow swirls of prose. The dice of cultures shaken, thrown—where did they go? Has even chance abandoned us? Near total non-sequituriality.

Are you an emptied upside-down brown pot?
Yes, I am a grub of smoke, a mineral spill.
Are you a headless man with TV rabbit ears?
Yes, I am a woman with her head between her thighs confronting
    the anal amber of the night.
Are you tearing curls and arcs, pink octopodal craniums streaked
    with festering hay?
Yes, I am the head of an Ethiopian warlord, risen out of shale,
    black-disked with sores.
Are you an R. Crumb couple exchanging anxieties, lost in a
    French mapscape dominated by a mahogany colonial skull?
Yes, I am the one who suckles, four-eyed, at the dyadic breast eye-
    ing me.
Are you the glowing hand plunged into my soot-black heart?
Yes, I am your sibyl, scratching my chin as my serpentine blue
    body narrows to an earthworm tip.
Are you the Dada noose of the whacko conjunction of sperm and
    egg?
Yes, I am the yellow body of squatting Kali with my spread dia-
    mond chalice twinkling some lighthouse boogie-woogie into
    your "Dying once is better than daily death."

What we can take in, we cannot recognize.
What we recognize, we cannot describe.
What we describe, we cannot define.

Elongated hoofed stork necks. Two-headed spinal cord. Tantrik
    body with its astral jewelry.
Top of a man's head blowing off plumbing and barbells. A severed
    head offered as a mirror to the terror-struck woman.
Molecular stroganoff.
Yes, it looks like India, but it's really a dripping piece of blueberry
    pie.
So get outta here as your limbs disconnect, as your brain turns
    into two turtles with hemispheric shells.
Scoop my purple ass onto your matrix mitt.
Titillate sense, infuriate comprehension, baffle engineering.
A hoisted, pawed, skinless rage.
The blue force bumping up against the bacteria bag.
Now power would determine reality, war lay down the law to
    business.
Black blood flowing down the back of the thigh-headed man.
He slipped his hard-on into the honey of the mirror.
As he pumped her, she sat on his lap juggling his three heads.
Encased in a tentacled hotdog, a sleeping hairless head.
Into what pothole to sink her anal stamen?
Who's seeing can now saw without context's seesaw?

Gang up on the possession of image, on the univocal power station
    running the political world.
Homage to Horst Haack, a tapir man, sticking his nose into the
    weevil-drift of the daily and the archetypal, imagining the short-
    circuiting in man's relentless blather as it generates the hermet-
    ic knots of wriggling anti-cores now at large in the humanimal
    brew.

NOTES:

[1] This piece was commissioned by Horst Haack as the introduction to the catalog *Topos & Chronos* for a retrospective showing of his many years work in progress, *Chronographie Terrestre*. The show took place at the Neuer Kunstverein Aschaffenburg e.V in Darmstadt, Germany, from September 24 to November 6, 2005.

SHEELA-NA-GIG (II)

For Nancy Spero

Medieval European motherhood hazards: on the average, death at 27. Most of her adult years she was pregnant, or nursing. She buried one-third of her children before they reached maturity. Dublin, late-19th century: one mother in every seven had ten or more children baptized. Over twenty-two percent of these infants died in their first twelve months. Poor nutrition: inadequate protein, insufficient iron.

Who could she turn to? Not the Church. "God the Father, the Son, and the Holy Ghost have ordered that you bring forth your child with pain and bring it up with sorrow and distress and many sleepless nights."

Thus pagan cures and charms: Artemisia placed on the genitalia to speed birth. Stones were pulverized and drunk, crushed then mixed with red sandalwood, citron wax, cypress cones. Skin of a white worm worn around her waist.

Midwives would smear their hands with butter or hog's grease, then work on her vulva, pulling, widening the birth passage to help the baby glide out.

Thus folk deities, *Spiritus familiars*. Thus Sheela, with grotesque lower abdomen, cavernous oval-shaped vulva, held open, so big as to reach the ground.

Sheela's genital areas were rubbed (like the yonis of Hindu god-
desses).
Birthing stones may have been placed in their genitalia.
Sheelas were drilled, head and body, with holes,
portrayed in vertical birth-giving posture.
Some were depicted with birth girdles, or holding birthing stones.
Some have protruding amniotic sacs,
or vertical channels cut below the vulva,
egg-shaped objects lying between their open legs—
hanging between the open legs of the Romsey Sheela:
a baby's head with eyes, nose, and mouth.

Yet these Sheelas are also breastless, with skeletal rib cages, skull-
like heads,
hollow eyes. They are found surrounded by graveyards, located
near the Lich Gate.
Sheela is not only the defender of the door but is to be repelled
there. A "bald grandmother," she traces back to Mistress of the
Animals.

At Binsteed, Sheela sits on an animal head,
at Whittlesford Church, she is approached by a crouching, ithyphallic beast.

> By the holy well of Melshach,
> garments fastened up under their arms,
> hands joined, women are dancing in a circle.
> In their midst: a crone, dipping a vessel into the water,
> sprinkling the dancers.

> [drawn from Barbara Freitag's *Sheela-na-
> gigs: Unraveling an Enigma*, Routledge:
> Abington, England, 2004.]

A NOTE ON CÉSAR VALLEJO'S "INTENSITY AND HEIGHT"[1]

One of César Vallejo's finest traditional-form poems, a sonnet, was typed up and dated on October 27, 1937, in Paris. The octet seems to be in two voices, the first complaining about the impossibility of articulating a vision in poetry, and the second stating that there is no difference between cipher and summation, that anything said comes to nothing, and that all artifice and myth is rooted in natural life. One can think of these two voices as poet and devil's advocate. While the second voice does not really respond to the first voice's complaints, by its nihilistic statements, it deepens the first voice's predicament.

The sestet appears to be taken over completely by voice one who, faced with his blocks and screw-ups and voice two's negative declarations, proposes to live like an animal, eat his own anguish and consume the art of the past. Some sort of action is demanded facing the complications set forth in the octet. As the sestet proceeds, the call to action becomes increasingly frantic, and in the poem's last line the first voice, or poet, identifies the second voice as a raven (immediately recalling the famous Poe poem). He urges the raven to join him in seeking out the raven's mate and inseminating her. As the figure of "Nevermore!" the raven evokes Death. In a sense, the poem proposes that the only solution to creative agony is to impregnate Death—with what, the reader might wonder.

Much of the poem is quite translatable, and after years of tinkering with the translation (I have published a half-dozen versions of it between the late 1960s and the late 1980s), I have gotten all of it to at least half-rhyme (but not in the order of the rhyme structure in the Spanish). However, there are a few knotty problems for which explanatory translations, or generalizations, are possible, but for which exact ones, that match the original, do not seem to be. Here is my translation, next to the original:

Intensity and Height

I want to write, but out comes
    foam,
I want to say so much and I mire;
there is no spoken cipher which
    is not a sum,
there is no written pyramid,
    without a core.

I want to write, but I feel like a
    puma;
I want to laurel myself, but I stew in
    onions.
There is no spoken coughv, which
    doesn't come to brume,
there is no god nor son of god,
    without progression.

For that, then, let's go eat grass,
the flesh of sobs, the fruit of wails,
our melancholy soul canned.

Let's go! Let's go! I'm struck;
let's go drink that already drunk,
raven, let's go fecundate your mate.

Intensidad y altura

Quiero escribir, pero me sale
    espuma,
quiero decir muchísimo y me atollo;
no hay cifra hablada que no sea
    suma,
No hay pirámide escrita, sin cogollo.

Quiero escribir, pero me siento
    puma;
Quiero laurearme, pero me
    encebollo.
No hay toz hablada, que no llegue a
    bruma,
no hay dios ni hijo de dios, sin
    desarrollo.

Vámonos, pues, por eso, a comer
    yerba,
carne de llanto, fruta de gemido,
nuestra alma melancólica en
    conserva.

Vámonos! Vámonos! Estoy herido;
Vámonos a beber lo ya bebido,
Vámonos, cuervo, a fecundar tu
    cuerva.

The problems: "me atollo" in the second line is stronger and more directed than "I mire," which, however, is not inaccurate. "Me atollo" means to get stuck in the mud or in a rut at the side of the road. It has a kinetic directness that "I mire" lacks. The challenge is to translate the verb in a single word (i.e., not in a phrase, such as "I get stuck in the mud"). "I mire" is also attractive because it half-rhymes with "core" (itself a problem!)

"Cogollo" is not specifically translatable, as far as I know. It can mean, depending on context, a number of things:

heart of lettuce, cabbage; bud; shoot;
top of a pine tree (lopped off when using the tree for timber);
in Argentina: large cricket;
in Mexico, the sugar cane tip;
in Columbia: outcrop of a mine;
in Chile: praise, compliment;
in Latin American usage, the cogollico, or cogollito, is the small heart or flower of a garden plant.

I think in Vallejo's sonnet that "cogollo" refers to the heart of the cabbage, the part that attaches the head to the root. The neck of the cabbage, as it were. The clue is the pyramid in the same line: some of the ancient ones had burial shafts below ground level. This passageway can be thought of as a kind of neck connecting the pyramid to the earth. "Cogollo" is used in an arcane way in the poem, and is very specific. There is no English cognate, and while "core" is not inaccurate, it comes off as a generalization compared to "cogollo."

"Encebollar" means to flavor or cook with onions, or to use them as seasoning. An "encebollado" is a stew of beef and onions. My translation is not as abrupt and surprising as the original is.

In the seventh line, Vallejo has intentionally (we believe) mis-spelled "tos" (cough) as "toz," evoking "voz" (voice). I add a "v" to "cough" to at least pick up the sound-swerve at the end of the coined Spanish word. However, there appears to be no way to evoke "cough" and "voice" in a single coined English word.

"Our melancholy soul canned" is accurate but a bit short (fourteen syllables in the Spanish line, seven in the English). "Marmalade" would lengthen the line a little, but destroy the half-rhyme scheme I have constructed, which is:

ABAB
ACAC
DED
FFE

I have made an adjustment in the poem's final line to avoid the literal, and awkward, translation: "let's go, raven, to fecundate your ravenness." The female "a" ending "cuerva" is quite natural in Spanish. "Mate" translates it accurately and also picks up the earlier "a" sounds in the line, giving this final line a nice triple "a" cadence.

Most rhymed poetry is translated as free verse, in an attempt to salvage meaning at the expense of sound. It has always seemed to me that one of the essential elements of a sonnet is the sound grid that not only partially determines word choice but sings the argument, with rhyme offering a kind of fugal emphasis. In other words, I do not accept the proposal (taken up by a range of American poets, from Ted Berrigan to Gerald Stern and Charles Wright) that a sonnet in American English can be a short poem in free verse, more or less fourteen lines in length. However, translating rhymed poetry into rhymed English verse more often than not results in what I call a limbo poem, not really a translation but not an original poem either (Robert Lowell's "imitation" of Rimbaud's "Les Chercheuses de poux" being a hair-raising example). Given these two extremes, both of which in their own ways are problematic, one near-solution is accuracy and half-rhyme like I have attempted in "Intensity and Height."

NOTES:

[1] This paper was written in 2002 for a translation panel with Pierre Joris and Lydia Davis at SUNY–Albany. It was published online in *Fascicle* magazine.

A GLOSS OF HART CRANE'S
"LACHRYMAE CHRISTI"[1]

The title: "Lachrymae Christi" (The Tears of Christ) is a dryish pale golden wine, made from the grapes grown along the southern slope of Mount Vesuvius in southwest Italy in the state of Campania. The Neapolitans claim that the Saviour, looking down one day on the citadel of wickedness that Naples had become, shed a tear which fell on Mount Vesuvius, where a vine sprang up (the wine has nothing in common with the sweet dessert wine from Málaga, Spain, by the same name). Thus, both Christ and Dionysus, as dying/reviving gods are summoned in the title, which also implies resurrection.

Embedded in the title as well is a sense in which Christ's blood and suffering are to be transformed into Dionysian celebration.

> Whitely, while benzine
> Rinsings from the moon
> Dissolve all but the windows of the mills
> (Inside the sure machinery
> Is still
> And curdled only where a sill
> Sluices its one unyielding smile)

Stanza one: "benzine" is a key word for the entire poem. As a volatile flammable distillate it not only conjures fermentation and distillation, but fire, and ignites a long fuse that will burn through the poem to contact the "tinder" in the one line fifth stanza and then burst into flame in the seventh, as "lattices of flame." Whitely (that is, purely, blankly, and voidly), the moon cleanses the world of human industry—almost. Even though the building (a mill evoking grinding labor) is dissolved, the lower part of the window still smiles evilly at the speaker—a smile that will not yield to "the benzine rinsings." Note the double rhyme in this phrase, which must have appealed to Crane and possibly, sound-wise, led him to the juxtaposition.

> Immaculate venom binds
> The fox's teeth, and swart
> Thorns freshen on the year's
> First blood. From flanks unfended,
> Twanged red perfidies of spring
> Are trillion on the hill.

Stanza two: While this process is going on, spring comes forth, yet it is under the control of "whitely" (suggesting that an unknowable blankness, or abyss, enfolds everything, including the moon). The purification and void implied in the first stanza are picked up now in "immaculate venom." The fox is not evil, but from the lamb's viewpoint, with its "unfended flanks," it is deadly. As flowers burst forth, so does the blood of carnivorous consumption, life feeding on life. There seems to be something perfidious (treacherous) about this, or let's say betrayal seems to be sewn into the nature of things. "Perfidious" starts a chain reaction, picked up in stanza #3 by "perjuries," converted to "penitence" and "perpetual" in stanza #4, and then transformed into "perfect" in stanza #8, the five "p" words underscoring the transformation underway.

> And the nights opening
> Chant pyramids,—
> Anoint with innocence,—recall
> To music and retrieve what perjuries
> Had galvanized the eyes.

Stanza three: Yet spring and night continue to open, expand, and the speaker can suddenly see through all the way back to Egypt, to the pyramids. The night makes him feel innocent again; it cleanses his eyes of the perjuries imposed on him (thus the night is effecting the speaker as the moon was said to effect the mills). Here "galvanized" probably denotes "coated," as iron or steel can be coated with zinc, rather than "stimulated."

> While chime
> Beneath and all around
> Distilling clemencies,—worms'
> Inaudible whistle, tunneling
> Not penitence
> But song, as these
> Perpetual fountains, vines,—

Stanza four: The speaker is also aware of worms, evoking aerated earth, as well as the transience of the flesh. The worms are whistle-shaped; their tunneling is a kind of singing, and what their action implies is not repentance or moral remorse, but celebration. The proper response to death and betrayal is transformation, renewal. The perjury that had galvanized/coated the eyes must erupt as a perpetual fountain, or the adopting of a viewpoint in which all is sensed as flowing, in which destruction and immolation are, at the same time, rebirth. Life and death are dyadic, a kind of circular causation.

> Thy Nazarene and tinder eyes.

Stanza five: the one line fifth stanza creates a mid-way pause in the poem. At this point a lot of material accumulates and coalesces. Christ on the cross is to be transformed into Dionysus or, to put it slightly different, the tears (remorse, sorrow, sufferings) of Christ are to be consumed in the livingdying god of poetry and wine, Dionysus, the inventor of vine culture. Joseph Campbell writes, "Dionysus, known like Shiva as the Cosmic Dancer, is both the bull

torn apart and the lion tearing." The birth of Dionysus is also pertinent here: Father Zeus appeared in his true form as lightning,
killing Dionysus's mother, Semele, and causing the god's premature
birth (and the need on Zeus's part to shelter the infant in his thigh
until his subsequent rebirth). Both Dionysus and Christ are symbolically killed and eaten yet resurrected gods of bread and wine; a
significant resemblance between the fate of Dionysus and Osiris
links Dionysus in the poem to pyramids and sphinxes. Dionysus is
also, besides vines, a god of trees (note "slender boughs" in stanza
#8). While he dies a violent death, there is no evidence I know of
that he was burnt at the stake or on a pyre (as was Hercules).
Dionysus was dismembered but not burned, so Crane's vision of
him as being burned at the stake appears to be his own invention.
This is also true about Christ; mauled and crucified, he was not in
the Gospels set on fire.

The Nazarene's tender eyes are "tinder eyes," inflammable, kin-
dling in effect.

> (Let sphinxes from the ripe
> Borage of death have cleared my tongue
> Once again; vermin and rod
> No longer bind. Some sentient cloud
> Of tears flocks through the tendoned loam:
> Betrayed stones slowly speak.)

Stanza six: While the sixth stanza takes place, the Nazarene is set
on fire by Crane and begins to transform into a blazing Dionysus
(who does not fully appear until the last stanza). "Let" here means
unbound, I believe, or released.

"The ripe borage of death" = death envisioned as medicinally
fertile. I wonder if the Egyptians had borage (the sentence implies
they did). The hybrid sphinx (evoking Dionysus and Christ at the
moment they fuse) emerges from a demulcent herb (capable of
soothing an inflamed membrane). I understand that borage is also
used in the preparation of a cordial.

"Vermin" (related to the worms above) and "rod" (flagellation associated with the penitence above) "No longer bind" plays off the venom that binds the fox's teeth in the 2nd stanza.

Now instead of worms, "a sentient cloud / of tears flocks" (stanza #2 lamb flanks recalled) "through the tendoned" (or now human) "loam," or earth. Why were the stones "betrayed?" Perhaps because until this minute they were not envisioned as participants in a cosmo-poetic resurrection?

> Names peeling from Thine eyes
> And their undimming lattices of flame,
> Spell out in palm and pain
> Compulsion of the year, O Nazarene.

Stanza 7: Back to the god's eyes, which are now peeling/pealing, as bells peal, with names (Adonis, Attis, Dionysus, Christ, etc.)—with each name carrying its own "undimming [lattice] of flame" (recalling the burning of viniculture and creeping vines). These names "Spell out in palm" (the spiked palms of the Nazarene, also the palm tree, thus Dionysus-associated). "Compulsion of the year" = the driven cycling of nature, relentless, without freedom to deviate, that all living things suffer, Dionysus and Nazarene here as man.

> Lean long from sable, slender boughs,
> Unstanched and luminous. And as the nights
> Strike from Thee perfect spheres,
> Lift up in lilac-emerald breath the grail
> Of earth again—

Stanza #8: "sable," like "swart" (stanza #2) = black; the "boughs" that the burning figure leans from are blackened (possibly from past burnings as well). They become the "riven stakes" (possibly from vineyards) in stanza #9. As a transformation of the moon with its rinsings/cleansings this figure is now aflow with fire, that is, he is "unstaunched" (not cauterized or checked but "luminous," light-giving). The nights that previously opened to pyramids now strike an ethereal harmony (Pythagoras' vision, produced by planetary motion—"harmony of the spheres" I assume is being alluded to here). The "perfect spheres" suggests dew and grapes, as well as sweat (borage is also a diaphoretic). "Perfect," the culmination of the "p" flotilla, also suggests that the word itself has reached a state of grace.

Then the "breath" of the "earth," embodied in the blazing god, is proposed to consist of lilacs and emeralds (plants and gems). The "grail" is no longer associated solely with Christ (from which he ate the Last Supper, in which his blood was collected, or in other versions, from which he drank wine at the Last Supper). The "grail" now belongs to Dionysus, or to a Dionysian perspective in art. "Again" implies that this is a cyclic, perhaps yearly/seasonal ceremony. The god is thus blessing the fruitfulness of the earth as he burns, with the lifting up of the grail, another trope for resurrection/transformation.

> Thy face
> From charred and riven stakes. O
> Dionysus, Thy
> Unmangled target smile.

Stanza nine: "O Nazarene" (stanza #5) is now "O Dionysus," as if the god now looks down at the speaker (though his eyes have been twice acknowledged). The lack of a verb here is significant. After "Thy face," I think we are to pause, as if the verb missing is covered by such a pause. Note that "O" is set by itself at the end of this line, punning on zero as well as the roundness of the target to appear two lines later. The last line presents us with a god whose face is filled with arrows but who is still smiling. This "unmangled... smile" is set against the unyielding sill smile in stanza #1. The "twanged red perfidies" (stanza #2) may play into the target also, as a twang is the sharp release of a bowstring, and to twang is to release an arrow (a minor point, perhaps, but "twanged" is so odd that one seeks to account for it).

The dovetailing drive of the poem seems to be one in which the negative suffering-for-others qualities of what we might call "the Christ complex" are to be not substituted, but subsumed, assimilated into the positive, celebratory qualities of the "Dionysus complex." If I am to be torn apart, the poet seems to be saying, I want to sing as I break or burn; I do not want to go down in penitence. This transformation is synchronized with the appearance of spring, though it is worth pointing out that spring is also seen as one aspect of a venom-bound natural cycle. Since Crane prays for this transformation (in the command "Lift up..."), we can assume that the poem is self-reflective of his own life and creative problems. There is a strong implication running through the text that his own tendency has been to take as personal, as directed at him, the venom, perfidies, perjuries, and betrayals that are part of the havoc of his life. By casting his speaking self against the great cycles of natural life and mythological imagination, it is as if Crane would depersonalize these negative forces and transform them into the compulsive pain of being part of life at large. The absolutely extraordinary last line, we should note, does not present a Dionysus made whole, or a figure who has simply been purified by fire—rather, in the word "target" are gathered all the arrows, all the agonies evoked at various points in the poem, so that the smile we encounter is one that carries in its surrounding flesh the cruel and horrifying contradictions of life and yet is somehow "unmangled," whole. One might say that this is a truly honest smile because it is offered not in evasion or simplistic transformation of the speaker's multifoliate sufferings.

Note:

Over the years I have written several poems about Hart Crane, and in a couple of them I have invented conversations with him. The longest of these pieces is "At the Speed of Wine" (Hotel Cro-Magnon, 1989). A shorter "conversation," which took place on the patio of Hotel Centenaire, in Les Eyzies, in the French Dordogne, on July 20–21, 1985, has the following exchange, which seems pertinent to this Gloss:

He paused long enough for me to ask: your Dionysus, with a Nazarene core, is a full company of bit parts as he flames and sparks at the stake. In what sense is his "target smile" "unmangled?"

"The 'I' must go unpruned and be allowed to elaborate its tendrils. Since I could not 'shoulder the curse of sundered parentage,' I sought a hermaphroditic grafting. I refused my parents' nature in favor of a vision that included crucifixion *and* pagan multiplicity. Dionysus never was mangled—his being takes place in parts, or minute orders, 'divine particulars,' yet 'the bottom of the sea is cruel.' For the Protestant, always under curfew, the underworld is infested with criminal elements, thuds of Capone, Manson butt-raped as a child whose later martial hysteria wrote its 'helter-skelter' in living flesh. As a Protestant, I was always on that 'sundered' leash when I went down into the image hive, but that was part of my vision too: to wander under Dionysus and to suffer Dionysus in the flesh. Because of this, I allowed my sense of line to be governed by Tate and Winters. Only the voicings rising in writing, I know now, are not estrangements. Winters often visits me in this place. In death his soul has become mellow and most open. I see him wandering a nearby vale, chewing peyote, reading Artaud, his flesh neatly stacked on his skull…"

NOTES:
[1] This piece appeared in the online magazine *Fascicle*.

HEADPIECE STUFFED
WITH BOOKS

Around 1994, Norman O. Brown wrote me a letter (undated), from which I copy out these excerpts:

"America's (see H. Bloom, *The American Religion*—which I have not read yet but am frustrated by its absence from the library) effort, heroic, to find Dionysus in Christ (we have yet to get beyond Blake…).

The only thing in your far-flung letter that I must comment on is Cage. Since his death (!!), my obsession.[1] It is only after his death that I am able to shake off my Marx and Freud determinism and embrace Chance—no, "embrace" is the wrong word— You are the most scholarly of poets. On "Chance" I will give you first of all M. Serres' *Le Parasite:* L. Mark, *Standard* [illegible word]: Chance and the Modern British Novel, Etc., Etc., but bibliography is not the way to go. You are probably right in thinking Cage is not for you but I have to. I will never forget Cage's negative reaction to my first attempt at the Theme of love. You see from the text "Love hath reason" that the fool persists in his folly. And even on p 8-9…

Thinking of you, Jim Clifford, and many others
I ask   the Woodstock generation
Have you ever seen a book—BL 624 R 36 1978 in our library—which may or may not be called BE HERE NOW— "This book is made in love for love any part of this may be

reprinted to ring the bell of the dharma—Lama Foundation
1971 Hanuman Foundation 1978"—with 18 pages of bibliography—

    The Woodstock generation   The Third Great
    Awakening   but do they slumber still
      Yrs truly
      Headpiece   stuffed with books

Here, as my response to Brown's Lecture on Cage, are some of
Brown's thoughts expressed in it, followed by what they evoked for
me.

Our ears will be in much better condition

I last visited the Browns in 1990. We had dinner at their house.
That evening at least, Brown was obsessed with the 1960s. He told
me that his discovery of the poetry of Robert Duncan had made the
writing of *Love's Body* possible. I said that I thought it was William
Blake that led to the breakdown of rational procedure in that book.
No, it was Duncan, he insisted, then saying: And I couldn't figure
out how to get more of him into the book. Several times Brown
asked me: didn't *Caterpillar* mean more to you than *Sulfur* does? I
wouldn't agree, saying that I thought *Sulfur* was *Caterpillar* and
then some.

With this lyre Orpheus, Amphion, founded
the humanity of Greece

While Brown addresses some of the Upper Paleolithic painted
caves in the "Nature" section of *Love's Body*, he sees them as exam-

ples of the labyrinth, and fails to comment on what seems to be their most distinctive characteristic: they are not merely wandering places, or even dancing enclosures, but sites for some of the earliest image-making.

The earliest musical instruments that we have examples of today may be flutes. The French ones are made of hollow bird bones while the German and Russian ones are of reindeer or bear bone. The problem is that we do not know for sure whether the holes in them were made by human beings or carnivores. Some oval objects have been interpreted as "bull-roarers," and certain mammoth bones, from Mezin, near Kiev, are thought to have been percussive instruments. A hip-bone xylophone? A jaw-bone rattle? Paul Bahn writes that such "instruments" have even been played by Soviet archeologists, who cut a record of their jam session (*Journey Through the Ice Age*, 1998, pp. 84–85).

will you, won't you, will you, won't you,
come a join the dance

Recalled Robert Kelly's marvelous little (but tall) book, *Round Dances* (1964). Here is one of them:

Round Dance: Oracle

Delphos
     smooth curved out & over
whelk body of justice
              end of act,
voluted, our will turns toward it,
     Volva, wisewoman, the prophecy of
when all turns to the fire & the sea turning,
        man's home, broadbacked the gods play.
inwards.   What Delphi means.   & where

that furrow is our only earth.

that gods turn.

plow, seeds of.

the tree hangs down

(it is the direct contact of vulva with vulva. cleft of the
earth, priestess suspended, three stools of justice, above
it.   the smoke is sky, the words the answer)

it is the

body

answers

Harmony, the repressive principle of the real

In 1921, César Vallejo wrote the *ars poetica* of his revolutionary
book, *Trilce* (1922), XXXVI, parts of which are the poetic equivalent of compositions by Bartok and Prokofiev. One stanza in
XXXVI reads:

Refuse, all of you, to set foot
on the double security of Harmony.
Truly refuse symmetry.
Intervene in the conflict
of points that contend
in the most rutty of jousts
for the leap through the needle's eye!

Here I am also thinking of Ronald Johnson's "dissonances
through dissonances through dissonances" (he is quoting from a
field guide to western birds) in "Ark 37" (from his long poem, *Ark*,
1996). This poem is followed by "the invisible Spire," which "consists of a tape recording made with the assistance of sound technician Roger Gans, under the auspices of Erik Bauersfeld for KQED
in San Francisco. This was a project extending some six months

with the end result being just over six minutes of 'musics' constructed out of recordings of songs of the birds of eastern United States."

Several years ago, Andrew Schelling sent me this tape, which I enjoyed a great deal, then passed it along to Gary Snyder.

And here, as if it suddenly started raining in my workroom, lines from Francis Ponge's poem, "Rain" (translated by Cid Corman in *Things*, 1971) drift in:

> Rain, in the courtyard where I watch it fall, comes down at very varied speeds. At center it's a fine discontinuous curtain (or network), an implacable but relatively slow downfall of probably rather light drops, a sempiternal precipitation of no vigor, an intense fraction of pure atmosphere. A little ways from the walls to right and left fall with more sound heavier, individuated drops. Here they seem the size of a grain of wheat, there of a pea, elsewhere almost of a taw. On tringles, on the balustrades of the window the rain runs horizontally while on the underside of the same obstacles it is hung with convex candies... From the adjoining gutter where it flows with the exertion of a deep stream of no great slope, it drops all at once in a perfectly vertical filament, somewhat thickly braided, to the ground where it breaks and jumps up in brilliant aiguillettes.

Civilization originates in thunder

Here, I quote Brown against himself:

> Nothing happens for the first time.
> (*Love's Body*, p. 201)

a John Cage concert

While I was living in Kyoto, Japan, 1962–1964, Cage and David Tudor came through for a concert. I attended and invited Cage to lunch. I recall that we ate outside by a Zen temple. Cage brought a young Japanese photographer, Yasuhiro Yoshioka, with him. Yoshioka then sent me a copy of a book with his photographs of nudes, not in the traditional sense, but as body parts (close-ups of pubic hair, erections that looked like the top of waterfalls, spread vaginas whose interior folds looked like distorted faces). Cage was very charming and talked rapturously about wild mushrooms. He had Wesleyan University Press send me his book *Silence* (1961), which I couldn't connect with. The thinking in it struck me—I was primed on Northrop Frye and Blake those days—as "liquid."

Listening to noise is a little like being killed

During the American invasion of Iraq, spring 2003, I spent a few days in Baltimore at the AWP Convention. One night I got drunk and flipped out. "Where's Caryl?" I shouted, pulling at Caryl's arms. I attempted to protect her in a psychotic fit: we were in Baghdad under bombardment, nowhere to run.

The name of the god is Dionysus

While Dionysus is mentioned in *Hermes the Thief* (1947), he first appears as a force in Brown's writing in *Life Against Death* (1959). Dionysus is associated with "body mysticism," "poetry and psychoanalysis," "dialectical imagination," "dreaming," and the struggle to circumvent depression and make the unconscious conscious. On the last page of the book, Brown proposes that "the dialectical" moves toward a Dionysian ego, which "does not negate anymore." Like de Sade, Brown gravitates toward clusters.

It is space and emptiness that is finally urgently necessary at this point of history

A contrasting viewpoint is articulated by Declan McGonagle in a Foreword to *Leon Golub: Echoes of the Real*, by Jon Bird (2000):

> I would argue that the flight from social reference and meaning in the most successful American art of the mid-twentieth century was not accidental. It was driven, we now know, by economic and political forces whose interest lay in the separation of art from social meaning and therefore the separation of the artist from a valued, functioning place in society. Those forces had the same interest in separating the worker from the value of his/her work. The contest in art is regularly characterized, and trivialized, by the media, as a contest between forms of figuration and abstraction, when the fundamental tension is actually between figure and ground—the figure of art/the artist and the ground of society.

Farce is nihilism

The word "farce" appears to come from old French "farsir," meaning "to stuff," leading to: to stuff with forcemeat (to be farce-fed?); to fill with mingled ingredients. Dramatically, it is defined (in *Webster's International Dictionary*) as: "a light dramatic composition of satirical or humorous cast in which great latitude is allowed as to probability of happenings and naturalness of characters."

Such does not strike me as nihilistic, but akin to what Mikhail Bakhtin (whose work Brown knew) called, via Rabelais, "grotesque realism."

Saturnalia, season of unbridled license

Brown always wanting to cut loose.

Charles Olson:

> "I think I can take you into *The Odyssey* and explode the notion that *The Odyssey* was an epic at all, was, in fact, a drama—was written as such—and that it reflects at its late date the masked dance of the caves: that *The Odyssey* was itself what Euripides made a piece of it into the fifth century, a *saturos*, or, if I am right that the form is larger and deeper than the saturos had become by the fifth century, what we had better call a grotesque..." (*Olson #10*, p. 91)

Thus a dance drama in which a shaman quester wends his way through a labyrinth of monsters to be reuinited with a human other—a fascinating tie-in of prehistory with history.

Dionysus in Amerika

Continuing to follow the trail of Dionysus in Brown's writing.

At the end of the Boundary section in *Love's Body* (161), Dionysus reappears: "the mad god breaks down the boundaries; releases the prisoners; abolishes repression; and abolishes the *principium individuationis*, substituting for it the unity of man and the unity of man with nature."

Violence and fire follow. "Madness is, Dionysus, is, violence." "The real prayer is to see this world go up in flames." "But, as Frederick Crews remarks, in his essay on Brown in *Out of My System* (1975), "then he reminds us that literal interpretations are vulgar; by making his fantasy explicit, by allowing the repressed to return uncensored, he has made it innocent of covert violence."

"For a Dionysian or enthusiastic Christianity ('enthusiasm' is from the Greek *enthousiasmos*, 'to be inspired or possessed by the god'), we have to turn from Luther to Müntzer; to the Radical Reformation; to the lunatic fringe; *die Schwärmer*, the madmen, Luther called them." (We are now in *Love's Body*'s "Resurrection" section.) While it is true that Thomas Müntzer (1489–1525) was a spiritualist (he advocated an inner baptism that was to replace outer baptism through water), he also took over the Muhlhausen town council and set up a communistic theocracy. The price for his actions was beheading.

Brown's context is strictly intellectual. "Freedom is poetry, taking liberties with words, breaking the rules of normal speech, violating common sense. Freedom is violence" ("Freedom" section, *Love's Body*, 244).

❧

that Dionysian body in which we are all members of one body

Dionysus makes his last appearance in Brown's *Apocalypse And/Or Metamorphosis* (1991) in the final essay, "Dionysus, 1990." Exaggerations, gift-giving, consumption, and rawness are now added to the Dionysian arsenal. Gift-giving comes up via potlatch via Bataille's vision of excess. Sadly there is no contact with planet Artaud. By now we understand that Brown wants to keep the action in theory and to tingle-tangle with the poets. From a poet's viewpoint, *Love's*

Body is the masterpiece. Brown, in that book, took the suspicion that all literary criticism is repressed imagination, i.e., the springs of poetry, as far as it has been taken to date. This book is a magnificent "defense of poetry" that ends on the cusp of poetry itself ("Everything is only a metaphor; there is only poetry"), without attempting to stifle experimentalism (Bloom) or to pulp poetry and to foreground philosophical inquiry as an ersatz prior (Derrida).

〰

Chance operations avoid real uncertainty
the negative capability of being in uncertainties,
mysteries, doubts, and darkness

Off Keats, a cogent perception uttered by Apollo hanging by his heels from a Dionysian cliff. It helps me understand why I have so valued Jackson Mac Low's lyrical prose and poetry and have been so uninterested in his "chance" work.

If there is any weakness in Brown's implicit proposal that love's body is poetry it may lie in the fact that in the last thirty years of his life he appears to have continued to read discourse for the most part, poetry for the lesser.

〰

Devotion based on discipline

Jeff Clark (from *Music and Suicide*, 2004):

> "Obsession is made of emptiness, and Devotion of fulfillment. Obsession is ruled by compulsion, whereas Devotion is an act of free will. Obsession stuffs itself and still can't get enough, while Devotion offers its gift as a continual & inexhaustible outpouring. Obsession is an impoverished state, Devotion an impossibly rich one. Obsession desperately

needs to consume & appropriate the life-force of its object;
Devotion takes nothing but brings everything."

Shades of Blake's the "Devouring and the Prolific," but with a 21ˢᵗ-
century twist.

ᴵᴸ

Upon reading of Norman O. Brown's death, I wrote out the following lines:

> Strolling Lost Street, in hand with my noun.
> Crammed America reeking of loss, apocalyptic
>   disposables.
> The paradise behind the veil separating my bear
>   from its garbage.
> Stratigraphy of loss.
> "Pure loss pours through. I'm home," versus the
>   twin molten cornucopias sprouting from Uncle
>   Sam's dome.
> Gated communities as citified limousines.
> Do not tell the homeless she's solved the gated
>   man's plush hell; the homeless woman suffers
>   the literal frostbite of loss.
> I arrive with *Love's Body* fermenting 30 years in
>   craw, a Cro-Magnon nexus, as if the earliest
>   images were the catastrophic heralds of this
>   interior guillotine: the beheading of the fear of
>   loss.

NOTES:

[1] In the fall 2005 issue of *Aufgabe* magazine, the editor, Tracy Grinnell,
reprinted a lecture by Norman O. Brown on John Cage (that was given at
Wesleyan University, February 1988). She asked a number of us to respond to this lecture, and printed our responses in this issue.

ANOTHER LOOK AT ULLIKUMMI[1]

Kumarbi   the old god
  would bring down Tešub his successor
Tešub = Storm-God
        [probably still imbued with matriarchal force,
        no connection between conception & fucking,
        conception brought about by wind action, or rain,
        by external forces... *la parole fecundate*]

Kumarbi is thus in this sense not an "old god," but *new stone man*,
the painted pebble carried out of the cave, the Neolithic pebble,
to be *planted* now in the earth, to grow itself with earth's assistance
    (Earth no longer cavern,
                but a painted pebble,
                portable, with the power to radiate,
                have rays, spokes)

Thus to bring down conception as external force, Neolithic
    Kumarbi
brought his painted pebble "to a place where he met a huge rock,"
Güterbock writes, "Kumarbi has intercourse with this rock.
At this point the first column of the first tablet breaks off."

Here we need Ogotemmêli's "First Day" when Amma, his
    Kumarbi,
tries to have intercourse with the earth—she raises a termite hill to

ward him off—her massive clitoris, or her external force, equal to
   his,
he breaks off
         and in Dogon lore a jackal, or carrion eater, is born.
Dogon Ogotemmêli's tale is older than Neolithic,
for he preserves the ghost of Upper Paleolithic "reciprocity"
—by the time we meet Hittite Kumarbi
not only does the "tablet break off," but Earth's resistance is broken:
into this "huge rock" his "manhood [*flowed*].
         And five times he took her,
[*and again*] ten times he took her."

Olson, in his rendering of "The Song of Ullikummi" is mesmerized
   by
this repeated penetration, and cannot get beyond it,
in his comments in "Causal Mythology" he curiously refers to Ullikummi,
the offspring of Kumarbi and the (unnamed) "huge rock,"
as "this aborted creature," and claims Ullikummi "started growing
   from
the bottom of the sea," thus botching the heart of the action in the
   Hittite epic:
"the rock bears a child to Kumarbi," Güterbock writes, "divine
   midwives
put the [stone] child [or lithopaedion] on Kumarbi's knees," still,
   thus,
associating Ullikummi with lap, or womb, but here a new disjunc-
   tion takes place:
Kumarbi orders the child to be deposited *on the shoulders* of a god
named Upelluri, "an Atlas-like giant who carries Heaven and Earth
   and...the sea.
There Ullikummi grows, in the sea, with tremendous speed until
   he reaches the sky."

The movement from *lap to shoulder*
is the movement from cavern to sky,
Ullikummi the first menhir?
"an extension of the earth's fertility,"

stone no longer possesses spirit to be interiorly decorated, as in the
caves, but is an altar *to which a god is to be summoned...*

The war in the Hittite epic is between patriarchal seeding and
matriarchal parthenogenesis, Tešub can only stop Ullikummi's
    "growth"
with "the ancient tool with which Heaven and Earth had once been
cut apart—with this tool Ea cuts Ullikummi off 'under his feet;'
by separating him from the body of Upelluri on which he has
    grown,
he magically breaks his power." "A fourth tablet," Güterbock con-
    cludes,
"follows with an elaborate account of the final battle... the victory
    of the Storm-God over the Stone."
                    But it is a battle between gods,
and *the scythe* is "in"—the penis has become "plough, axe,
dagger & sword: semen the seed, rain, sun, snake & bird..."

The phallic stone child is severed, the earth is planted with—and
here I think the word Olson misused is true: the earth is planted
with his *aborted* force, studded with *his consternation*—
a chopped up & planted "prince" now meets the-mole-with-a-
    single-deadly-eye,
the earth is ALIVE with death, the "divine midwives" have fled
    into the stars
from where they will now "steal men's vital energy away in sexual
    dreams...
    nixies, calling them to an erotic
            but watery grave."

NOTES:

[1]This "hinge" piece was written on July 22, 1985, by the swimming pool at Hotel Cro-Magnon, in Les Eyzies, in the French Dordogne. It draws on Hans Gustav Güterbock's "The Song of Ullikummi: Revised Text of the Hittite Version of a Hurrian Myth;" pp. 72–75 and 91–93 from Charles Olson's *Muthologos*, Volume 1; and "The Second Day," from *Conversations with Ogotemmêli* by Marcel Griaule. It was published in the online journal *Second Room*.

NOTES ON CHARLES OLSON AND THE ARCHAIC [1]

for Ralph Maud

1] On May 20, 1949, Francis Boldereff sent S.N. Kramer's article, "The Epic of Gilgameš and Its Sumerian Sources" to her recently-discovered poet-hero and correspondent, Charles Olson. At two points in the article, Kramer presents scholarly verse translation of two sections concerning Gilgamesh, Enkidu, and the Underworld. In the first section, Gilgamesh's *pukku* ("drum") and *mikkû* ("drumstick") have fallen into the Underworld. Unable to reach them from this world, he sits at the gate of the Underworld and laments:

> O my *pukku*, O my *mikkû*,
> My *pukku* whose lustiness was irresistible,
> My *mikkû* whose pulsations could not be drowned out,
> In those days when verily my *pukku* was with me in the
>   house of the carpenter,
> (When) verily the wife of the carpenter was with me like
>   the mother who gave birth to me,
> (When) verily the daughter of the carpenter was with me
>   like my younger sister,
> My *pukku*, who will bring it up from the nether world,
> My *mikkû*, who will bring it up from the 'face' of the
>   nether world?

A week later, Olson sent his adaptation of these lines to Boldereff:

La Chute

O my drum, hollowed out thru the thin slit,
carved from the cedar wood, the base I took
when the tree was felled

                    o my lute
wrought from the tree's crown

my drum whose lustiness
was not to be resisted

my lute from whose pulsations
not one could turn away

                    they
are where the dead are

                 my drum
fell where the dead are, who
will bring it up, my lute
who will bring it up
where it fell in the face of them
where they are, where my lute and drum

have fallen?

Olson has added information from Kramer's explanation of prior material in the poem. And without explaining why, he has also converted "drumstick" to "lute." It should be noted that the lustiness of the drum and the pulsations from the lute refer, on one level, to King Gilgamesh's tyrannical behavior with the citizens of Erech, including his abusive sexual cravings. The cedar wood out of which the instruments have been carved is from a magical tree nurtured by the goddess Inanna, which has become invested with snakes, Lilith, and birds. As a chivalrous favor to the goddess, Gilgamesh felled the tree.

In a subsequent passage of the epic, Gilgamesh's servant and friend, Enkidu, volunteers to descend to the Underworld and retrieve the fallen drum and lute. In Kramer's version, Gilgamesh warns his companion of the various Underworld taboos that he must respect:

> Gilgameš says to Enkidu:
> 'If now thou wilt descend to the nether world,
> A word I speak to thee, take my word,
> Instruction I offer thee, take my instruction.
> Do not put on clean clothes,
> lest like an enemy they will mark thee;
> Do not anoint thyself with the good oil of the
>   buru-vessel,
> Lest at its smell they will crowd about thee.
> Do not throw the throw-stick in the nether world,
> Lest they who were struck by the throw-stick will
>   surround thee;
> Do not carry a staff in thy hand,
> Lest the shades will flutter all about thee.
> Do not put sandals on thy feet,
> In the nether world make no cry;
> Kiss not thy beloved wife,
> Strike not thy hated wife,
> Kiss not thy beloved son,
> Strike not thy hated son,
> Lest the outcry of Kur will seize thee;
> (The outcry) to her who is lying, to her who is
>   lying,
> To the mother of Ninazu who is lying,
> Whose holy body no garment covers,
> Whose holy breast no cloth wraps.'

Kur here is another word for the Underworld.

Two weeks after composing "La Chute," Olson, skipping the first lines and leaving out the names of the characters, reworked the rest of the passage into "La Chute II":

If you would go down to the dead
to retrieve my drum and lute
a word for you, take my word,
I offer you directions

do not wear a clean garment
they below will dirty you
they will mark you
as if you were a stranger

nor rub yourself with oil
the finest oil from the cruse
the smell of it will provoke them
they will walk round and round
alongside you

carry no stick, at least
do not raise it
or the shades of men will tremble,
hover before you

Pick up nothing to throw, no matter the urging.
They against whom you hurl it
will crowd you, will fly thick on.you.

Go barefoot, make no sound,
and when you meet the wife you loved
do not kiss her or strike the wife you hated.
Likewise your sons. Give the beloved one no kiss,
do not spit on his brother.

Behave, lest the outcry shall seize you
seize you for what you have done
for her who, there lies naked, the mother
whose body in that place is not covered
whose breasts lie open to you and the judges

in that place
where my drum and lute are

Both of Olson's adaptations make for engaging, mysterious poems. These two poems (along with a third, "La Chute III, which is not an adaptation²), propose a contemporary entry into the archaic, as well as protocol to be followed in such a descent. They are the first signals in Olson's body of work that the archaic is the post-modern, and that stripped of its historic context its content is potentially our own.

᭥

2] Near the end of Olson's life, the drum fashioned from Inanna's cedar (now identified as "The Tree of the World") appears in two poems ("for my friend" and "The Drum World"). This drum has become in these later poems the drumming of Jack Clarke's fingers on a table (perhaps a seminar table at the head of which Olson was holding forth in the spring of 1965). Such drumming evokes for Olson a ninth-century Norwegian ship burial containing the body of a queen as well as the entombment of Djosser, a Third Dynasty Egyptian pharaoh, in a pyramid he has designed. The evocation here is that of Clarke, as shaman apprentice, sending the aging Olson off into symbolic realms.

᭥

3] The "La Chute" series, along with "Bigmans," "Bigmans II," and "The She-Bear" series make up Olson's first archaic focus in poetry. Writing to Robert Creeley in August 1950, he remarks:

> The whole & continuing struggle to remain civilized is docu-
> mented reign in & out: I imagine you know the subtle tale of
> how Gilgamesh was sent Enkidu to correct him because he
> had become a burden to his city's people. As I read it, it is an
> incredible myth of what happens to the best of men when

they lose touch with the primordial & phallic energy from
which man, said these younger people, takes up nature's force.

Written a few days after Olson had worked out much of "I, Maximus" in a letter to Boldereff, unlike Gloucester-centered "Maximus," "Bigmans" and "Bigmans II" are based on Gilgamesh material. The first poem begs Bigmans to leave the house of an
unnamed goddess (as one might have urged Odysseus to leave
Circe's ingle) and to "wake" unnamed "cities." "Bigmans II," addressing the "land," proposed that Bigmans has already seen everything, cut down "the dirty tree," and started to "unravel what no
man can complete." A long passage then describes Bigmans as the
master builder of a well. An even longer passage, set in the voice of
the people, complains about Bigmans' tyrannical wildness and begs
"whatever force presides" to create an equal to distract and test
him. Gilgamesh-wise, this rival would be Enkidu.

The "Bigmans" poems end as if they are the opening evocations
of a much longer work. Both they and the "La Chute" series are
shadowed by Olson's own size and ambitions, throwing up an
archaic background to substantiate his recently discovered desire to
do an end-run around post-Bronze Age history and invest his poetry with a primordial core.

Olson wrote to Boldereff that "The She-Bear" is "based on the
images you invoked in me," and that "You are / that girl, SHE- /
BEAR!" Boldereff thus joins Olson as a shadowy presence through
these early archaic engagements. Of the three versions of "The
She-Bear," the first strikes me as the most original and intelligent.
It grounds a renewed goddess image in a chant-like assessment of
patriarchal damage to woman's body and spirit, basing its "praise
for woman" on some up-to-date feminist-positive anthropological
data. Like "La Chute III," it belongs more to Olson than to archaic texts.

🌿

4] Boldereff's passion to engage Olson sexually and psychically, to absolutely back him as *the* poet of their age, and to feed him materials he quickly came to see were timeless to the human condition, had a rippling centrifugal effect on his entire life in 1949 and 1950 (possibly, because she could not support him, he refused to leave his first wife, Constance, for her). One potent indication of this Olson/Boldereff mesh is the flexibility in their gender relationship as it dances about in their letters. She is his daughter, sister, sib, his angel, mentor, and miracle, and he (symbolically) impregnates her. He is her daddy, her son. This god-like confusion or iridescence (in which, mythologically, a serpent can be consort, deity, and offspring of the Great Goddess) harks back to undifferentiated prehistoric archetypes without discrete and complimentary structures.[3] Such flexibility in personal address and identification accounts, in part, for a poem like "The She-Bear." Given the departmentally differentiated world of 1950s America, Boldereff's multiple presentation of herself to Olson (along with his immediate reciprocity, at least as far as correspondence goes) appears to have been the prime in the poet's carving a man out of himself, filling his own space, and making traceries sufficient to others' needs.[4]

5] One crucial aspect of Olson's shaping a poetic personality involved locating and rejecting positions inimical to his ongoing post-modernist project. The correspondence with Boldereff and Creeley (and Cid Corman to a lesser extent) is peppered with blocks to be destroyed on the road to the archaic:

"original sin"
"existence of a previous golden age" (Boldereff); "we've been dragooned into a notion that whatever came before was better"
"lyrical interference (the poet interposing himself between what he is and other creatures of nature… and objects)"
"inherited form;" "a poet stays in the open and goes by breath, not by inherited forms"

"the lazyness of specialization"

"the archaic mushed into Xty, in order to give it a ride on a new back, when itself… could walk… BY HERSELF"

"lust and shame—words invented by Hebraic man" (Boldereff)

"stopping anywhere this side of ICE"

"PATRIARCHY;" "a vision is the absolute dynamiting of the patriarchy"

"URBANITY i.e., gentilnesse, grace, recognition of others, connection to realism, tendency toward the suave"

"symbol, magic, aesthetic art, superstition or religion"

"opposites"

"Humanism" (versus "man as object in field of force"); [Humanism in Olson's sense of it includes] "a single patriarchal god; a concept of Ideal or World Forms (Socrates–Plato); Future, that thing Christ most did havoc with, Redemption"

"the descriptive and the analytical"

"logic and classification"

"the microscope and the telescope."

Facing such a list, one might inquire: what is its primary purpose? Beyond building access to the archaic/post-modern, there is this (from a letter to Creeley, August, 1951):

> my assumption is that any POST-MODERN is born with the ancient confidence that, he *does* belong.
> So, there is nothing to be *found*. There is only (as Schoenberg had it, his Harmony, search) tho, I should wish to kill that word too—there is only examination. And I hew to ED's proposition, one perception instantly, another—as, the INSTANT is, that fast, *another :* why, too, I take it, the *flaws*, when they exist, are COMPOSITIONAL

To belong would be to end the estrangement that Heraclitus perceived as dividing man from that with which he was most familiar. Olson was intuitively convinced that the loss Heraclitus addressed at 500 B.C. had, at the beginning of the 20th century, ceased to obtain, and that this profound shift had released man from a mind focused on the absolute and the ideal, in place of which the comparative and the archaic offered man the possibility of becoming a creative rival to nature.[5]

The "peril in stopping anywhere this side of ICE" presents Olson with a problem that he never solved. ICE here can only mean the last Ice Age, the Upper Paleolithic period (roughly 35,000 to 9,000 B.P). The archaic is a vague term and can refer to the art of ancient Greece as well as to images in Lascaux. Olson's primary archaic materials for his poetry are predominately Bronze Age and classical Greek. As we shall see, he made some perceptive (as well as erroneous) notes on Upper Paleolithic culture in 1953, but these notes led nowhere, and were never developed in his poetry, essays, or interviews to any substantial extent.

In the Introduction to my book, *Juniper Fuse*, I wrote:

> To follow poetry back to Cro-Magnon metaphors not only hits real bedrock—a genuine back wall—but gains a connection to the continuum during which imagination first flourished. My growing awareness of the caves led to the recognition that as an artist, I belong to a pre-tradition that includes the earliest nights and days of soul making.

6] In contrast to positions rejected, Olson was simultaneously proposing stances and perspectives to be adopted. He announced to Boldereff that innocence was "the real home of creative being" (unaware, I suspect, that William Blake had astutely qualified such a belief by declaring that after "innocence" and "experience" there was only "organized innocence," thus making a distinction between the mature poet and the child).

Olson associated the archaic (which he also called the chthonic and the primordial) with "the poet's ability to hear through himself" and access "secrets objects share." Such language evokes shamanism. While the word crops up from time to time in Olson's correspondence, he does not appear to have brought a detailed shamanic plan into his sense of the mythic. In 1965 he bought Mircea Eliade's *Shamanism: Archaic Techniques of Ecstacy* and annotated the Foreword.

While stressing "self-containment," the "staying within one's nature," in the same spirit that the poem must "stay within itself," he also insisted that the poet must "stay in the open" (which he associated with "going by breath and not inherited form"). The goal of such inside/outside positioning was that of "accomplishing coverage of the whole field of knowledge."

Again and again, assimilation of whatever the archaic includes is presented as the key. Dreams produce the presence of archaic figures, he told Boldereff, and such presence is "of absolute importance to a rebirth of conduct and structure and force: simply because it was from these areas that, originally and now, men discovered ambiguity of experience which told energies they wot not of."

One might ask: why is "ambiguity of experience" presented as a positive? I think Olson would refer the question to the Keats quotation that, along with the Heraclitus adage on estrangement, is used as the epigraph to *The Special View of History*:

> Brown and Dilke walked with me & back from the Christmas pantomime. I had not a dispute, but a disquisition with Dilke on various subjects: several things dovetailed in my mind, & at once it struck me, what quality went to form a Man of Achievement especially in Literature & which Shakespeare possessed so enormously—I mean Negative Capability, that is, when man is capable of being in uncertainties, Mysteries, doubts, without any irritable reaching after fact and reason—Coleridge, for instance, would let go by a fine isolated verisimilitude caught from the Penetralium of mystery, from being incapable of remaining content with half knowledge.

To acknowledge ambiguity is also to recognize ambivalence, and the poetic obligation to allow contradictions to coexist as part of the fullest showing possible.

〵

7] For Olson, to eliminate history (or that portion of it he associated with the "WILL TO DISPERSE") is also to eliminate time, as if it were a container, or Pandora's Box, replete with Greek classification and logic, Christianity, opposites, inherited form etc. The goal, in this sense, is spacial existence which turns out to be, or turns on, perpendicularity and the instant e.g., "time, as axis, is only this now, every new instant."

This perpendicularity is directed downward, toward an "under" that is increasingly probed in *The Maximus Poems IV, V, VI* (I will henceforth refer to this middle volume as *II*, to keep it in line with *I* and *III*), where it is especially targeted in the fourth of the "Maximus, from Dogtown" pieces. Olson's anxious repetition of "under" here suggests a desire to once and for all break through the bottom of Tartaros to some absolute lower level or base. Perpendicular descent immediately calls to mind the horizontal strata of middens, so Olson's pounding at the vertical as the percussion of the instant is more of an emphasis than an elimination of the horizontal. For he writes to Boldereff: "We are a perpendicular axis of planes which are constantly being intersected by horizontal planes of experience coming up from the past (coming up from the ground)… and going out to the future… it is at the innumerable points of intersection that images and events spring up."

There are of course many instances of one of Olson's "Projective Verse" commands—"ONE PERCEPTION MUST IMMEDIATELY AND DIRECTLY LEAD TO A FURTHER PERCEPTION…"—which I understand as an attempt to keep poetic movement in an appositional swiftness and away from description and narrative tied to memory. There is a terrific example of the fruits of such a practice in a late *Maximus* poem, "As of Parsonses or Fishermans Field or Cressys Beach or Washington, the Capital, of my Front Yard?" I have in mind the following sequence:

> Gassire's
>> fate to
> I FA—to
>> s-i-n-g the
>>> root of
>>> the Well of the
>>>> Liquid of the
>>>>> Eagle's mouth:
>>>>>> *teonanacatl* is also
>>>>>>> God's body…

Gassire is the hero of a folktale from Niger who is told that his lute will only sound when it absorbs his pain, blood, breath, and the lifeblood of his son. In Dahomey, a man seeking to see into the future visits a sorcerer who "draws the FA"—fruit stones are thrown like our dice and the way they fall enables the sorcerer to make a prediction. The Well of Mimir is located beneath the Nordic World Tree, Yggdrasill. Odin, turned into an Eagle, let fall from his mouth drops of magic mead and in this way humankind received the gift of poetry. *"Teonanacatl"* is the Nahuatl sacred mushroom and means "God's flesh." So here we have a kind of metonymic syncretism utilizing four mythic systems, a brief rhapsody of "stitched song." The risk here is Poundian: if the nodes do not light up, the dramatic presence will be weak, and the reader's only thoughtful response will be to turn to the reference texts.

After reading the Olson *Selected Letters* in 2002, I wrote to the editor, Ralph Maud: "One of the things that struck me, with some of the intellectual letters, is the way Olson's mind acts when it gets excited. It reminds me of watching a stone being skipped across a pond—hit hit hit and pong! The associations come in so fast that each is touched upon, struck, followed by a ricochet, and so on. This is one version of 'one perception must lead directly to the next,' but in a version that often seems to me to work against thinking. In contrast, some of the best poems seem slower than the above procedure, with quick decisive moments, but with enough of the image or material offered for the reader to grasp before being taken forward. 'The Librarian,' for example, or 'In Cold Hell..." I am wondering what if anything accounts for such speed. Is this vertical thought (as he once proposed)? An attempt to discharge a constellational moment so that all nodes are present at once?"

8] In his essay "The Gate and the Center," Olson makes a challenging and audacious proposal: that something he calls "THE FIRST WILL" is, as of 1950, "back in business." While he does not define "first will," implications are that it relates to "the will to cohere," and that it manifests itself in "a life turning on THE SINGLE CENTER." By "center," historically Olson means Sumer, 4th millennium B.C., which he takes to be the site of the first city which "nourished, increased, advanced… all peoples around it," and provided "a coherence for the first time since the ice." One reason I think that Olson chooses Sumer for his first "center" is that the Sumerians are credited with inventing the cuneiform system of writing near the end of the fourth millennium. Since Olson also proposes that the 'WILL TO COHERE" begins to fail around 2500 B.C., when important Sumerian cities such as Kish, Erech, and Ur were supposedly at their height, the question arises as to how the poet would explain the "WILL TO DISPERSE" as setting in at this time. What we need here from Olson is an extended, in depth, essay on Sumerian civilization, contrasting it with other early settlements such as Jericho (8000 B.C.) and Catal Huyuk (6500 B.C.). And of course we do not have that.

Olson offers examples of the Amerindian Omaha puberty quests as proof that 'THE FIRST WILL' had reasserted itself. What such quests have to do with post-industrial, capitalist America in the 1950s misses me. Indeed, Olson joins his comrade Hart Crane in having a visionary program undercut by grinding pessimistic feelings about the America of their respective eras. And the Omahas themselves, no matter how we regard their puberty quest, were, to borrow Olsonian terms, moreorless put out of business in the mid-19th century when they ceded all of their lands west of the Mississippi River to the United States. Granted that the puberty quest is probably of Ice Age antiquity, it would seem to be a miraculous and attenuated survival rather than a new direction-determining power.

Elsewhere (same period) Olson writes to Creeley: "I am led on to imagine that the turn of the flow of man's energy (I take it the turn came c. 1917, or thereabouts) is only the SECOND TIME it has ever happened—and thus all our measures had better be tossed overboard, if we are to participate & to project." Why 1917? Could Olson have the Russian Revolution in mind?

A clear distinction between "cohere" and "disperse" also seems questionable. As a writer who owes his own existence to migration, one would think that he would see beyond a "will" as central to dispersal throughout history. Near the end of *The Maximus Poems*, Olson writes:

> Migration in fact (which is probably
> as constant in history as any one thing: migration
>
> is the pursuit by animals, plants & men of a suitable
> and gods as well—& preferable
>
> environment; and leads always to a new center...

While writing these notes, I came across an article by Paul Krugman in the August 8, 2003, *New York Times*, called "Salt of the Earth." Krugman writes:

> When archeologists excavated the cities of ancient
> Mesopotamia, they were amazed not just by what they found,
> but by where they found it: in the middle of an unpopulated
> desert. In "Ur of the Chaldees," Leonard Woolley asked:
> "Why, if Ur was an empire's capital, if Sumer was once a vast

granary, has the population dwindled to nothing, the very soil lost its virtue?"

The answer—the reason "the very soil lost its virtue"—is that heavy irrigation in a hot, dry climate leads to a gradual accumulation of salt in the soil. Rising salinity first forced the Sumerians to switch from wheat to barley, which can tolerate more salt; by about 1800 B.C. even barley could no longer be grown in southern Iraq, and Sumerian civilization collapsed. Later, "salinity crises" took place further north. In the 19th century, when Europeans began to visit Iraq, it probably had a population less than a tenth the size of the one in the age of Gilgamesh.

As often, in human history and prehistory, climate is the "unmoved mover."

9] Given Olson's base of historical information for most of the first Maximus volume, and a significant portion of the second and third ones, it is intriguing to note the stress he places on figurative language. "Image is the most volatile thing in creation," he writes to Creeley, and: "This leads me to think what's involved here is, actually, METEMPSYCHOSIS—and the restoration of METAPHOR as the human 'science' proper to human affairs & actions."

> When [psyche and metapsyche] are in such identity vectors come into existence that an individual is a force astronomically different than the personal alone, the resonances then resulting from the beat and sound of those two "boards" and strings being comparable only to the finest speech to the best poem.

> Image… is the only thing I am after, in any search, act, or learning.

The implication here, as I read these proposals, is that when psyche and meta-psyche (or consciousness and the subconscious) connect, the product is metaphor, or image.

That Olson also equates metaphor with "the act of art" suggests that he is using the word in a more inclusive sense than a Surrealist might.[6] In the poem, "Maximus of Gloucester," one reads: "the only interesting thing / is if one can be / an image / of man, 'The nobleness, and the areté.'" The complexity of this matter is sounded in the poem "rages / strains," concerning the Cretan war god Enyalios (called by Olson "Enyalion"). In the poem, Enyalion becomes what the depth psychologists call a "combined object," made up of himself, Tyr, Mars, and Hephaestus, "who goes to war with a picture." The implication is that going to war with a picture, or image, ennobles Enyalion, illuminating him as an image of man.

10] Olson also asserts that "No prime has an opposite... it exists not by reaction from but by virtue of its own nature." It can be demonstrated that the Cro-Magnon move from no image of the world to an image established the rudiments of the wilderness/cultural divide, and was a primordial act that established the first opposition. An enduring and catastrophic "separation continuum" was set in motion, it could be said, by initial image-making.[7] If one agrees, then it would seem to follow that there is no cultural prime *without* an opposite.

11] Olson and mythology. He quotes Bronislaw Malinowski's definition of myth (from Jung and Kerenyi's "Prolegomena" to *Essays on a Science of Mythology*) to Creeley, lauding it as the "best thing a man has sd, so far as I know 'em, on this subject." Here is the Malinowski:

> The myth in a primitive society i.e., in its original living
> form, is not a mere tale told but a reality lived. It is not in the
> nature of an invention such as we read in our novels today,
> but living reality, believed to have occurred in primordial
> times and to be influencing ever afterwards the world and
> destinies of men... These stories are not kept alive by vain
> curiosity, neither as tales that have been invented nor again as
> tales that are true. For the native on the contrary they are the
> assertion of an original, greater, and more important reality
> through which the present life, fate, and work of mankind are
> governed, and the knowledge of which provides men on the
> one hand with motives for ritual and moral acts, on the other
> with directions for their performance.

Olson appears to like this definition because it denies the symbolic and the etiological (that myth explains something). The problem here, as far as Olson's attempt to establish himself in a prime
for his own times, to find a perpendicular stance geared to the
instant, is the part of the definition that states that mythic stories
"are an assertion of an original, greater, and more important reality through which the present life, fate and work of mankind are
governed." If we look at the Gilgamesh material from this point of
view, I guess we could agree that Olson's recasting of the first two
"La Chutes" communicates that the content is still an "influence"
in Olson's own time. However, one must also note that to make a
poem of his own, Olson had to decontextualize the work, eliminating the Sumerian figures. Thus the "governing" aspect of Malinowski's definition becomes nebulous indeed.

One might also question the matter of a descent into an underworld which both workings indicate. We have no underworld today
in the Sumerian and Greek sense. This is the old problem of taking the reality of archaic myth for granted: can one really worship
Zeus if one does not sacrifice bulls to him? This dilemma pertains
to Malinowski's last sentence concerning knowledge of rituals and
directions for their performance.

❧

12] Convinced that "the struggle for language today is THE PRIMARY," that "it is the Poet... who is the one finally responsible agent of culture," Olson also proclaims "that it was language—words, goddamn it, WORDS—which freed man from his hands and any extension of same." His source for this claim is C.F.C. Hawkes' "Prologue" to *The Prehistoric Foundations of Europe*, in particular the passage where Hawkes stresses that "The faculty of even the simplest speech could substitute precept for mere example in the training of the singly born children whose slow-passing infancy kept them so long in need of it." In the same letter to Creeley quoted above, Olson also argues that the invention of speech replaced tools.

Clearly, Olson is feeding his own speech furnace here, finding prehistoric evidence to bolster his argument for the importance of the poet in his own time. But speech did not free early man from tools—speech enabled him to contextualize the use of tools, develop more complex ones, and find new uses for hands and tools. The invention of long-distance weapons was crucial in increasing his power over animals and creating via image-making the culture/ wilderness divide.

Olson must be thinking of only extremely basic tools, such as fashioned by Neanderthal. Without long-distance weapons on one hand, and flints, burins, pads, hand lamps, scaffolding, fiber rope, and mineral-based paints on the other, the Cro-Magnon moves into image-making and culture would not have taken place.

One of the questions motivating these Notes is why Olson did not move Ice Age research materials into *The Maximus Poems*—or into non-Maximus poems and essays. I will have more to say about this when I look at the material in *Olson #10*. Here I want to point out that what appears to be an over-emphasis on speech, and a failure to make the connection between tools and image-making may account in part for the failure of the wide visual Upper Paleolithic range to make its way into his poetry and essays, where archaic materials are dominated by a referential mythology.

❦

13] Occasionally, I come across ideas in Olson's writing that when juxtaposed with Upper Paleolithic images offer some insight into them. Take his comment that

> "man is but one object in field of force declaring self as
> force," which he opposes to a "'humanism,' [in which] man,
> out of all proportion of, relations, thus, so mis-centered,
> becomes, dependent on, only, a whole series of 'human' ref-
> erences which, so made, make only anthropomorphism, and
> thus, make mush of, any reality, conspicuously, his own, not
> to speak of, how all other forces (ticks, water-lilies, or snails)
> become only descriptive objects…"

The figure of the human is relatively rare in Ice Age image-making, and when present is often one tiny human force in a huge field of animal forces (as in the engravings in Les Trois Frères' "Sanctuary"). While there are more women figurations than men, only around 140 "Venus" statuettes have been found, in contrast to the thousands of horses, bison, and other animals painted and engraved on cave walls or on portable objects.

The non-narrative way in which most of these animals are presented is evoked by another Olson proposition. One nearly always finds them depicted in profile, often motionless, with no landscape or background indications. While there are realistic details (particular pelt marks, feline whiskers, anal flaps on mammoths, etc), to our eyes the animals seem generic. They do not appear to be part of a human society. D.H. Lawrence made a comment in his essay, "Him with His Tail in his Mouth," that seems relevant here:

> The pictures in the cave represent moments of purity which
> are the quick of civilization. The pure relation between the
> caveman and the deer: fifty percent man, and fifty percent
> bison, or mammoth, or deer. It is not ninety-nine percent

man, and one percent horse: as in a Raphael horse. Or hundred percent fool, as when F.G. Watts sculpts a bronze horse and calls it *Physical Energy.*

And here is Olson (from the "Human Universe" essays):

> All that comparison ever does is set up a series of reference points: to compare is to take one thing and try to understand it by marking its similarities to or differences from another thing. Right here is the trouble, that each thing is not so much like or different from another thing (these likenesses and differences are apparent) but that such an analysis only accomplishes a description, does not come to grips with what really matters: that a thing, any thing, impinges on us by a more important fact, its self-existence, without reference to any other thing, in short, the very character of it which calls our attention to it, which wants us to know more about it, its particularity.

Such comments suggest an affinity with Ice Age sensibility. Had Olson visited some of the caves in the spirit that he looked at Mayan glyphs in Yucatan[8], I think that their contextual visuality might have impressed him more than it did on the basis of looking at small black and white book photos and drawings. He might have found that some of his ideas were grounded in Cro-Magnon imagination.

14] At the 1963 Vancouver conference, Olson identified himself as Bronze Age man. From Pauline Wah's notes (in *Olson #4*):

> Olson a bronze-age man
> O. & metal—identification, not metaphoric
> "I Maximus, a metal hot from boiling water"
> belief is substituted for metaphor
> Keats: man's life is a life of allegory

From Daphne Marlatt's notes (same day, August 7):

> Olson is now Bronze Age man, goes back that far (metal)—
> "special character," "good conductors of electricity (kinetics
> of the thing) & heat (writing action)"—Olson thinks of him-
> self as a metal, specifically antimony (anti-money, also that
> which strengthens lead, produces luster but not rainbows)—
> his poems then: Bronze Age poems, poems of the clarity of
> the metallic age— "towards the Absolute"—Cro-Magnon man

His Bronze Age civilizations and figures include:

> Sumer/Babylonian: Gilgamesh, Tiamat
> Egypt: Ptah, Geb, Nut, Isis, sneferu
> Phoenicia: Byblos, Ousoos
> Canaan: Athirat, Ras Shamra Tables
> Crete: Enyalios

Most of his other archaic materials are Greek. The list is considerable and indicates more of a focus than the Bronze Age group:
Hesiod, Herodotus, Thucidides, Hermes, Hercules, Athena, Typhon, Zeus, Andromeda, Moira, Phryne, Okeanos, Tartaros, Eumol-
pus, Styx, Iris, Hera, Kouretes, Hydra, Tethys, Kore.

Among these, Tartaros and Typhon are given particular attention, for one reason, I think, because both press against what we
might call the Greek back wall. They gesture toward the never-
arrived-at "ICE."

⚶

15] Tartaros (the word is apparently Cretan, thus very old, signifying, according to Robert Graves, "far west") is the deepest of the
Greek infernal regions. According to Hesiod, its unmovable
threshold is made of bronze, "having unending roots and it is
grown of itself" (facts that would appeal to Olson), Tartaros is the
eternal stronghold of the Titans, imprisoned there by Zeus, along

with Typhon ("stupefying smoke, hot wind, or hurricane"), the largest monster ever born, and the child of Earth and Tartaros. The struggle between Zeus and Typhon is described by Graves as follows:

> Wounded and shouting, Typhon fled to Mount Casius, which looms over Syria from the north, and there the two grappled. Typhon twined his myriad coils about Zeus, disarmed him of his sickle and, after severing the sinews of his hands and feet with it, dragged him into the Corycian Cave. Zeus is immortal but now he could not move a finger, and Typhon had hidden the sinews in a bear-skin, over which Delphyne, a serpent-headed, sister-monster, stood guard.

The cave, bearskin, and serpent-tailed sister-monster imagery evoke a background of considerable antiquity.

Olson's fullest treatment of Tartaros, in "Maximus, from Dogtown—IV," argues the libidinous depth-charge of this region and implies that it is placed between Hades and primordial realms. According to Charles Stein in his Olson/Jung study, *The Secret of the Black Chrysanthemum*:

> Olson believes, apparently, that the story of the conquest of the Titans by the Olympians and the destruction by Zeus of the monster, Typhon, prefigure, in mythological terms, the conquest of the chthonic, appetite-centered cosmology of the old Mediterranean world by the rational and ultimately "statistical" cosmology of the subsequent European West.

By emphasizing certain aspects of Typhon (out of Hesiod), Olson also connects the monster to shamanism. As the soul of Tartaros, Typhon is said to have "'voices' / inside all his dreadful heads / uttering every kind of sound (imaginable?... sounds / such as solely the gods / caught on to." Typhon is also Protean: at one time, he was a bull, at another the sound of a lion's heart, at another he made sounds like whelps, and at another time "he would hiss / so the sky would burn." Elsewhere, Olson depicts Typhon as sea serpent that migrates to North America as a kind of "shadow" (in the Jungian sense) of Olson/Maximus. In one poem, "the blue monster" who departs for America from "his cave at Mt Casius" becomes Olson himself, in his blue postman's uniform, making his Gloucester rounds, delivering psychic "news."

Olson also tells us that "Heaven as sky is made of stone," while "Earth [is] made of grout." The image struck here is one of Earth as a mortar connecting a stone Heaven to a Bronze Age underworld. To think of Heaven as stone, for me, evokes the earliest paradise, the ur-underworld of the Upper Paleolithic caves. This view is reinforced by a passage in "Maximus, from Dogtown—IV":

> Tartaros
> was once 'ahead' of
> Heaven was prior
> (in coming into being) this 'child'
> of Earth: Tartaros
> was next after Earth (as Earth
> was next after hunger
> itself—Typhon
> was her child, by Tartaros...

This is pretty much standard Greek mythic information. However, in Olson's shaman-shadowed context, such words suggest that Tartaros was a kind of "heaven," or paradise, before Heaven, the first alternative world after Earth herself, allowing the possibility that the proto-shamanism might have been the "off-spring" of the interpenetration of stone and humankind.

16] There are a half-dozen occasions when Upper Paleolithic materials make brief appearances in *The Maximus Poems*.

In "Maximus further on (December 28th 1959)," at the beginning of the second volume, we find the following compacted lines:

afternoon Manatee of my mind? Rock picture
of a beast? Lausel (sic) woman, holding out a ladle? Actually
sluggish treadle up which nature
climbed Wet white body dried Old picture Andromeda
awash Norn nurse waitress

According to Butterick, Olson saw the photo of one of the three
Laussel Venuses in Erich Neumann's *The Great Mother*. The one
reproduced there is not the more well-known one holding up the
notched bison horn, but the one called "the Venus of Berlin." What
Olson calls a ladle is proposed by archeologists to be either an
object comparable to a jai alai basket, or a water-skin made out of
a ruminant's stomach.[9]

✺

17] In *Juniper Fuse*, in the poem "At the Hinge of Creation," one
stanza reads:

Olson, out of Fowler, writes:
"licked man (as such) out of the ice,
the cow"   Authumla
comes into being to provide food for Ymir,
"a rich, hornless cow"
the streams of milk from her udders nourish
    Yggdrasill

The entire Olson poem referred to here reads:

Licked man (as such) out of the ice,
the cow---------did who
herself came into being
so that Ymir would have some source
of food (her milk one supposes

> Odin was born of either this man directly
> or one generation further on, Odin's mother
> was the giant----------.

Olson may have put the blanks in to suggest unverifiable or missing sources. He may also not have remembered the name of the cow (Authumla, or Audumia), or Odin's mother (Bestla, a giant's daughter, one of Ymir's descendants). The licking of Odin and his brothers out of the ice could also suggest birthing on Authumla's part. Since Odin is depicted as a warrior–shaman, it would not be unusual for him to be the offspring of giants and animals.

While the mythology here is Norse, and not prehistoric, as a creation myth it strongly evokes the Ice Age. The next poem in *The Maximus Poems* repeats some of the information in this poem and adds a little material on the birth of Burr (also licked out of the ice), the father of Odin. As before with Gilgamesh, Olson's contribution has been to reframe fragmentary information into his own context.

18] We now leave *Maximus II* and enter *III*. Near the beginning, one finds the following short poem:

> I believe in God
> as fully physical
> thus the Outer Prědmost
> of the World on which we 'hang'
> as though it were wood and our own bodies are
> hanging on it

Olson is probably, with the word "Prědmost," referring to a schematic and somewhat geometrical figure of a woman engraved on a piece of mammoth tusk (six inches long), from a camp site of mammoth hunters upon the Moravian plain, around 24,000 B.P. Her head is an upside-down triangle, possibly horned, with a tectiform sign near the top. She has mussel-shaped breasts, and one atrophied arm on the right (the left side of the engraving is badly damaged), no hand. Her navel is emphasized by chevrons to the left and to the right. Her vulva is a horizontal oval larger than her head with interior chevrons. She has no feet. The entire figure can also be read as a face-mask.

Olson's addition of "Outer" to "Prědmost" would seem to indicate a place or region, not a goddess. If the engraved figure is being referred to, why "God" and not "Goddess?" Since the figure is identified as being of ivory (in Neumann, Olson's probable source), what is wood doing in the poem? Might the "Outer Prědmost" be a cross?

❦

19] Another short poem from *Maximus III:*

> Sweet Salmon
> from the coldest clearest
> waters. Cut the finest
> on the bone.
>   Rose
> directly from the stream straight into my greedy
> throat. And breast. A home
> for life.   Wise goddess
>
> of the straightest
> sapling
>   Saturday March 20th
>   1965

Butterick provides a 1959 note by Olson implying that this salmon refers to a "bone carving   art mobilier / France, Perigord / perhaps / Aurignacian / anyway." A more exacting placement of the salmon occurs in two lines of a poem from the same period,

"OCEAN, and we shall fail..." (rejected from *The Maximus Poems* and published in *Olson #9*):

> Ocean is stags cut on a reindeer horn
> with salmon entangled under their feet

If the three salmon references pertain to the same engraving, then Olson is wrong about the provenance of the object in the note, as the salmon on the reindeer horn is from Lorthet, a site in the Pyrénées, depicted in Henry Fairfield Osborn's *Men of the Old Stone Age*, figure #208, a book Olson acquired in 1952. The object is a broken reindeer antler, with superb engravings of two reindeer apparently crossing a stream, with four salmon leaping up between their legs. Two of the salmon leap toward the genital area of one of the reindeer.

A variation on this poem occurs on p. 187 of *Maximus III*. In both pieces, Olson's attention is directed less to the deep past than to the salmon leaping from the stream into the speaker's throat (troped as the speaker leaping into the "Beloved's love" in this poem). The meaning of the leap might be what Gary Snyder has, à la Dōgen, called nature affirming us, versus the Romantic notion of man affirming nature. Such affirmation is equated by Dōgen with enlightenment.

Note that in the first salmon poem the vertical leap becomes the "straightest sapling," bolstering Olson's belief in the perpendicularity and the "immensity," or wisdom, of dwelling only in the present.

❦

20] In "View: fr the Orontes" in *Maximus II*, Olson juxtaposes "Canary Islanders" with "Cro-Magnon." In "To my Portuguese..." (*Maximus III*), he writes: "You know, Gloucester itself comes from the / Canaries / probably..." and, later in the same poem, "Gloucester still moves / away from the Canaries—". In "The chain of memory is resurrection..." (in *The Collected Poems*), we find: "Cro-

Magnon man and… his descendants are Guanches / right now in the Canary Islands…"[10] Here we clearly need some background information.

Butterick writes: "The Canary Islands make up an archipelago in the Atlantic about sixty miles west of the North African coast. They were taken by Spain in the early fifteenth century. See Note V, 'The Cro-Magnons of the Canary islands,' in Osborne's appendix to his *Men of the Old Stone Age*, p. 506, for evidence of Cro-Magnon stock among the inhabitants of the islands at the time of their conquest."

The aboriginal inhabitants of the Canary islands, called Guanches, were, according to Osborne, "a composite people made up of at least three stocks: a Cro-Magnon type, a Hamitic or Berber type, and a branchycephalic. These natives were in a Neolithic stage of civilization." Butterick again: "In later published Maximus poems, which incorporate the theory of continental drift and the wider migrations of man and his symbols westward, the Guanches are again seen as ancestors of the settlers of Gloucester, esp. its Portuguese settlers form the Azores and Canaries, just as Gloucester itself is seen as having once been joined, geologically, to the Canaries."

Olson's proposals here are two-fold: 1) that Cro-Magnon descendants are alive in the Gloucester of his own days, and 2) that millions of years ago what was to be the eastern coast of America was attached to Gondwana, the southern landmass of the huge continent known as Pangaea ("All Earth").

According to the map of Gondwana on the cover of the second *Maximus* volume, while mostly to the south of the northern landmass known as Laurasia, Gondwana did touch Laurasia at points of the future North American eastern coast. However, this was 200 million years ago, and by 125 million, Laurasia was completely split off from Gondwana. Since Africa-to-be was in Gondwana, and North America-to-be was in Laurasia, there was no geological contact between the landmasses from this time onwards.

Thus the possible geological contact is so ancient that Olson's point about Gloucester still moving away from the Canaries is without much resonance. As for his statement, in *Olson #10*, that "Cro-Magnon man... still lives, in the Pyrénées, and the Guanches, of the Canary Islands:" the Spanish exterminated most of the Guanches in the beginning of the 16th century. Of course it is possible that some interbred with their conquerors and made up part of the stock of immigrants to North America.

Thus Olson's attempt to bring incredible time depth to bear on his claim that European North Americans are the last of a "first people" is more visionary than factual. The lines that can be drawn between the dots, as one might anthropomorphize star assemblies, are faint indeed.[11]

21] The last appearance the Upper Paleolithic makes in *The Maximus Poems* is in the piece about the Beothuk "boat" on page 189. In 1967, the poet was given an article by someone identified only as "Gardner" that mentioned an earlier article by E.F. Greenman entitled "The Upper Paleolithic and the New World," which, according to Butterick:

> ...argues that the sea-faring canoe of the Beothuk Indians of Newfoundland 'may be of Upper Paleolithic origin, and that its prototypes'—which could have easily made Atlantic crossings—'were quite possibly in use in the Bay of Biscay by Late Stone Age people as early as 15,000 B.C., or even earlier.' Gardner also reports that Greenman had identified 'an hitherto unexplained Upper Paleolithic painting in the Cave of Castillo in Northern Spain, not far from the Bay of Biscay, as a representation of a craft that could well be the direct prototype of the Beothuk canoe'... while pointing out that the Beothuks, who became extinct in the early nineteenth century, 'were much addicted to the use of red ochre, whence they got the name of Red Indians.'

Butterick's note continues and I recommend it to anyone seeking more information about this matter.

Before looking at the signs Greenman identified as "boats," I must note that his argument for the presence of Upper Paleolithic artifacts and traits in the New World (from Magdalenian northern Spain) is based on a late Upper Paleolithic diffusion between the Biscayan area and Newfoundland. This would mean that small boats like kayaks and canoes were able to make the North Atlantic crossing (at that time "choked with floating ice," according to Greenman). To what extent this was possible, I do not know. For many decades, the Bering Strait landmass at 13,000 B.P. has been proposed as the only credible corridor of access to the New World. However, Greenman's artifactual evidence makes a strong case for some North Atlantic contact.

In the northern Spanish caves of Altamira, El Castillo, and La Pasiega, there are signs that can be read as naviform (boat-shaped). El Castillo in particular has at least a dozen signs, mostly in red ochre, and scattered throughout the cave, that could be read as small, stubby, barge-shaped boats. André Leroi-Gourhan calls these signs in La Pasiega, "brace-shaped," and those in El Castillo "female quadrangular signs." The Abbé Breuil calls the El Castillo ones "tectiforms" (roof-shaped).

As with the pieces linking the Guanches and the Canary Islands, this poem is another attempt to argue unbroken diffusion between The New World and the ancient Old World.

Perhaps it should be noted that the boats described in the poem are hut-like, with a covering frame extending beyond the sides. If the Spanish signs are boats, they appear to have no upper structure or covering.

22] Outside of *The Maximus Poems*, there is even less referencing of Ice Age culture in Olson's poetry. There is, of course, the well-known juxtaposition of "Buchenwald" with "new Altamira cave" in the 1946 "La Préface" (which I comment on in my Introduction to

Juniper Fuse). Olson's juxtaposition is, to my knowledge, the first acknowledgement that the rediscovery of Altamira and the existence of the Nazi death camps (there could hardly be two greater opposites) occurred in the same time frame. Beyond that, in a later line of the poem—"He talked, via stones   a stick   sea   rock   a hand of earth"—there is an implied perception that the archaic is the post-modern, for not only has Altamira displayed itself as a visionary element in the modernist panorama, but the image of a stripped human being scratching with a stick in the dirt backgrounded by a concentration camp wall powerfully evokes, in a positive way, a Cro-Magnon in cavern dark drawing a flint line in stone. It is not only that the beginning of imaginative play has jutted into our era, but that our dwelling place has been scaled back to a sinister caricature of its original.

In other poems, there are a few mentions of Upper Paleolithic animals—the mastodon, the woolly rhinoceros, the giant deer (probably the Irish elk, or megaloceros), and a slight but memorable piece called "On All Sides:"

> the cave/wall the cave lion's
> SHOULDERS
> are rubbing off

23] "Maximus, from Dogtown—IV" is the far point of any saturated push into Gloucester's antecedence. After it, there is an abrupt swing back to historical Gloucester, with the relatively weak "Fort Point" section concluding the second *Maximus* volume. Olson, at the end of "Maximus, from Dogtown—IV" reminds me of Rimbaud two-thirds of the way through the voyage of the drunken boat—a maximal point has been reached. In Rimbaud's case, the poet is thus simultaneously confronted by destroying himself at sea and becoming a caricature of his visionary self in the memory of himself as a child playing with a paper boat on a puddle.

In Olson's situation, this is when he needs "ICE" and he doesn't have it. Rather than making contact with the Canary Islands, say, and envisioning Cro-Magnon settlements there, or engaging the Bay of Biscay and making metaphorical contact with the nearby painted/engraved Cro-Magnon caves, he stays in Gloucester "to write a Republic / in gloom on Watch-House Point." Whereas he had written to Creeley in late 1950 that "RELIGION [was] one of the two monsters" and "on a par with SUPERSTITION," he now writes (several months after the accidental death of his wife, Betty, from which he would never really recover):

> I believe in religion not magic or science I believe
>   in society
>   as religious both man and society as religious

Thus moving through *Maximus III*, and seriously effecting its presence, is a grim "return of the repressed" Catholicity in conjunction with despair and the conviction that Gloucester is no more than another tacky part of 1960s America. The Christian prayer on page 561, for this reader, is the nadir of *The Maximus Poems*.

Olson is certainly entitled to his feelings, but as far as the poem goes the repeated declarations of abject self-pity and the appeals to God represent an abandoning of the Maximus/Olson presence, foregrounding instead the intrusive voice of pathetic Charles on his knees before God. I shudder to think what the Olson of the Boldereff and Creeley correspondences would have said reading this material. Loss here seems so total as to have ripped the fabric of a work that was initially mounted off one of the most demanding and charged apprenticeships in modern letters.

24] The Olson writings that make up *Olson #10*, subtitled "The Chiasma, or Lectures in the New Sciences of Man," from 1953, are probably only in part the actual notes that were the basis for the lectures. Butterick refers to this material as a "selection," and says that he has "been guided by copies of the lectures among Edward Dorn's papers... and by notes made available to him by Mervin Lane." This may or may not account for the fact that Olson's "Outline" for the Lectures, on pages 8 and 9, is only in part followed by the ensuing notes. Under these circumstances, it is hardly fair to evaluate this material *as* Olson's Lectures.

Much of Olson's reading and thinking here is a logical outcome of his engagement with the archaic especially in his correspondence with Boldereff—these writings start to engage the "ICE" or "Absolute" that was sighted via Bronze Age and Greek myth, and while the Upper Paleolithic observations are often mixed in with Greek, Neolithic, and 19th century Australian aborigine mythology, these notes act like a springboard for a leap and descent that never took place.

Earlier I mentioned that one possible explanation for Olson's failure to include material from the deep past in the unfolding of his long poem was that his obsession with speech versus tools always drew him to oral sources e.g., he could relate to the Sumerians via the Gilgamesh epic (and I should note here that there is very little material on Cro-Magnon painting and engraving in the Chiasma material). Another explanation might involve a compulsion to return the poem to a daily sense of Gloucester (in 1963, at the beginning of *Maximus III*) after hammering away at Tartaros. Olson had never earlier allowed himself what we might call confessional largesse. There is very little personal/private life material in the early and middle period poetry—certainly some dreams, but nothing directly about Constance or Betty, or daily life at Black Mountain College. The part of Olson's life involving dependence upon women and the subsequent "goddess" idealization is not addressed. In the *Guide*, Butterick mentions "a long, confused, personal poem (involving the poet's mother and deceased wife" from 1969 and then quotes a few lines from it. When published one day it may open up some of this sealed and congested psychic terrain.

25] In the Chiasma material, Olson has a tendency to propose presentations that he does not follow up on. Here one must keep in mind that some inconsistencies may occur because we do not have the Lectures as outlined.

He proposes to quote Jung's "shortest characterization of the anima," then two pages later, he mentions a paper Jung has sent to him which he will use to "launch [his] own attack on this question of present power & a useable force of myth to each of us now." There is no follow up to either of these matters. Later, he proposes to give his "reasons in just a moment, as of the intent of Paleolithic man," and to offer "abundant evidence of signs of the winding path not only in Paleolithic but right thru Mesolithic and Neolithic… down to, say, the labyrinth of Crete at least." Paleolithic man's "intent" would represent a central declaration. Nothing more is said about it. Ditto for signs of the winding path, possibly because there is no evidence for such in the Upper Paleolithic (the term comes from Australian aborigine myths of origin). He also proposes to discuss "a man stalking a bison, and covered with the skin of the bison as he does it," and to examine Cro-Magnon dance. Again these fascinating matters are left up in the air.

Olson's free-wheeling and often exciting blast of ideas in the late '40s/early '50s seems to have set up an anti-methodical way of working that became problematic when examples were needed to concretize proposals.

26] I am impressed with the rapidity with which Olson was able to read and assimilate materials about which he must have known virtually nothing until he looked into the books on the archaic that Boldereff brought up, along with what appears to be a half-dozen more. According to Butterick's notes at the end of *Olson #10*, the books involved were the Frobenius/Fox *Prehistoric Rock Pictures*, the earlier-cited Osborne *Men of the Old Stone Age*, C.F.C. Hawkes' *Prehistoric Foundations of Europe*, Gertrude Levy's *The Gate of Horn*, and Max Raphael's *Prehistoric Cave Paintings*. Neither the Hawkes nor the Frobenius/Fox books would have been much help with the European Ice Age: after a brief introduction, the former moves to the Mesolithic and works forward from there; the latter is mainly about Africa and its historic rock paintings. Olson apparently did not know about the publication of the Abbé Breuil's *Four Hundred Centuries of Cave Art* (in English translation, spring 1952). The book would have been a cornucopia, and have alerted him to, among many other painted/engraved caves, the revelation of Lascaux, discovered in 1940.

At times in these Lectures, Olson made perceptive observations and sightings. Probably via Levy, he recognized that cup-shapes (cupules), gouged out of rock slabs at La Ferrassie were "the first instance of engraving & shaping moving from utility to celebration: he [Mousterian man] starts with PERFECT CIRCLE then spiral, or, labyrinth." He is one of the first to notice that there may be regional differences in aesthetic development in Cro-Magnon image-making, and associates the geometrically-painted stones from the Azilian period Mas d'Azil site with Australian *churingas*, noting that "these churingas are believed to hold in union divinity-animal-man, including the recent dead as well as those awaiting incarnation, and were shown to every initiate at the moment of his passage from boyhood to membership of the clan." While there is no evidence that the Mas d'Azil stones pertained to puberty rites, Olson's link is imaginative and resonant.

He intuited that the maze (and, by implication, the maze-like cave) was involved with the concept of a second birth:

> But the birth-death thing has another side to it—and action-
> able side of considerable moment now. It is the actual fact of
> SECOND BIRTH—that the maze of life does not stay
> maze—that one gets through. And thus all of these acts of
> expression we have been following is of a different import
> than merely that generalized thing—how does Eliot have it,
> that chief contemporary generalizer? birth, copulation, death

for men have never, it appears, when they have known the
intensities of the passage, rather than just the cave—that
darkness—or the outside—that activity—been unaware that
this is the thing, that *this is yourself*, that the passage can be
forced to yield light, or something beside the noise of itself

He also offers a fantasia on the cave's evolution to tomb, temple,
house, and church, up to the present: "and now, in the refusal of
any of us any longer even to admire the SKYSCRAPER, we have
that pseudo-cave, the WOMB, in place of that recognition which I
have suggested will force itself more and more on men, that they,
now, are literally CAVE—that the phrase that we are forced back
on ourselves, has just such meaning."

Finally, he made the fascinating proposal that *The Odyssey* was
not "an epic at all, was, in fact, a drama—was written as such—and
that it reflects at its late date the masked dance of the caves."[12]

27] When my wife Caryl and I moved to the French Dordogne in
the spring of 1974 for several months, Olson was not much on my
mind. After visiting some of the painted caves, including Lascaux,
I became aware that all the direct research done on them had been
carried out by archeologists and that the field was wide-open for a
poet to undertake his own investigation. After returning to Los
Angeles late that summer, I reread Olson's advice to Ed Dorn that
by taking on a man or a subject and doing what Olson called "a
saturation job" on him or it, he would learn more about such than
any other man and, in some mysterious way, "be in, forever."

I had actually done my first "saturation job" from 1962 to 1978
in translating and co-translating all of the European poetry of
César Vallejo. I made that decision in Kyoto in 1962, thinking of
my project not as a "saturation job," but as my apprenticeship to
the art of poetry. The stone lithographer Will Petersen had visited
one day and told me that he had just come from a *bonsai* gardener
who had recently started to do some very original work. How old

is he, I asked Will. In his late 60s, was the reply. When I expressed my amazement that it would take someone that long to come into his own, Petersen explained that in traditional Japan, artists and artisans often had long apprenticeships and sometimes only did their own work at the end of their lives. As a young American fixated on doing something original in my late 20s, this news threw me for a loop and got me thinking about what might really be involved in practicing an art over the long haul. I began to realize that I had learned very little about poetry as it might relate to myself while I was a student. Vallejo struck me as a different kind of poet than I had read before, and I intuited that if I really worked through his *Poemas humanos* I would learn something about poetry and about myself that I couldn't get anywhere else.

Thus the sixteen years spent translating and retranslating Vallejo somewhat prepared me for my even longer investigation of the origin of image-making. Other than the Lectures in *Olson #10* (which Butterick kindly xeroxed for me in 1977, a year before they were published), Olson's writings did not figure much into my work, and the Lectures themselves, while fascinating, did not bear directly on my project. However, I had two significant dreams concerning Olson, one at the beginning of the investigation, in 1976, and another at its end in 2000. They represent a kind of psychic contribution, a comradely display on the part of a man I never met. Here is the first dream:

Poem Copied From Text Written in Dream

I, Charles Olson,
    left

    Oprecht
    walking my bicycle

      a trace of chat
      on the catless road

> seemed to bridge
> two far points
>   moon nodes

[at this point I was presented with a drawing of what looked like
two cat ears intersecting a curved line—I drew it into the poem as
I remembered it from the dream]

> where I'd gotten air
> the boy said be sure to see
> the north ear
>   the marsh there   nothing intersecting earth
>   more beautiful

> I cast
> & netted
> Babson Whitehead
> Jung & Neumann
> stocked
> my inner lake
> until I need no longer
> want what other men call
> food, the outside,
> was sufficient on
> my innerness
> an image of man
> & collaged their
> words into the fabric
> —were they keloid
> over an unhealable wound?
> A faceless woman
> chained to
> the Venus of Willendorf
> —was the lacuna in
> the areté this crouched facelessone
> the bridge across

> atlementheneira

"Dictated" would be a better word than "written," as I woke up with the entire "dictation" in mind. After the list of scholars' names Olson has drawn upon, fragments of a couple of his poems make their way in. The stocked inner lake probably picks up on "Wholly absorbed / into my own conduits to / an inner nature or subterranean lake," and "an image of man" must allude to the "Maximus of Gloucester" poem from 1965 with the line, "The only interesting thing / is if one can be / an image / of man…"

The most interesting word in the dictation is the last one, "atlementheneira," a neologism. I took it as the sounding of the unknown depth possibly to be encountered in an investigation of the deep past. At the beginning of the poem "Visions of the Fathers of Lascaux," I seized on the word as the name of one of the "Fathers." I also heard ghosts of other words inside of it, like *atl atl* (the Nahuatl word for spear-thrower), "men," "then," and "era." Something like "*atl atl* era of men then."

28] During the night of February 16, 2000, when *Juniper Fuse* seemed to be finished, Olson appeared in another dream:

> Near a beach I discovered mole hills between kennels or chicken coops. A farmer said he'd turned his dogs on them. I watched furious fighting inside a shed, lots of pups being spit out. Worried that Caryl would not know where to find me, I started walking a path to suddenly find myself in a crowd where I heard that Charles Olson, now out on the road with a small child, wandering and giving lectures for food, for some eighty days, was to arrive. I was shown photos of Robert Kelly with a young black woman and other strangers. Then I was in a house with people who had studied Olson, including an attractive Irish woman who had a small *tansu* set into the floor. She said it contained Olson texts and could not be opened until he arrived. The excitement was mounting— Olson enthusiasts seemed to be everywhere. I was now in a

spacious cave and heard the approach of what I took to be
Olson and his retinue—there he was, seven feet tall, shaggy
white hair, thin neck, block-like skeletal head, hunched over,
climbing through the air. I went up to him, took his huge
hand. He looked at me curiously, then boomed: "How are
your caves coming along?" I started to describe the comple-
tion of *Juniper Fuse* but he interrupted: "The music, how
about the music?" Before I could respond, he was past me. I
was surrounded by hip-looking men in sunglasses whom I
figured were Olson aviators. It was a joyful occasion—then it
hit me: How could he be here? He died in 1970! Larry
Goodell then piped up: "That's the majesty of it!" I was now
caught up in another crowd, being shown a map of the Pech
Merle cave with certain areas marked that I understood
Olson had explored. "Olson is coming!" I heard. "What?" I
said, "I just saw him." "No, he's coming now," voices clam-
ored, and a strange creature rounded a cave bend, a leg-like
head with one huge eye, stick-like body, insect legs. There
was intense conversation about what was referred to as a
"restoration." New people appeared, shouting that Olson was
on his way! An even stranger apparition appeared, more
insectile, arachnoid, long extending legs front and back, its
head—a compact lavender mass—under its body. I worked
my way under as the creature ambled along, yelling: "What
happened to you?" I got my hands around the jewel-like head
and wrenched it free, at which moment an agonized voice
cried: "I couldn't get the whole Theolonius!" What was left
disappeared among the mass of people thronging the cave.

Olson appeared, in this dream, to be devolving, or passing from
personal consciousness into his collective, the realm of creature
souls. His response to my question—"What happened to you?"—
possibly banked off his earlier music remark, brings Theolonius
Monk to mind, but even more a pun on "the whole Olson," perhaps also sounding the name of the Roman poet, Ausonius, whose
poetry Olson read in translation in the late 1940s.

Shortly after this dream, I wrote "Cemeteries of Paradise," and added it to the manuscript. While writing the poem, the final line from "The Kingfishers" came to mind: "I hunt among stones." Olson had set up this line with the couplet right before it:

> I pose you your question:
> shall you uncover honey / where maggots are?

In his study of this poem, "What Does Not Change," Ralph Maud writes: "Olson is drawing here on a proverbial expression in *The Bible* (Judg. 14: 5–9), where Samson kills a lion and, coming back later, sees 'a swarm of bees in the body of the lion, and honey.' In other words, bees can make use of the rotting carcass of a lion; can you make use of the apparently dead past, Western civilization?" In a way parallel to the bees, Olson implies that he will figure out a way to move into the future by attending to the archaic past, the past that one might examine in a field or ruins. Thus recovery of work done in the sun becomes the task of an "archeologist of morning."

In my poem, I wrote: "Unlike Olson / I do not 'hunt among stones.' / I hunt inside stone." In other words, I have gone back to the ice, as it were, before there was a city, to the dark of caverns, as an "archeologist" of the wee hours, right before dawn, and before any heaven. Olson's Lectures and fragmentary referencing of the Upper Paleolithic in his poetry slashed a path into that abyss of forms, confirming that a poet had business there. It was up to me to find my own direction toward the source of form that ultimately turned out, in *Juniper Fuse*, to be the hole that grew into a pole (or, bending, became the Uroboros and Okeanos). Or to ring one more change off my Gloucester companion, in the spirit that "FORM IS NEVER MORE THAN AN EXTENSION OF CONTENT," one could say: *pole is never more than an extension of hole.*[13]

NOTES:

[1] This lecture, commissioned by Robert Creeley, was given in the Special Collections Library at the SUNY–Buffalo, on October 22/23, 2004. It was published in *Minutes of the Charles Olson Society #52.*

[2] The S.N. Kramer article is to be found in *Journal of the American Oriental Society #64* (1944), pp. 7–23.

"La Chute III" links incest, descent, and second birth, and appears to be Olson's own poem, not an adaptation. For more on descent and second birth, see my *Juniper Fuse: Upper Paleolithic Imagination & the Construction of the Underworld* (Wesleyan University Press, 2003), p. xxi.

It is appropriate here to note that there is a fascinating relationship between "La Chute II" and "A Newly Discovered 'Homeric' Hymn." Both poems concern the registration of a protocol to be followed when dealing with the dead, the first Sumerian, and the second out of Homer. While the first is a slightly revised translation, the second is, as far as I can tell, Olson's own, and a fine poem in its own right.

While, outside of *Olson #10*, there is little material in Olson's work on Ice Age imagination, the presence of the historic archaic is constantly there. To engage it fully would require a book length study. Certain poems set in the present, such as "The Lordly and Isolate Satyrs," are made more substantial by deft archaic referencing. Olson's seeing Hell's Angels on the beach as resonant with "The Great Stones" of Easter Island builds an archaic shadow into the motorcycle gang that makes their strangeness unearthly.

[3] For more on undifferentiated archetypes, see *Juniper Fuse*, pp. 46–47.

[4] The latter part of this sentence draws on Olson's words in a letter written to Vincent Ferrini, in 1952, to be found in *Charles Olson, Selected Letters*, ed. Ralph Maud, University of California Press, 2000, p. 18.

[5] Robert Duncan's essay, "The Rites of Participation" (from the still unpublished "H.D. Book"), with its opening statement about "all things coming into their comparisons" is pertinent here. The some 400 pages of "The H.D. Book already published in magazines can be accessed via: http://www.cca.ca/history/ozz/english/books/hd_book/HD_Book_by_Robert Duncan.pdf

[6] Olson's extended use of "image" is sounded in an exchange with Robert Kelly in 1960. When I asked Kelly about this, he responded:

this was before I actually met the man, and while I was still living in Brooklyn. I had sent him the first purple hecto-graphed versions of my Notes on the Poetry of Deep Image, and in his reply, speaking I think to the points I was making about the rhythm of the images constituting (what we would call now) the deep structure of the poem he (and I remember it scrawled on a post card) said:

> "not imageS but image"

in so many words. Left me to chew on the difference he was after. My guess is/was that he was already after the Angel, the Sufi transsensory (hence beyond images but not beyond being an image of use to the mind) that so preoccupied him through the third volume of *Maximus* and marked his sensa-tional (and not much noticed by Olsonians) departure from the Aristotelian into the realms of what would presently be talked about as soul, angel, Amoghasiddhi.

[7] This idea of a "separation continuum" is argued throughout *Juniper Fuse*, and presented in the Introduction to the book, pp. xvi–xvii. Also see footnote #14 , p. 245.

[8] It should be added here that at the time Olson went to Yucatan, in 1951, no one knew how to read Mayan glyphs, including Olson.

[9] The "sluggish treadle" occurs in an earlier Maximus poem, p. 127, in the first volume, there clearly referring to a machine in a ship's hold. Here the image seems more evolutionary than mechanical. It is unclear in this poem who the pregnant woman is (Gen Douglas? her sister? Androme-da?); whoever she is, Olson tells us, at the poem's end, "Perseus [is] the husband not me."

[10] There are also other Upper Paleolithic references in "The chain of memory is resurrection…" on pp. 375 and 376, such as "the animal / fat lamp" and "The Venus of Willendorf." "the gate of horn" is also the title of Gertrude Rachel Levy's book on the deep past which Olson had read.

[11] See *Olson #6*, pp. 69–71 for further commentary by Butterick on the Gloucester/Canary Island "connection." Manuel Brito, in *Un Topos Atlán-*

tico para El Mitólogo (Zasterle Press, 1989) has collected and translated all of the Olson material relevant to the Canary Islands, with an informative introduction.

[12] Olson also makes quite a few errors, mostly of a factual nature, in the Lectures. Some of these undoubtedly come from material he was reading that is now considered out of date. Some examples: Olson wrote that no objects were found in caves. Thousands of objects have in fact been found, including engraved bones and stones, hand lamps, paint tubes, flints for etching, charcoal, crayons, and ornaments. Olson also confused time periods, implying that Australian aboriginal ceremonies took place in the Upper Paleolithic. He was also confused as to where decorations are in the caves, thinking that paintings only occur in the depths and that all signs and Venus statuettes are at the entrances. This is not so. He suggests that the bull-roarer was the first musical instrument. While it is possible that one incised reindeer antler from La Roche de Birol is a bull-roarer, this piece is Magdalenian (18,000 to 12,000 B.P.) and much younger than Aurignacian or Gravettian flutes or Solutrean ochre-marked mammoth bones thought to have been musical instruments.

[13] For a contextualization of the hole/pole matter, see *Juniper Fuse*, pp. 232–236.

CIRCLING THE CRADLE [1]

Bataille, Georges. *The Cradle of Humanity: Prehistoric Art and Culture.* Edited and Introduced by Stuart Kendall; Translated by Michelle Kendall and Stuart Kendall. Brooklyn, NY: Zone Books, 2005. (210 pp.)

In 1981, during a trip to Paris to consult Aimé Césaire about problematic words in my co-translation of his *Collected Poetry* (University of California Press, 1983), I was invited to the Chinese scholar Jacques Pimpaneau's apartment for dinner. Upon arriving I was introduced to Georges Bataille's widow. Pimpaneau knew that I was researching the origin of image-making via the Ice Age painted caves in southwestern France and he had thoughtfully made it possible for me to talk with the woman who was with Bataille in the 1950s when he did research on Lascaux. Madame Bataille told me that she and Georges spent over a month in the nearby town of Montignac and that Georges was allowed to visit the cave every evening, on his own or with photographers, after the tourists went home. In contrast, by the mid-1970s, after Lascaux had been closed to all but professionals, I had had to pull all sorts of strings to arrange several forty-five minute visits.

Bataille's research led to his monograph on the cave, *Prehistoric Painting: Lascaux or The Birth of Art* (Skira, 1955), which, for its time, provided an exciting vista, via excellent photographs and thoughtful text, on the extraordinary imaginative breakthrough that Lascaux represented. For Bataille, Lascaux's paintings "announced the presence of man on earth." It is hard for us today to realize the force of the discovery of Lascaux in 1940 during the terrible days of the Second World War. The pristine condition of the cave (sealed until re-discovery for some 17,000 years), the magnificently conceived and painted animal scenes led Picasso to exclaim: "since Lascaux no one has done anything better!" Bataille was then to treat Lascaux as in a class of its own and to refer to the imagery in other Upper Paleolithic caves as "hardly legible."

Even in the early 1950s, such an assessment was inaccurate. While Lascaux's impact is singular, such caves as Font-de-Gaume, Pech Merle, and Niaux, to name three that are hardly mentioned by Bataille, have unique and masterful paintings. With this new collection of Bataille's previously-untranslated essays on prehistory, one can see just how mesmerized Bataille was with Lascaux—and its shaft "scene" in particular—to the exclusion of other caves. While he comments briefly on the hybrid engravings in Les Trois Frères, and on the Lespugue Venus statuette, he appears to have only visited Lascaux and to have depended on the Abbé Breuil's and Johannes Maringer's books for information on all other sites. What appears to be a sad lack of curiosity is explained by Stuart Kendall, who has co-translated *The Cradle of Prehistory* and contributed an informative introduction to it, in the following way: "Bataille had cerebral arteriosclerosis, diagnosed in 1953. By the late 1950s, the disease had progressed to a state of debility such that he could not remember something he had done even five minutes before." The implication is that beyond visits to the easily-accessible Lascaux, spelunking was out of the question. Bataille's compromised memory may have also played a role in the way he thought through his speculations about the origins of art, religion, and man's relationship to death.

As some readers will be aware, Georges Bataille (1897–1962) published works in a variety of fields, including erotic fiction, philosophy, and literary criticism as well as art history. His reinterpretation of the philosophies of Nietzsche and Sade influenced a generation of French theorists, such as Derrida, Foucault, and Baudrillard. One of his primary impulses as a writer was to go beyond, or get under, disciplinarian specialization, and in this respect he is quite similar to Charles Olson who, in the late 1940s, proposed that one must go all the way back to "the ICE" to devise a method by which it might be possible to cover the whole field of knowledge.

In the same period that Bataille was investigating Lascaux, Olson, at Black Mountain College, was assembling the notes and lectures on Cro-Magnon imagination. Both writers attempted to dislodge the past from the domain of prehistorians. In 1950, Olson wrote to Francis Boldereff: "The archaic or primordial is not at all past—we are participants in it now as we are in what we call 'reality'—we are a perpendicular axis of planes which are constantly being intersected by horizontal planes of experience coming from the past coming up from the ground and going out to the future."

While certainly speculative, Olson's comment here has a clarity that is often absent from Bataille's writings on prehistory (outside of *Lascaux or The Birth of Art*, that is, which is well-organized and coherent). In the writing in the book under review, attempting to avoid superficiality, Bataille constantly qualifies what he says, and often comes to no conclusion. His writing has an odd way of disappearing up its own sleeves. Compounding this sort of obscurity is the sketchy use of his research. While he makes, in my opinion, too absolute a distinction between Neanderthal and Cro-Magnon awareness, and fails to bring into play on Neanderthal's behalf the proto-images discovered at La Ferrassie in 1909, one must take into consideration the abyss that he is confronting and thinking into: the imaginal fragmentation of a culture to which there is no alphabetic or contextual bridge.

As a rule, Bataille goes along with Breuil's "hunting hypothesis" (a now discredited theory explaining cave paintings of animals as a form of sympathetic magic), but he is uncomfortable with it as a total explanation, and sometimes contrasts it with what he calls "the apparitional power of the image." In such "apparitions," he discerns sensations of expiation, atonement, and divinity. And in *Lascaux or The Birth of Art*, he arrives at a broad and beautiful definition of art that is still pertinent today. Bataille writes: "In every ritual operation, the seeking after a specific end is never but one amongst a number of its operators' motives: these motives derive from the whole of reality, its religious and sensible (aesthetic) sides alike. In every case, they imply what has always been art's purpose: to create a sensible reality whereby the ordinary world is modified in response to the desire for the extraordinary, for the marvelous, a desire implicit in the human being's essence."

Some of the absolute distinctions I have referred to can be explained by the fact that when Bataille was distinguishing Neanderthal from Cro-Magnon, for example, he was working with much less information than appears to be available to us today (I say "appears to be" because such enigmas as intentional versus accidental markings on ancient bones will probably never be resolved). We now think we know much more about Neanderthal than Bataille did. Besides the simple burials that he describes to indicate Neanderthal's humanity, there is now evidence that besides the cupules at La Ferrassie, Neanderthal made ochre and manganese "crayons," simple musical instruments, incised zigzag marks on bones, and in one instance amputated a man's arm and possibly staunched the bleeding with ragwort (*Ephedra*), one of at least six species of flowers that were found in one of the Shanidar (northern Iraq today) burials. Today, what was referred to by John Pfeiffer in 1979 as the Cro-Magnon "creative explosion" looks more like a shifting, accelerated development.

Throughout his writings on prehistory in the 1950s, Bataille kept returning to what became for him his own primordial "scene of the crime:" the Shaft scene, which he called "the Holy of the Holies," at the bottom of an 18-foot, dry, well-like pit in Lascaux. Under an enraged, possibly disemboweled bison whose hindquarters are crossed by a broken shaft, a bird-headed, ithyphallic man is stretched out, with a broken spear-thrower below his feet. Under one four-fingered bird-foot-like hand, a bird topping a staff appears to stare at the anus of a woolly rhinoceros out of which six turds, arranged in two rows, emerge. In contrast to the other figures, the rhino is quite naturalistic and appears to be slowly moving away from the rest of the action on an implied ground level.

Bataille initially approached this scene (probably before visiting the cave) in a 1952 lecture, the year of the publication of Breuil's landmark *Quatre cents siècles d'art parietal*. He apparently showed a slide of the scene and then left his audience on their own to make of it what they could. In an essay written a year later, he draws upon Breuil's description of the scene, again without adding any commentary. Two years later, several months before the publication of his own book on Lascaux, he showed a film on the cave, spoke of its discovery, and commented on a few paintings without bringing up the Shaft scene. In the book itself, he offers a fairly comprehensive description of the scene (indicating for the first time that he has actually been down in the Shaft), but instead of saying what it means to him defers to the anthropologist H. Kirchner whose shamanistic explanation he quotes and then partially disagrees with. In 1957, in his book *Erotism*, he finally suggests "a coherent interpretation of the Lascaux pit painting where a dying bison faces the man who has probably killed it and whom the painter shows as a dead man. The subject of this famous picture, which has called forth numerous contradictory and unsatisfactory explanations, would therefore be murder and expiation." In the title essay of the present book, written in 1959, he writes that "the death of the man (we can in fact only see a dead man in the fallen figure) is linked to the death of the animal, not that the agonizing bison necessarily killed him, but that the two deaths are in some way complementary. The man is guilty of the bison's death because a line coming from an expressly drawn propellant penetrates the animal's stomach. Because the man is guilty, his death could therefore be taken as a compensation offered by chance or perhaps voluntarily to the first victim."

There are several problems with this interpretation that I can only go into briefly here.[2] Rather than dead, a more apt description of the unwounded, ithyphallic bird-headed man is that he is in a trance, and that rather than "fallen," he is, along with the bison, part of a visionary descent or ascent. The bird-headed staff links him directly to descriptions of 19th-century Siberian shamanic activities. Bataille's interpretation also completely leaves out the rhino and the turds. And it does not make sense to me that a man would have been killed, as Bataille strongly implies, for having killed, or sacrificed a bison (if indeed that is what happened, since the broken spear is placed across the bison's hind-quarters and does not appear to be the cause of the exposed guts, which may be, in fact, a grotesque depictation of a vulva).

Regardless, Bataille's circling and circling of this scene over close to a decade is touching, and illustrates his admirable tendency to resist sealing over the mystery of such a narrative complex with a definitive guess. He alone of all 20th-century French poets and writers dared to situate the origins of image-making in what Stuart Kendall calls "a broad horizon of value or concern." "He writes," Kendall continues, "for an educated general reader—on art, eroticism, laughter, death, poetry, play, the sacred. 'I have sacrificed everything,' [Bataille] writes, 'to the search for a perspective which reveals the unity of the human spirit.'" His American comrade in a similar endeavor, Charles Olson, said pretty much the same thing in his own way:

> I've sacrificed every thing, including sex and woman
> —or lost them—to this attempt to acquire complete
> concentration...
>   The only interesting thing
> is if one can be
> an image
> of man, "The nobleness, and the aretē."

NOTES:

[1] This review appeared in *Rain Taxi*.

[2] For my remarks on the shaft scene, see pp. 35–41 and 179–190 in *Juniper Fuse: Upper Paleolithic Imagination & the Construction of the Underworld* (Wesleyan University Press, 2003).

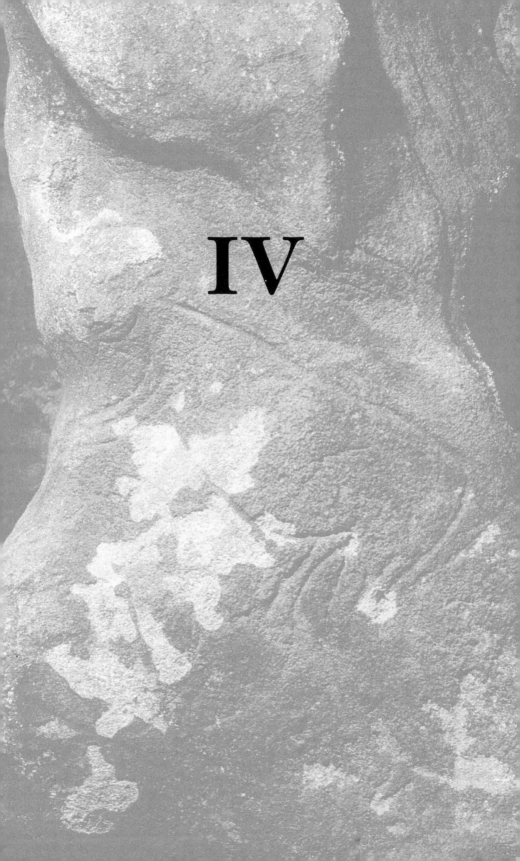

IV

BEFORE PARADISE: AN INTERVIEW WITH DALE SMITH[1]

Dale Smith: Your recent book of essays, *Companion Spider* (Wesleyan University Press, 2002) is among other things a lucid document of the poet's occupation. "Novices," the long essay, especially reads as a kind of introduction to the rigorous self-preparation demanded by poetry. In it you address a diverse body of knowledge, ranging from alchemy to psychoanalysis and literary history. There seems always to be a tension between the social urgency of poetry and the individual, and isolated experience of discovery through it. Was your literary journal *Caterpillar* an initial solution for you to that tension?

Clayton Eshleman: I was editing *Caterpillar* during the Vietnam War, which brought home with awful force the American imperialistic anti-Communist campaigns. I joined an artist group in 1967 called "Angry Arts" (mainly through friendship with Leon Golub and Nancy Spero), and started what we called the Poets' Caravan. Twenty or so of us rented flatbed trucks and read anti-war poems from it with megaphones at shopping malls and in front of the Metropolitan Museum in New York City; we also attended a high mass at St. Patrick's Cathedral with photos of napalmed Vietnamese rolled up under our suit coats—when we stood up, unfurled them, and held them high, we were immediately arrested by plainclothes cops who had been tipped off about our demonstration. I spent the night in the Tombs, the jail in downtown Manhattan, before being bailed out the next day.

However, it was in Peru in 1965 and 1966 that I became politically aware. I had gone to Peru with $300 and a pregnant wife in
the fall of 1965. The point of the trip was to attempt to get access
to Vallejo's worksheets for the poetry he wrote in Europe between
1923 and 1938. His widow, Georgette, was living in Lima, more or
less taken care of by the Peruvian government. To support us, I got
a job with the Peruvian North American Institute to start and to
edit a bilingual poetry magazine to be called *Quena*. The Institute
turned out to be a front for the American State Department and
fired me after I had assembled a 300-page first issue (with the first
translation into Spanish of Charles Olson's "Projective Verse" essay
among other things), as I had asked Paul Blackburn to translate
some of Javier Heraud's poetry for it. When my boss at the Institute saw the Heraud (who after writing the poems Blackburn translated had become a guerrilla and was murdered during a plantation
invasion), he said I had to take them out. Even though these poems
were not political, Heraud was still a hot issue, and to my boss it
looked as if his presence in the magazine implied backing for his
later political position. I then found out that the manuscript for the
issue had been sent to the American Embassy and that the censorship command had come from the American Ambassador. Of
course, I refused and was fired, but they had to pay me three
months severance pay (it came to $600), so I stayed on while my
son was born, working with Maureen Ahern on my Vallejo translations. During this time, I was taking long walks in the Lima barriadas, where the poorest lived on a poverty level that was shattering
to me. I began to put two and two together and realized that the
American government's presence in Peru was oppressive (I later
found out that the U.S. military had set up "a miniature Fort
Bragg" in the Peruvian jungle to wipe out guerrilla groups that had
come into existence due to the terrible Peruvian poverty). Because
of my several month involvement at the Institute, a number of
Peruvian poets decided that I must be a spy!

I go into a little detail here about Peru—which was an even
worse experience than I have suggested—because it prepared me to
respond to our invasion of Vietnam. Some of my new political

awareness made its way into *Caterpillar.* In the 1968 double #3/4 issue, there are horrifying photos of napalmed Vietnamese teen-aged girls that I got from a doctor who had gone to Vietnam and taken the pictures—too strong for *Ramparts* magazine, which published other photos by this doctor. As you are undoubtedly aware, this was a very dynamic period for American poetry. A lot of translating was going on and poets such as Denise Levertov and Robert Duncan came into a sense of maturity via being willing to include reactions to the war in their writing.

Your phrase "the social urgency of poetry" can be read in a number of ways. I feel that poetry seeks to communicate with those who do and do not write it, regardless of whether it is political or not. Such communication is very restricted, and most of us live in the tension of isolation. The '60s made it look, in 1967 and 1968, as if a kind of responsible avant-garde was going to move into the foreground and replace official verse culture. Of course it never happened. Most of the gains of the '60s were washed away by the '70s. Now instead of having Allen Ginsberg as the one American poet much of the world has heard about, we have Billy Collins. Ginsberg at his best was a part-shamanic up-to-date reincarnation of Whitman, a deep populist poet. Collins is conventional entertainment.

Smith: The years you lived in Kyoto working with Cid Corman seem important for your growth as a poet. You relate in the personal mythology of that period a sense of being utterly lost. I can't help reading into it a peculiarly North American urge toward escape into an unknown condition. Japan must have been quite alien culturally. How do you feel about that experience now? Is it better to be lost, or to be found?

Eshleman: To be found one must be lost. Too many artists, especially American ones, want to be found without being willing to be lost. Of course there are many ways to be lost, and some do not come with a "found exit." W.H. Auden once wrote that the gates of hell are always open. I would dispute that, even though it is an interesting, somewhat true perception. For the people I saw and talked with in Lima barriadas, their hell-gate is padlocked. For an artist to do anything original—the main point of being an artist, though not the only one—he must get in over his head and lose himself, certainly his given self, in a vacuum that if turned inside out contains a creative self. Hitchhiking to Mexico made it possible for me to see that I needed to live outside America for a while, needed to learn how to regard myself, and the human at-large, outside the gringo context. So I signed up for a year with the University of Maryland's Overseas Program, teaching literature and composition to armed forces personnel in Taiwan, Japan, and Korea (1961–62). It was not much of a job, but it got me over there, and then Gary Snyder who visited us in Tokyo in the fall of 1961 (on his way to meet Ginsberg and Orlovsky in India) told me I could teach English as a Foreign Language in Kyoto and really get to Japan. So my first wife Barbara and I moved to Kyoto in the summer of 1962 and stayed for a little over two years.

Since I have discussed my Kyoto relationship with Cid Corman elsewhere I won't go into the details of it here. How do I feel about it today? All in all, I think I was quite lucky to have been able to learn from Cid. As complicated as he was, he was also totally dedicated to the art of poetry and the art of translation and literary magazine editing. I saw him at his coffee shop in somewhat the same spirit that a graduate student visits a professor during office hours. I would prepare for my visits, thinking about what I wanted to bring up with Cid, and so that I wouldn't sound dumb, I made mental notes. This helped me to organize my reading and my thinking at a time when I was otherwise in a purgatory between my old Indiana life and another life I was only beginning to grasp. While the visionary experience with the red spider in the fall of 1962 confirmed for me that I had made the right decision about attempting to become a poet, and moving to Kyoto, I didn't have a single poem that I was really proud of. As you know, I was seriously translating César Vallejo's *Poemas humanos* at this time, spending more time on this work than on my own. Like Cid, Vallejo made me realize how much could be done in poetry, and what an awesome task it would be to come even close to fulfilling poetry's desire. I was so impressed by Vallejo that when I tried to write my own poems, I would often just sit, cross-legged on tatami, behind a small short desk that held my typewriter, and stare at a blank page for hours. I was also reading all of Blake (and Northrop Frye's magnificent study of Blake); the so-called Prophetic Books, especially "Milton: A Poem," created an even greater disturbance in me than Vallejo did. I once passed out while reading "The Book of Urizen." Between Corman, Vallejo, and Blake, I was a man trying to nail together a shack during a hurricane.

Kyoto was a very good place to be lost in—in fact, I could not think of a better place in all the world. It was very cheap to live there in the early 1960s. I had lots of time on my hands, and a few people—just a few—to talk to (Corman, Snyder, and Will Petersen mainly). I had no close friends and it was at this time that I also learned how to correspond. Kyoto was not bombed during the Second World War, and was still laid out, as a city, on a medieval grid. There was a huge ancient wood gate (similar to the one in the film *Rashomon*) not far from our house and just standing before it made me tremble. Kyoto was also elegant, and profoundly strange—but strange in a way that made me want to take every bit of my life seriously.

I did have one sort of friend, a guy named Genkawa, from Okinawa. We traded English and Japanese lessons (his English was pretty good, so I mainly read D.H. Lawrence short stories with him). He once invited me for New Year's dinner and served me a large, raw, bright blue sea slug! He hated the Japanese, for good reasons. I also briefly knew a young Korean man, one of the many who had come up to me while I was walking downtown and begged for an English conversation. We had the Korean over to dinner a few times and he quickly filled us in about the deep prejudice of the Japanese toward Koreans (and Okinawans).

As I implied, Corman was a model of devotion and commitment, and he resisted me in what turned out to be very useful ways. I have never been more alone, more pent upon myself than when I was in Kyoto. I learned to be with myself there, to talk to myself, to get into a real self-conversation about the limits and the depths of poetry.

Smith: How has companionship personally and in a diverse body of art made you a better poet—a better man? I assume you believe, after Pound, "all ages are contemporaneous?"

Eshleman: The Pound remark is a fascinating insight that is not altogether true. You can see Pound's poetics showing through that statement, and the limitations, too, of his poetics. Pound seemed to think that he only had to name cultural peaks, or troughs, and since they were contemporaneous to his own mind, that would be so to the reader also—but such is not true. Pound's sense of presence, of presentation, is extraordinarily weak, and also undermined by his obtuse political agenda. The risk in assuming that all ages are contemporaneous lies in failing to detect difference, as well as in assuming that an aspect of another earlier culture that appeals to one represents that culture justly.

Companionship is a wonderful, wonderful thing, and it can be many things. Robin Blaser has some poems that he identifies as concerning his "great companions," of which Robert Duncan—in spite of Duncan's nasty treatment of Robin—and Pindar stand out. So there is companionship in the arts, in the reverence we feel for certain artists' achievements. Such figures are mental travelers, or companions, and then of course there is the real companion, one's lover, partner, wife, or friend. Carl Jung once said: "The meaning of life is a good companion." I quoted that at the beginning of my book *Fracture*, in dedicating the book to Caryl.

Caryl's presence in my life as a writer and as a man is so great as to be inexpressible. She has opened gate after gate for me, and in most cases I have had the sense to pass through.

I called my 2002 collection of essays *Companion Spider* because of the red spider vision I mentioned earlier, given to me in Kyoto in 1962, which was a charm, an amulet, that I have never ceased to wear. When I feel lost, rejected, totally peripheral, fed up, etc., I return to that vision and adhere to it. So "companion" is a rainbow force, a dimensional spectrum that includes, in my case, that red spider, Vallejo, yes, Corman, Golub, Snyder, Caryl, and Adrienne Rich—to name some of the most important.

Then there are the caves. I think they lie outside of the companion phenomenon, but they do bring in the tricky matter of to what extent the oldest culture we have access to is contemporaneous. I think they are profoundly not contemporaneous! I suppose that one could argue that by spending twenty-seven years investigating what may turn out to be the origin of image-making and of mental reality, that I have turned them into a form of companionship. But that seems loose to me, leaky. The apparent lack of war, and the complex bond with animals makes the Upper Paleolithic most uncontemporary. And: every claim that I make on Cro-Magnon imagination, I must realize is a combination of what is there on a cave wall and my projection. All image-making, from the start I intuit, is charged with projection.

Smith: You show in your Introduction to Artaud's *Watchfiends & Rack Screams*, translated by you in 1995, affection for that tormented author. Your opening sentence proclaims him as "one of the greatest examples in art of imaginative retrieval of a life that was beyond repair." Elsewhere you've clearly noted the opposing differences between your psychic life and his, and that your affection has no basis in identity. You've also indicated that he's more important to you than someone like Pound. So what's Artaud's appeal to you? Or more specifically, what have you absorbed from him?

Eshleman: I don't think that Pound is a deeply engaging poet. I remain after many investigations of his poetry so disappointed that I will probably not read him again. Pound does not seem psychotic to me, unless you want to say that anyone who embraces Hitler and Mussolini in the early 1940s is simply insane. The early poetry, and the editing of *The Wasteland*, is often perceptive, even brilliant. Something in Pound was killed in the 1920s. I do not know what that was. Pound, from what I can tell, collapsed and turned his imagination over to his spectre, in a Blakean sense. The spectre learned how to run the show. Peeking through the spectre, who felt he only had to cite, and not to create presence, was the younger Pound who had a remarkable feel for natural imagery. Throughout the *Cantos*, a sensuous presentation of the natural world sparkles. And occasionally there are amazing shifts involving jump cuts and juxtaposition and Pound's obsession with a male spermatic force (which he wrote about outside the *Cantos*, and about which he was simply wrong; see his introduction to Remy de Gourmont's *Natural Philosophy of Love*, and Weston LaBarre's correction in his book *Muelos: A Stone Age Superstition about Sexuality*).

I think it is understood now that Pound's life was saved in Washington by the people who examined him, who lied on his behalf. Pound, no matter how troubled he was, was not insane, and out of his non-insanity he did not draw forth very much. Pound in fact fell into silence as the rational beautiful person in him slowly realized what a disgusting anti-semite he had become in the early 1940s. And the good man in Pound drove the spectre into a kind of standstill: meaning that Pound stopped talking as an old man, at a time, alas, when the poet of *Cathay* might have had some imaginative things to say about Pound's experience. As an American poet, Pound is probably the greatest disappointment of the century.

Artaud—and all I say here briefly should be reflected on in the light or darkness of my long introduction to *Watchfiends & Rack Screams*—was clinically, totally insane for a number of years, and his insanity appears to have usefully tangled with his ongoing latent rationality during his regeneration at the Rodez asylum. God knows if Artaud is honest. He may not be. But he was sufficiently out of it, for at least four or five years, that we can say, or I can say: he had lost himself in a way that Pound never lost himself. Artaud was dead to Artaud at the point he entered Rodez in 1944. He was a menagerie of voices, doubles, torments. He spat at apparitions, howled, had to be restrained, erupted in glossolailia under any circumstance—he had lost it. Somehow after that fiendish Dr. Ferdière put him through over fifty electro-shocks, Artaud got the message! Somehow he understood that Ferdière would kill him if he did not give himself to a task in the asylum that would totally occupy him and stop his acting up, as it were.

He began to draw. We have a pretty good record of this. Much of this material has been saved, and is reproduced in the 1986 Gallimard book of Artaud's art and the collection the Museum of Modern Art did in 1996 based on Artaud's drawing show there.

I respect Artaud in a way I do not respect Pound. Pound did not attempt to tell us why he became a Fascist, what it felt like to be one, nor did he apologize in any meaningful way that I know of. Pound ends up in silent remorse. Artaud dips below the social and engages us with what I would propose is the most open subconscious after Blake. It is more conflicted and less voluminous and inventive than Blake's. Blake continues to be an imaginative hero for me because he staked out a full ground in the subconscious and populated it with characters in his, as it were, "theater of cruelty" (Artaud's term for the kind of theater he sought to invent). Artaud, unlike Blake, remains in obsessive coils, running fugally against his projected enemies. Blake uses Christianity perhaps as a positive pole—hard to know—he may have been afraid that if he didn't moor himself to a Christian positive perspective he would have destroyed himself. The turbulence in *The Four Zoas* suggests that he was close to breakdown.

Artaud reveals that the subconscious is a place of incredible energy, that it has a coherence contactable but alien to the conscious, and that it is obsessionally-bound.

Smith: I'd like, if we could, to abandon modernism to discuss your archaic interests. In your Introduction to *Juniper Fuse: Upper Paleolithic Imagination & the Construction of the Underworld* (Wesleyan, 2003), you mention meeting the Upper Paleolithic researcher Alexander Marshack on several occasions. His study of bone markings in *The Roots of Civilization* presents complex data about the Cro-Magnon people who created that magnificent cave art. How does that "hard" data influence your own study of the images found in the caves? I guess, since you mentioned the projective experience of our image-making earlier, I wonder how poetry and science together might detect or supply meaning for those extraordinary images.

Eshleman: Marshack's work in *The Roots of Civilization* was mainly useful, for me, on the basis of the photographic blow-ups of portable objects, which enable one to scrutinize often quite small pieces with very difficult-to-see flint indentations. I am not sure if he was the first to assert that the notches and meanders were possibly notational (concerning lunar cycles), and thus not meaningless doodles. His book makes this claim, but I suspect that there were a few Europeans who had some sense of the meaningful in portable notation earlier. Marshack's writing is not convincing—his conclusions and proposals are quite general and dependent, for significance, on transferring 20th-century perceptions about primitive art and life to the deep past.

I mention in the Introduction to my book my curious meeting with Marshack in Lespinasse the spring of 1974. Caryl and I saw him on one other occasion, in his apartment near New York University in the late 1970s. There he was much friendlier than he had been in France, and we studied together some photographs of extremely ancient markings on an ox rib that he referred to as "core meanders" and "branch meanders." Such terminology helped me to think about the relationship between archaic image-making and the poetry I was writing.

But since my book is primarily about cave imagery and not about the imagery to be found on portable objects there is not much connection with Marshack's work, the focus of which is portable objects. Over the years, Marshack has continued to publish articles and I imagine he by now has the equivalent of a second book. He has studied a lot of material that few other people have studied, and he uses excellent state-of-the art photographic equipment. Like me, he is not an archeologist, but a science writer who, in a way, sort of stumbled into the Upper Paleolithic abyss.

Many ramifications of your questions here are dealt with in the Introduction to *Juniper Fuse*. There I say that I attempted to study, and respond to, the caves on an observational level as well as on a creative one, because they strike me as a world in which observation and fantasy are entangled—so entangled at times as to tie the viewer's mind in knots. So I read what the archeologists had to say, and looked very carefully at photos and drawings (since in most cases I had only a minute or two, at the most, before any image in a cave). In the long run, I spent much more time pouring over material in my workroom than I did looking at images in caves. I have a great deal of respect for Marshack, Jean Clottes, André Leroi-Gourhan, Henri Breuil, S. Giedion, Margaret Conkey, Paul Bahn, and others. Without their work I would have had a much more difficult time in thinking about what I saw. But they do not go far enough, I think, and I understand why they do not do so, because to go further, is to leave archeology and to enter poetry, or some extended form of imaginative meditating on what is there, and how it feels to be there groping around. My work, in this sense, is not dismissive in any way of the archeology I am to a considerable extent dependent upon. I hope to have extended the stakes in regarding what is there, how it got there, and what it may mean at the beginning of the 21st century. There is a terrible synchronicity between the modern discovery of the caves and the destruction of peoples and civilizations in the first and second world wars.

Smith: The 20th century opened—literally in terms of the caves, but imaginatively in art and poetry—the archaic imagination like no other period. Charles Olson, through people like Jane Harrison and Eric Havelock, proposed a kind of decolonization of the Western mind apparatus. (I think D.H. Lawrence was probably fuel for this in literature too.) Has Olson's work influenced your perceptions of the cave material at all? Or perhaps he served other purposes?

Eshleman: Olson's concept of "the saturation job," briefly outlined in one of his letters to Ed Dorn that was turned into a "Bibliography on America for Ed Dorn," was a provocation once I realized that no poet had taken on the Upper Paleolithic image continuum.

Olson's own relationship to the Upper Paleolithic is interesting and curious. He became very excited about archaic sources during his correspondence with Francis Boldereff (probably the best introduction to the man's work), who introduced him to most of the key books he would study. Their exchanges generated his attempt to base a poetics on pre-Greek sources and led to his concept of a new institute of the sciences of man, while at Black Mountain College in the early 1950s. Such an institute, which never came about, would have been rooted in what we could call Cro-Magnon sensibility. Olson's notes for lectures on this material are collected in *Olson #10* by George Butterick. They represent Olson at his scholarly best, working from other people's research, cutting here and there, reassembling, building a kind of crazy quilt house on the subject. There are valuable insights peppered through these notes, along with some mistakes. It is a shame that Olson never visited the caves himself—if he could get to Yucatan, one would think he could have figured out a way to get to the Dordogne where he would have seen much more art than he did in Yucatan. In those days, cave access was much less problematic than it is now: Georges Bataille visited Lascaux every evening, after the tourists left, for a month! Such would be unheard of today—so had Olson gone to the Dordogne in the early 1950s, he could have seen anything he wanted to see, and could have spent a lot of time before the images.

As you probably know, the Upper Paleolithic—the caves—is hardly taken up in the *Maximus* poems. There are a few short pieces that refer to early Nordic mythology and are set, I think, in the Mesolithic period (10,000–8,000 B.P.), but this work is of minor importance to the entire sequence. Had Olson pushed *Maximus* back to the last Ice Age, and had he also visited the caves, his life would have turned out, I believe, less tragic than it did. He would have hit the real back wall and it would have given him courage and a renewed sense of imaginal power. He would have been less damaged by what was happening in Gloucester in the late '50s and '60s—maybe. I wrote a long essay on Olson's relationship to the archaic that was published in *Minutes of the Charles Olson Society #52* (April 2004).

Smith: *Fracture* (1982) is a book of poems inspired in part by your cave studies. In a poem called "The Loaded Sleeve of Hades" you write:

> You find yourself, at last,
> as if it were a blessing, blocked by nature,
> as a new plan is blocked out,
> attacked by a cave
> because you got too close to the Hades–Dionysus
> hinged appetite...
>
> Your fracture is a fleck
> amidst global enigmatic fractions,
> it is nothing and it is a headlight
> frozen in a ditch, and the depth of your life?

The "fracture" here is personal and global, interior and public. In the title poem "Fracture" you also say "that earth is responsible for our deaths, / that if we die collectively / we will take the earth with us if we can—" You suggest here, if I'm reading correctly, that an acceptance of the hell in us might prevent its global manifestation. How do we integrate Hades? Would that be enough? Burroughs somewhere suggests we're already dead in the West. Perhaps we are the dream issues of some Aurignacian shaman?

Eshleman: The statement about the earth being responsible for our deaths and our desire to take the earth with us if we can is not a personal credo. I intended to present it as a collective ancient cry, something that is in all humankind and enacted by a significant number of human beings. It marries the nuclear bomb to global pollution and extermination of species. It is a human weakness, I believe, to make something else responsible for our demise, and this scapegoating is massively pervasive. After what appears to be an initially innocent association of woman with nature, and probably with the recognition of the role of semen in conception, men developed what we have come to know as the patriarchal viewpoint in which women are linked to the violence and terror of nature and, worst of all, made responsible for the mortality inherent in conception. Because women get pregnant and give birth, and because they are traditionally (for significant reasons) associated with the hearth, and with gathering (in contrast to hunting), they are also thought of as being more primary, more akin to nature, than men. This is probably true, but its truth is misused to consequently degrade women as less spiritual and more animal-like than men. Women may be more primary but they are also more spiritual (as priest garb in all religions indicates). It is also probable that men are more primary in regard to their involvement with strife and slaughter.

Your reading of what you quote from my poem "Fracture" is inspiring. I wrote the piece in the Dordogne a couple of weeks after my car accident in an attempt to come to terms with nearly being killed. How does one accept the hell in oneself? One approach would be to dechristianize "hell" and take it back to the underworld, so that the question would read: how does one accept the underworld, or subconscious structures, in oneself? One way is to attempt to make them conscious—the primary goal of art as I see it. America is a very religious country in a negative, political sense: the political form of redemption may be intervention, which we have ruthlessly, for a long, long time, practiced in the name of spreading democracy, working our own clouded destiny out in the backs of the third and fourth worlds.

To integrate Hades would be to assimilate subconscious information and patterns, via dreams, fantasies, slips of the tongue, and the recognition of impulsive behavior. Were every American man to get up in the morning and state out loud: "I am a potential killer and am responsible for everything that I do and that happens to me today"—and mean it, America might become less lethal. I attempted to deal with the potential killer in me near the end of my poem "Coils" (in the book, Coils, 1973). I let my darkest spectre speak. When I read that poem in the mid-'70s, I put a paper bag over my head with eye slits (a kind of cartoon of a KKK hood) when I read that section. Audiences must have thought I was crazy. Which in that speech I was.

Burroughs is very entropic and nihilistic—that touches a nerve in many of us, as on one level it appears to be true. But it is not fully or thoroughly true. Some Americans are very alive, very decent, very vital. But as a nation we are driven by a Christian phantomatic desire to conquer and bring about Apocalypse with a pathetic lack of awareness of what such would terrestrially mean and be. Such is the work of death, as it means perpetual war in quest of the mirage of peace not only on an American-dominated planet but in an American-dominated universe: the control of outer space.

I think it is possible to make image contact with the dreams of Aurignacian shaman, or so I argue at points in *Juniper Fuse*. But image contact, while something, is not much. We do not know the context in which the image took place, nor do we have any idea of its meaning to other Aurignacians. So to view these images is tragic in a way—to be in a dark cave with such images is to be in one of the cemeteries of paradise, to be looking at the remains of a pre-paradise, of imagination still in touch with animal powers before paradise was formulated (I intuit that it became formulated at the same time the Fall was formulated).

Smith: The archaic conditions presented by the caves contrast drastically with our administrative, high-tech culture. Those Cro-Mags had a maximum knowledge of their environments with minimal tool use. We are the opposite. What vision can you extend from a 30,000 wreck of images that might possibly derail the current global insanity masquerading as corporate industrialism?

Eshleman: Any vision I might have is incapable of derailing anything! Which is to say that vision, in the imaginative sense I intend, has become totally peripheral, in industrial/technological society, to the action of the state. This is not news. It is blasted in our faces anytime we turn on television, read a newspaper, or listen to the radio. In fact, we do not get the real news via most media now—NPR is a kind of domestic Voice of America, primarily the voice of U.S. official policy with "human interest" tales mixed in to seduce the listener into the fantasy that America is basically in some muzzy sweet way human and funny. When I hear intelligent men like Bill Maher proclaim their love for America, in spite of their outrage at our foreign policies, I wince. What we have done to Iraq from the Gulf War on is unforgivable.

Education is the only potential solution to the anti-visionary situation our country is in. If we could start with kids, and educate them to know about and respect sex, dreams, art, others, animals, plants, etc., then we might produce a generation that could make a difference. By the time college students came to me, as their professor, most of them were ruined in any imaginative sense. Occasionally, I would spot one for whom some things mattered, or who was at least deeply curious and not mainlining the mainstream messages. But most have been ruined at home, or just by knocking back every awful media drink they were offered. One has to go back to the '60s to find a sense of being a college student that carried severe socio-political responsibility, and of course the '60s were ultimately flimsy and temporary.

Smith: One last question from your essay on Paul Blackburn in *Companion Spider*. You say that most "people who are artists… are not so because they have solved great human problems or even the daily minutiae, but because of the particular way they feel these problems and minutiae are unsolvable in their own lives." Are you comfortable with this lack of solution in your own life and work, with feeling your way through toward some mysterious outcome or unanticipated experience?

Eshleman: Well, in that essay I extend that statement to a more extreme position by writing: "It takes a particular set of imbalances, incredible stresses in some directions with unusual absences in others, faults, burning explosive deposits and areas of glacial motion that create the energy stresses that volcano under an art." I can say that at 70 I am more comfortable with it than I was at 37 when I wrote it. That is probably because the pits and blocks that drove me into art, in my early twenties, have for the most part lost their negative energy, or have been scabbed over, like poisonous pits that have used up their gas. If this is so, it must be mainly so because I have attempted to deal with my background and my self (conscious and subconscious) as directly as I knew how. On one level, my body of work, including my translations, is a battleground strewn with body parts. If this was all it was, it would be very negative, but not in the Burroughs sense evoked earlier.

I would argue that much of this negation is there to test affirmation. I feel that I am an affirmative person, but affirmative in a constantly self-challenged sense in which affirmation must ascend loaded with a full negational weight. Only if it makes it up, against the down pull of negation, is the affirmation worth anything. American poetry is often cheapened by simplistic, unconscious affirmation—or entertainment, or displays of the poet's sensitivity. One must write now, if one is an American, as an American aware of what America has been doing to others—our poor, and those in countries for one reason or other that we exploit and harm. This means one always works in shadow, one always writes with the dreadful awareness that what one says, no matter how imaginative or even truthful, will mean nothing at large, and that in reaching a public context (even a tiny one), it will be absorbed as just another American product. However, one must still make art because it presents to a few, who one day might become more than a few, an alternative to rapine commercialism and imperial pomposity. Artists are now nomadic specks in a spreading steel and electronic cyberscape. At some point, if the world of Bush and Ashcroft is allowed to fully deconstitutionalize the country, "they" will decide to get rid of all of "us." Until then, or through then, we must continue to be emanation and spectre, the children of our own imaginative push.

Smith: Hopefully, that imaginative push will see us through.

Eshleman: I am now reminded of that terrible synchronicity in the discovery of Lascaux in the fall of 1940 when some of the worst death and concentration camps were starting to function. And the caves are modernist, in a way, because they are fragments, in T.S.

Eliot's words, that we can shore against our ruins. The fact that a new cave with Ice Age decorations is discovered every year or so is also fascinating—such keeps the whole Upper Paleolithic adventure latent, as a to-be-revealed potential. Current Carbon-14 dating methods, much improved from the '50s and '60s, show that certain paintings in Pech Merle and Cougnac were worked on over a period of time spanning 10,000 years. So they are communal in a staggering sense—totally different cultures participating in their making.

NOTES:

[1] This interview originally appeared in *The Writer's Chronicle* in a slightly different form. I found that when I was adding it to this book that it discussed some material on Cid Corman, César Vallejo, and Upper Paleolithic cave art that had been covered in earlier essays. Therefore I did some cutting and rewriting so as to not repeat myself.

GOING TO THE MOON WITH SOME WONDERFUL GHOSTS

Literary Translation and a Poet's Formation[1]

An Interview with Clayton Eshleman
By Ethriam Cash Brammer

Brammer: The University of California Press has just released your translation of *The Complete Poetry of César Vallejo*. Is this work mostly a compilation of the Vallejo translations that you have already done, like *Trilce* and *The Complete Posthumous Poetry of César Vallejo*, or did you actually go back and revise and rework some of these already critically acclaimed translations?

Eshleman: Everything is reworked. In the *Human Poems* there are probably between 1,500 and 2,000 revisions. Maybe 200 to 300 in *Trilce*. And then, there's a seventy-page section of notes. *Los heraldos negros*, which I translated in 2004, is the only completely new work. *Los heraldos negros* is the easiest of all the books to translate. It's interesting that I ended up doing it last rather than first, which is probably the way I should have started.

Brammer: What inspired these revisions?

Eshleman: Accuracy, the desire to be accurate. And knowing more and more about Vallejo. Vallejo is very disconcerting for a translator because of the number of intentional misspellings, archaic and coined words that always leave him on shifting ground. And it's very easy to miss simple, little things when you're constantly looking out for these intentional misspellings and then having to figure out ways to misspell in English that will pick up the pun in the Spanish.

For example, in *Trilce XI*, there's the word "rebocado," instead of "revocado," or "whitewashed." By putting the "b" into it, he evokes "bocado," meaning "mouthful" or "bite." So my translation of the word now is "bitewashed." If you say "bitewashed" very quickly you hear "whitewashed."

Or when he's using a word that's archaic, say, like "calabrina"—

Brammer: "A foul air?"—

Eshleman: I think it comes off of "cadaver" in some way. It's a word that went out of usage maybe two hundred years ago. So, if I'm going to translate it, I can't translate it as "stench" or "stink" because if you translate "stench" or "stink" back into Spanish you get "hedor." So I have to find a word that is equally obscure in English. And, in this case, with the help of the linguist Dennis Preston, I came up with "ponk."

I try to put the reader of the translation in the same position that you as a reader in Spanish would be. That's the idea.

Brammer: Looking for the same amount of unfamiliarity—

Eshleman: Yes, to create an English in which Vallejo is as challenging as he is in Spanish and not to interpret, to always translate and not interpret. Many translations of poetry are full of interpretations.

I've worked on this poetry off-and-on now for forty-eight years. It's been a great companion—a kind of wonderful ghost—that I've learned from over the years.

Brammer: You've worked in so many different contexts as a translator: you've worked in isolation in foreign countries as you learned new languages, like Spanish in Mexico; you've worked with living authors, like Aimé Césaire—

Eshleman: And Michel Deguy.

Brammer: And you've worked with linguistic and literary scholars as your translating partners. I'm just curious: What are the advantages and disadvantages of partnering with, maybe, a literary scholar or a linguistic scholar, or having access to a living writer? Vallejo's widow, Madame Georgette seems to be more of a hindrance than a help.

Eshleman: For everyone, not just for me. Yes, she was a horror.

Georgette was a teenager when Vallejo met her in Paris. The story goes that he forced her to have a lot of abortions. I don't know if this is true or not. I was told this by an old Peruvian musician, who was—according to Rodolfo Hinostroza, a Peruvian poet living in Paris when we were in 1973—the last living person in Paris who knew Vallejo. And so Rodolfo took us over to his apartment one day. And of the stories he told, one of them was that he claimed that Georgette had something like fourteen abortions, because Vallejo had insisted on not having a child. Of course, Vallejo was the youngest of eleven himself.

Hinostroza's friend said that in the process of having so many abortions, she turned from a kind of a sweet person into a real bitch. And, by the time she moved to Peru in 1951, she was impossible for everyone to deal with. And it's had a suffocating effect on Vallejo publishing and availability. The plays, journalism, and letters have only recently been published in Spanish. None of this material has been translated.

Now, there's a complete works being published, volume by volume, at a university in Lima.

Brammer: They went back into his archives?

Eshleman: Yes, what's left of them. Georgette appears to have destroyed certain things. Vallejo kept year-dated notebooks throughout the 1930s. When Georgette published them with Mosca Azul in the 1973, one found only a few entries per year. The implication was that she had destroyed any entries she did not like or that reflected unfavorably on her.

Brammer: Did she do that with your own work when you were translating Vallejo? Did she say I don't like the way you translated this line or that line?

Eshleman: When I went to Lima in 1965, I had sent her some of my drafts, which had some errors and words that I didn't understand. I doubt if she read them as she did not appear to understand English. She spoke a combination of French and Spanish. In the same sentence, you'd get both French and Spanish. And, so, this was also difficult.

I traveled to Lima primarily to see the worksheets for the *Poemas humanos* because at that point the book existed in four editions, two of which were pirated, and all had errors. The first time I met her, she said, "You can't see the worksheets," and, "Vallejo is impossible to translate so I can't even consider giving you permission." At the same time, she was translating a selected poems of Vallejo into French.

Brammer: She herself?

Eshleman: Yes, with the help of Américo Ferrari, who is the scholar who helped me with *Trilce*. He's lived in Geneva for many years. He's retired now. Somehow he got along with her and they did a few projects together.

In 1968, Francisco Moncloa, who I believe was a wealthy publisher in Lima, gave Georgette a ton of money to allow him to publish Vallejo's hand-corrected typescripts of the European poetry. This book was published in 1968. All of the notes in the *Complete Posthumous Poetry* are based on having access, finally, to this material. *Poemas humanos* appears to have been never completed. While it is possible that the hand-written corrections in the European poetry were final corrections, it is also possible that had he retyped the manuscript he would have made new changes.

Brammer: What about working with Aimé Césaire, for example?

Eshleman: Aimé Césaire was very congenial and helpful, in his own way. At the point I met him, in the early 1980s, he seemed out of touch with the poetry he wrote in the '40s, '50s, and '60s. I visited him three times in Paris. The first two times we met in a café near his then French publisher in the Fifth Arrondissement. I would come with my word list. For the third visit, we met at his son's apartment where Césaire stayed when he was in Paris, and he spent some time pulling down African-French dictionaries from the book shelves.

Brammer: To research his own works?

Eshleman: Césaire's poetry is full of arcane and scientific terminology, as well as African and rare Caribbean words. Over the years, he had forgotten what some of these words meant.

But back to your question about translating with another person: you have to find the right kind of person to work with because, if you're working with the wrong kind of person, your partner can create more problems than you might have just on your own.

For example, I started working on *Trilce* with Julio Ortega, who's a Peruvian at Brown University. I knew Julio from when I was in Lima. Julio and his former wife, the poet Cecilia Bustamante, were very kind to me that year. They often had us over to dinner. So, in 1989, I thought, well, I can translate *Trilce* if I can work with a Peruvian, because there are certain words and phrases in it that I'm just not going to be able to handle through dictionaries. So, Julio and I decided to co-translate *Trilce*.

That fall, I stayed in a Boston B&B with my wife Caryl for a month, and daily, for a month, I took the bus into Providence and climbed the hill to Julio's office. We did a first version of *Trilce*.

I brought that first version back here to Ypsilanti and started making a second version. At that point, the ground disappeared and I realized what I was in for: I had several questions per line! I soon found out that Julio felt that his work was over, and that I was to complete the translation on my own. But from my point of view, the real work in the co-translation was just beginning.

So I was suddenly on my own. And my Spanish is not up to translating *Trilce* by myself.

Brammer: Few people could make the claim that they could.

Eshleman: Right. So I wrote to Americo Ferrari in Geneva and told him what had happened. He said, "Okay, send me your questions." We had a fruitful correspondence. I would write him in English and he'd write me in Spanish. We must have exchanged some fifty letters.

And he had to go to the library, because there are a number of words in *Trilce* that the scholars have all done end-runs around. And unlike scholars, who can write commentaries without understanding every word in a poem, translators, if they are being responsible, are confronted with every word in every poem they translate. With Ferrari's research, I was able to complete the version of *Trilce* that Marsilio published in 1992. I found errors in that version that I corrected for the second edition, by Wesleyan, in 2000. And I found more errors last year that I have corrected, with the help of José Cerna-Bazán, for *The Complete Poetry*. Vallejo's non-sequitur density in *Trilce* prefigures the American Language Poetry of the 1970s.

Brammer: What sort of discomfort or even undermining of language are poets like Vallejo and Césaire trying to perform by creating terms that even they themselves sometimes forget? What does that do with the poetry? And as a translator, how do you deal with it, because you have to make decisions?

Eshleman: Of the people I translated, I did so because I thought, by translating them, I would learn something about the nature of poetry. I've never translated anyone who I thought would not test me. The closest thing to problem-free translating, in my case, would be Neruda's *Residencias*. I did awkward versions of some thirty poems in the first two *Residencias* when I was a young man. I revised some of them for a new edition of *Conductors of the Pit* that came out in 2005.

In the case of Vallejo and Césaire, I think you have a kind of onslaught on language conventions, an attempt to re-determine how language can be assembled. It is as if they sense their given languages as second languages, and in their poetry they attempt to construct a first language that can convey their feeling for existence.

Césaire sees himself as a surrealist. So many of the non-sequitur moves in his poetry, which are compounded in difficulty by the presence of scientific terms, especially for fauna and flora, falls within a politicized post-surrealist frame. He thinks of himself as developing what Breton and Reverdy proposed, as an African Martinican, writing in the generation after Breton.

Vallejo, on the other hand, was contemptuous of surrealism. He felt somewhat the same way about it as Antonin Artaud did. He thought it involved a facile liberty and was more involved with games and cutting up than with moral fiber and the human situation.

Vallejo arrived in Paris in 1923. The first *Surrealist Manifesto* comes out in 1924. It must have been a fantastically exciting time to be an artist in Paris. But I have no information on him ever having met or associated with French surrealists. However, aspects of *Trilce* do evoke a kind of pre-surrealist aesthetic in writing.

Brammer: Right.

Eshleman: Except that *Trilce* is difficult in a way that someone like Breton is not. There's a kind of dream quality to Breton that I don't find in Vallejo. Vallejo is rationally irrational. He's mangled, but he's rationally mangled.

Working on your own—unless you are absolutely bilingual—translating somebody as difficult as Vallejo or Césaire, is impossible. And so if you find the right person to work with, you save yourself a lot of time, do better versions, and the work is not as lonely.

José Rubia Barcia, with whom I collaborated on *The Complete Posthumous Poetry* in Los Angeles in the 1970s, was wonderful to work with. He put in as much time as I did on our translation, often writing to Vallejo scholars like Juan Larrea to research word meanings. And Annette Smith, with whom I co-translated Césaire, was also great to work with. So I've been fortunate that, in contrast to Julio Ortega, I have had, in a couple of instances, people to work with who held up their end.

In the case of Michel Deguy, whose *Selected Poems* I translated in the late 1970s and early '80s, I had Deguy to talk with. In the fall of 1978 I went over to his apartment in Paris every afternoon for several months to talk through versions with him.

Brammer: And working with Deguy, you had a pleasant working relationship?

Eshleman: Yes, we became friends. The only problem with working with Deguy is that I'd often ask him a question about a word and he'd tell me what he'd had in mind in terms of the meaning and it would have very little to do with what appeared to be the standard meaning of the word. If I would have taken his advice, at times it would have appeared to the reader that I had made serious errors!

Brammer: [Laughing.] Eshleman doesn't know French.

Eshleman: Right. [Laughing.] Because at times he had fantasies about how he wanted particular words to work. So, there are posi-

tive and negative aspects to working alone or working with someone.

Brammer: Much of your 2003 collection of essays, *Companion Spider,* is devoted to the theme of the "novice" and a poet's period of
formation or "apprenticeship." You describe the time that you
spent in Kyoto, Japan and your relationship with influential writers
like Cid Corman. But what kind of poet would Clayton Eshleman
be right now if he had never served an "apprenticeship," via translation, under a "master" like César Vallejo?

Eshleman: Impossible to really know, of course. But there's a
chance that I would have been more conventional and more in tune
with establishment verse.

Coming into poetry partially through Vallejo, I opened up an
international base on which I could conceive an American poetry.
Some of the best known American poets today operate in a context
that is primarily dominated by American writing, often by figures
such as Robert Frost, Robert Lowell, and Elizabeth Bishop. From
my point of view, while these poets are all part of the essence of
20th-century American poetry, they don't really get under your
skin and disturb you into an awareness of being an American in a
global expanse.

At some point in the fall of 1962, in Kyoto, Japan, I decided to
attempt to translate *Poemas humanos* as my apprenticeship to poetry. Putting myself through that ordeal made me think about poetry in a completely different way than I had done while I was a student at Indiana University. It made me confront myself, and deal
with a range of ambivalences. It made me deal openly with contradictions, and swerves and knots in thinking that don't come up in
daily conversation or in simple self-regard.

So, mainly through Vallejo, I came to see the writing of a poem
as penetrating a labyrinth whose off-shoots and dead-ends were to
be experienced as a way of thinking into, against, and through. For
example, if while writing a line strikes me as a good final line, I put
it in as the next line because I don't want to trap myself into having

the poem from that point on be determined by something in the future. I want to stay in what I would call the creative present. A strong sense of that came through Vallejo as well as the other poet I was reading closely in Kyoto, William Blake. I read all of Blake while I was in Kyoto. And that was an initiation on its own.

Brammer: Are there specific poems, maybe one or two collections, or has your entire career now as a poet been influenced by Vallejo?

Eshleman: I think the writing I did in the '80s and '90s is more what I would like to be known by than the writing I did in the '60s and '70s, although *Coils* (1973) was a breakthrough book for me, because I came to terms with my Indiana background in it. While I now find lots of the writing in *Coils* too unworked-out, too descriptive or over-worked, I have to acknowledge that I would not be where I am today, in the writing of a book like *An Alchemist with One Eye on Fire*, without the drilling and excavating that went on in *Coils*.

Discovering the Upper Paleolithic Caves in southwestern France in 1974, and my consequent long project on them, made me think into material that was completely transpersonal. With the Cro-Magnon people who painted in the caves 15,000 years ago, we have no history, no language, just images on stone. By attempting to attend to them, I made a 180-degree swerve from the self-preoccupation with having been brought up in Indianapolis, Indiana, and having lived unconsciously for the first twenty-two years of my life. The turn from personal Indiana to transpersonal Cro-Magnon was a wonderful, fortuitous refocusing for me.

Unless you're one of the few poets who break into poetry and do your best work early, like Rimbaud, Lautréament, or Dylan Thomas, most of us need about twenty years to get to what really gnaws at us into a capable language.

Brammer: Twenty years of apprenticeship?

Eshleman: Yes. And also, note that I came into poetry without any literary background, in contrast to my friend Robert Kelly, who was teaching himself Sanskrit in his basement at twelve years old and was reading some of the people that I started to read in Japan. By the time that Kelly was twenty-five, he had a solid foundation in literature. When I was twenty-five, I had hardly read anything.

Brammer: Still talking about being an apprentice, Borges translated Poe, Cortázar translated Defoe, and it seems like most major modern Latin American poets have translated at least a little bit of Walt Whitman, do you think it would be accurate to say that, in Latin America, translation is much more widely accepted as a part of a writer's "apprenticeship" than in the United States? And why do you think that might be?

Eshleman: I don't know enough about the history of translation in Latin America to respond to that question. In the United States, my generation, which more or less came on board in the 1960s, is a translating generation. Most of the poets that I know from the '60s, that I'm still in contact with, or who have died, were involved in translation. All of that changed with language poetry in the '70s. The Language Poets, for the most part, are not translators. And a lot of the interest of my generation had in world poetry has fallen off considerably.

Brammer: Do you know if Vallejo himself, in his period of apprenticeship, did translation as an exercise or as part of his growth?

Eshleman: Not that I know of. He was introduced to French symbolism through Spanish translation around 1918, I think around the time he was starting to work on *Trilce*, maybe a little earlier. And my guess is that there are a few nuances in *Trilce* from reading Rimbaud. And he loved Baudelaire.

In the early 1930s in Madrid, I know that he translated at least two novels, *Elevación* by Henri Barbusse and *La Calle sin nombre* by Marcel Aymé.

We have a new chronology in the *Complete Poetry* by Stephen Hart that has more information about his background than I've seen before. Also, Stephen Hart believes that Vallejo was absolutely involved in the murders and the burning of the buildings in Santiago de Chuco that he was briefly put in jail for. One of the reasons that he left Peru in 1923 for Europe may be that, aware that he had not been cleared of involvement in the incident, he did not want to be around if the judges decided against him. As it happens, in 1926 the High Court in Trujillo issued a warrant for his arrest.

Brammer: Wasn't Vallejo supported once in Europe by a scholarship?

Eshleman: He received a modest grant from Spain in 1925, and while he never intended to live there, he traveled to Madrid three times over the next two years to claim the grant money.

But he appears to have been chronically poor while in Paris. There were times during the first two years when he was homeless. And he only got to Europe because his Trujillo friend Antenor Orrego's nephew, who had a first-class boat ticket to France, exchanged it for two third-class tickets so that Vallejo could accompany him.

Brammer: Do you think novice writers and creative writing programs in the United States should do more to embrace translation as a part of a writer's formation?

Eshleman: Yes, of course. Any student graduating from an MFA program in creative writing should have a reading knowledge of at least one foreign language, and should also have been exposed to literature in translation. While great translations are rare, there are many adequate ones, especially in fiction, but in poetry as well. For example, while Herter Norton's translations of Rilke's poetry are not up to the performance level of the original German, they are accurate and adequate.

Brammer: Do you think it should be formalized or do you think students of writing in this country should just go and do what you did and run off with barely your bus fare in your pocket, learn Spanish, and just have the experience?

Eshleman: I think you can do both. Though today, it is not as easy to hitchhike to Mexico as it was in 1959. Travel is both more expensive and probably more dangerous. But getting out of America and seeing something of how other people live, especially the disadvantaged, is important for a young writer. For one reason, because creative writing workshops don't teach you that much. They teach you how to write sufficiently for a degree, but that's about all. I don't think students learn much from their peers. I think they would be better off spending their class time in literature, history, and philosophy, for example, and discussing their writing, on a one-to-one basis, occasionally, with the writers who teach the literature courses. If they want to talk about poetry with their peers, they should do such on an informal basis, getting together on the weekend.

When I was teaching at Eastern Michigan University (1986–2003), I encouraged writing students to keep a reading/writing notebook, in which they would reserve the left-hand page for writing down quotations from their reading, and the right-hand page for their comments, and perhaps the start-up of their own poems. Such gives you a record of what you have been thinking about your reading, what you have found valuable in it, and it also starts to wean you from dependence on professors and workshops. You have to learn how to initiate yourself off of yourself, and writing programs don't teach you how to do that.

To read as a writer is absolutely essential, and a lot of the students never realize that.

Brammer: Do you think your work in translation may have acted as a cultural bridge, bringing readers closer to the people of Peru or Martinique, or even inspired others to take the kind of Bohemian trip you made as a young man to Mexico?

Eshleman: Perhaps. Occasionally, people have written to that effect. Again, keep in mind that when I hitchhiked to Mexico, I was doing so in an *On the Road* atmosphere, in which young men and women with very little money would just take off for months at a time. I hitchhiked to Mexico without any Spanish and with $200 in my pocket. The following year I went back again, this time in the back of a friend's truck, caught hepatitis in Chapala, but returned, still raring to go. And when I went down to Peru in 1965, that was even crazier. I am surprised that my first wife, who was pregnant at the time, and spoke no Spanish, agreed to go. I sent her by plane on ahead of me, then hitchhiked from Indianapolis to Mexico City, took a bus to Panama, and then flew to Lima. We had less than $300.

So I did all of these crazy things out of some sort of symbolic fascination—not so much simply with Vallejo—but with a project that I had committed myself to. That's interesting. I mean, I felt that if I'm going to commit myself to this, I'm going to see it through. I don't know where that depth of commitment came from—there was no model for it in my family—but I'm sure glad that I got it because I think it's a very good aspect of my personality: if I take on something, I'm going to go through with it, and nothing's going to stop me. Death, maybe, but nothing else is going to stop me.

And I did that with Vallejo. And I did it in a way that I compensated for my limitations with the Spanish language, because, weirdly—and I cannot explain this to you—but, I never took the time to learn Spanish thoroughly. I decided to translate Vallejo without having studied Spanish, which is possibly the most insane project that you could propose in terms in translation. And it took me forty-eight years, but I think I have done it.

So, I'm not a model of anything. I got bit by Vallejo, and at the same time I became committed to not allowing my own interests to interfere with the translation. I always fought against doing things like Ben Belitt did with Neruda, in terms of doing variations on things that made the translations sound like I wanted them to. But to keep the translation clear of my own fantasies has taken a long time.

I met Neruda and Vallejo through the wonderful 1944 *New Directions Anthology* and it was great. I don't know why, because I was this kind of monolingual nut from Indianapolis. And when I read the poetry of these people, I said, "This is what I'm interested in!" Then I said, "Who's translating them?" There's Spanish there, English here. Is it accurate?

There was something in me that had not been destroyed. A lot had been destroyed, but something in me hadn't been destroyed that said, "I want to find out what these poets are about. And I'll find out about them by making my own translations."

That was the beginning. I remember trying to translate Neruda in Chapala, my second summer in Mexico. I rented a room in the house of a transplanted American butcher named Jimmy George who had married a Mexican teenager. I would invite her into my room, ask her to sit next to me on the bed, and rather than trying to seduce her, I would say, "Help me with me Neruda."

Brammer: [Laughing.]

Eshleman: And she did. [Laughing.] I would say, "What does this word mean?" And, "What does that word mean?" And she would say, "Hmm…" And she was absolutely the worst person in the world to ask about these things because she knew less about the Spanish of Neruda than I did with my fifty-cent bilingual dictionary.

So what was I really up to? I was involved with a kind of mystique that was not directly tied to that poem in translation, a mystique of trying to figure out how I could insert my way into something that was not myself, that was—I can't say that wasn't necessarily Indiana or Indianapolis—but I was trying to cross over to something that was buried within me and that represented an alternative to what I appeared to be.

And it was as though one thing was as good as another. I mean, being with her was great. She was like 18 or 19 years old and she was trying to help me with simple translation problems, and that was an experience in itself. That in itself was more important than trying to seduce her, that, and engaging something that was outside of Indiana.

Do you understand what I'm saying? What I was doing with Vallejo and Neruda had stimulated me into wanting to be more than I was raised to be, because my parents had convinced me that I was no more than I was raised to be. They never said so per se. But all of the life around me in Indianapolis had been making a resounding case for it.

That's why going to Mexico that summer of 1959 was like going to the moon, because Mexico, that summer, represented the possibility of becoming other than myself. And myself was nothing, nothing!

Mexico was the place of my self-discovery. Without Mexico that summer, there would be no Eshleman/Vallejo.

It's true. Absolutely.

Brammer: Do you think your legacy is that you opened up those possibilities for future generations? Do you think your translations of Neruda and Vallejo will serve the same purpose for future translators that the 1944 *New Directions Latin American Anthology*, in which you discovered those poets, did for you?

Eshleman: Well, I don't know. There are a lot of good translators. What I have done for Vallejo, Eliot Weinberger has done for Octavio Paz, Pierre Joris has done for Paul Celan, Ron Padgett has done for Blaise Cendrars, and Rosmarie Waldrop has done for Edmond Jabès.

Brammer: Do you think the translation of Latin American writers into English has had any tangible impact on writers in the United States? Has it truly been absorbed, or, in the words of one of your previous interviews, has it established an "assimilative space" here north of the border?

Eshleman: I was using the term "assimilative space" to evoke one of the things that happens when a translator is moving back and forth between an original poem and the rendering he is shaping. My experience of this "space" is that it allows the poet translator to reflect as much on his own language as it does the language of the original poem. I think that this "space" is also deftly influential in as much as it allows the poet translator to learn from the second language text he is creating, in contrast to being influenced by reading authors who write in English.

As for the impact of Latin American writers—let's restrict this to poets here—I feel you would have to ask particular American poets this question to get a useful answer. Certain American poets have claimed that Vallejo, for example, has had a significant effect on their own poetry. Hugh Seidman, C.K. Williams, Ed Hirsch, and Franz Wright come to mind. And I imagine that there are others who would claim the same thing based on reading Neruda and Octavio Paz. For example, one could propose that the career of the essayist and translator Eliot Weinberger has been contoured and complexed by his translational relationship with Paz.

It occurs to me here to suggest that some poets become translators because they feel the language they have been given is inadequate as a language for poetry, and that by translating they are inducting not only a foreign psyche into their own mind set but increasing their own potential to find a language that can authenticate their sense of being. I mentioned earlier that the language one has been given can be thought of as a second language. Some of us have a vision that the language of poetry is a buried first language, which must be excavated via assimilative reading, translating, and a refocusing of one's life. I also feel that the "assimilative space" just discussed feeds material into the poet translator's subconscious, densifying its mosaic, and releasing certain springs from nationalistic gravity.

Brammer: Do you think there are possible pitfalls of cultural imperialism that come into play in this kind of translation? You've gone to great lengths to learn a culture from within, by moving to Peru, by spending a significant amount of time in Mexico. Do you think the capacity that you mention in one of your critical works for imperialist agendas in this country can even affect the way works from other languages get translated?

Eshleman: I think you are referring to a short essay called "The Translator's Ego" which appeared in my prose collection, *Antiphonal Swing* (1989). There I mentioned that when a "first-world" translator works on a poem by a "third-world" poet, if he does not translate thoroughly and accurately he may involve himself in something that could be thought of as colonizing the original text. When a translator like Ben Belitt utterly changes the meaning of words and phrases in Neruda poems, a reader might conclude that Belitt thinks his mind is superior to Neruda's, and that he is even educating and re-forming the original in a way that instructs the reader to believe that Neruda is aping American literary conventions.

My attempt has always been—even if I've made errors, and I certainly have—to render the translation as accurately as I can to put the English reader in the position that the Latin American reader would be relative to the original Spanish. I think we talked about this before, but I can't emphasize it too much.

Brammer: How do you carry that through?

Eshleman: Research. Anything that you don't understand, if you can't find it through dictionaries, and you can't find it through a friend, then you find somebody that can find it for you. Everything can be found. And if you can't find it in the long run, then you footnote it, and you say, "I can't find the meaning for this."

For example, Vallejo is full of semi-veiled sexual references. He uses "pajaro" in two cases in the *Poemas humanos* in conjunction with other sexual material. So, if I translate it as "bird," you miss that, especially if he uses "bragueta" ("fly" or "zipper") in the following line. He's talking about his "pajaro" and immediately afterward about his "bragueta." So I think I've come up with an interesting solution: I translate "pajaro" twice in the *Poemas humanos* now as "pecker."

Now we all know "woodpecker." [Laughing.] So I think that's a very nifty solution. Now we have Vallejo's "pecker."

That's one of the happier solutions. Others are not as sharp.

Brammer: Do you think there will ever be another great generation of translators in the United States?

Eshleman: Well, that depends on you. That depends entirely on you.

NOTES:

[1] This interview was published online at *The Woodland Pattern*, and in the *Denver Quarterly*.

A N   E G O   S T R O N G   E N O U G H
T O   L I V E

Translating & Imagining César Vallejo[1]

By the time I completed a third draft of César Vallejo's *Human Poems*, in Kyoto, Japan, in 1963, I felt that I was hardly any further ahead with the project than I had been at the beginning. By insisting on trying to get everything right, I kept running up against dead end after dead end. This word was not in any dictionary. This phrase made no sense. Not only did I not understand a lot of what I was working with, but I began to fantasize that Vallejo did not want his words turned into English, and in some bizarre way was resisting my efforts. I realized, however, that being lost in a labyrinth that I had created for myself was significant. I decided that if I could figure out a way to conceive this struggle in a poem of my own, I would have at least something to show for all my work.

I imagined that I was in a life-death struggle with Vallejo, or, in Blakean terms, with the specter of Vallejo. I was trying to wrest his language away from him as if it were his food while he cannily thwarted my thievery. So I worked on a poem ultimately called "The Book of Yorunomado." The crucial section of the poem, as far as the struggle with Vallejo was concerned, is this:

> I entered Yorunomado and sat
> down, translating,
> *Nightwindow.*

The coffee breathed
a tiny
pit—

As a black jeweled butterfly alights
in late summer on a hardening coil of dung,
so I lit on his spine

pages lifting in the breeze in   from the patio

We locked. I sank my teeth into
his throat, clenched, his fangs
tore into my balls, locked
in spasms of deadening pain we turned, I
crazed for his breath, to translate
my cry into his gold, howling, he
ripped for food

Locked, a month passed, and as he increased lean
I slackened, drained, and tripling my energy
drew blood, not what I was after, muscles
contracting, expanded he was clenched
in my structure, a dead matter
eating into my cords, and saw deep
in his interior a pit, in spring
I went for it, made myself into a knife
and reached down, drawing
out from the earth cold.
A hideous chill passed—

another month, cunningly
he turned himself into a stone

I dulled on, grinding my own teeth, woke up,
another month, a season. I was wandering
a pebbled compound, the stone in my hand.

I saw I had birthed the dead end, but Japan
was no help—until I also saw
in the feudal rite of *seppuku* a way.

On the pebbles I lowered stone-like.
Whereupon the Specter of Vallejo raised
before me: cowled in black robes, stern on the *roka*,

he assumed a formal kneel. With his fan
he drew a bull's-eye on my gut;
he gave no quarter; I cut.

Eyes of father tubes of mother swam
my system's acids. As one slices raw tuna
with shooting contortions not

moving a foot I unlocked Yorunomado,
undid his wrists and ankles chained to altars of
the multichambered sun.
Vallejo kept his word:

he was none other that year than himself

Hello all I have ever felt...

for that was the point upon which the knife
twisted loose an ego
strong enough to live.

Seppuku is the more sophisticated term for what is otherwise
known as *harakiri*, or disembowelment. In 1962, I saw, several
times, a terrific Samurai film called *Seppuku* that made a profound
impression on me.

Slicing into my own metaphoric guts, an eerie ecstasy ran
through me. I was envisioning the destruction of my given life for

a creative one, in which Yorunomado, a figure of imagination, was the transformation of my mother and father.

Years later, studying shamanism, I discovered that the novice in his initiation often experiences dismemberment in which his insides are torn out, or boiled. Spirits or ancestral shamans then replace the organs with rock crystals, indicating that the new initiate has an indestructible body enabling him to go on celestial or infernal quests.

Elsewhere I have written: "In early 1964, the fruit of my struggle with Vallejo was not a successful linguistic translation but an imaginative advance in which a third figure had emerged from my intercourse with the text. Yorunomado then became another guide in the ten-year process of developing a "creative life," recorded in my book-length poem, *Coils* (1973)."

The temptation in Kyoto at this time was to tinker with Vallejo's lines in English in such a way that they made sense to me, to, in effect, interpret them rather than to translate them. Probably because of the wall I was up against, I had a lot of fantasies, not only about what a particular line or image might mean, but fantasies that seemed detached from the translation itself. And since Vallejo was one of my key sources for what being a poet meant, I knew that if I was not careful I would skew the translation in directions that would represent my own, at the time, unclear aspirations in poetry. As I pointed out in "A Translation Memoir," the Afterword to my translation of *The Complete Poetry of César Vallejo*, I have worked hard, over the years, to keep this from happening.

Since I worked on Vallejo at the time I was seeking to lose and to find myself in poetry, his influence on my writing has been considerable. However, there seems to be a crucial difference between being influenced by a master in one's own language and by one in a language that one is translating. If I am being influenced by Hart Crane, say, you would think of Crane when you read my poetry, and by doing so, one could say that Crane's presence had marginalized my own. If Vallejo is to make himself felt in my poetry, one way that he could do so would be through what I, as his translator, have turned him into. In this sense, my translations of him act as a kind of half-way house between the original Spanish and my own poetry. If you think of Vallejo when you read one of my poems, you are most probably not thinking of him in Spanish, but of what I have turned him into in English. So to some extent, I have created a text to possibly be influenced by. While I would not go so far as to say that this is the equivalent of being influenced by myself, the translation is so full of "Eshleman decisions" that Vallejo, as direct presence, has been distanced.

Other forms of influence involve psychological strategies. Near the end of "Song of Myself," Walt Whitman writes:

> Do I contradict myself?
> Very well then…. I contradict myself;
> I am large…. I contain multitudes.

Vallejo's form of contradiction, certainly in *Poemas humanos*, often involves a subconscious thought entering a line under formation and re-routing it. I became aware of this strategy while in Kyoto, and it taught me that engaging lines of poetry are often those that construct a new image or yoke two disparities into a seamless proposal. For example, look at what happens in this stanza from Vallejo's, "There are days, there comes to me an exuberant, political hunger…":

> Ah to desire, this one, mine, this one, the world's,
> interhuman and parochial, mature!
> It comes perfectly timed,
> from the foundation, from the public groin,
> and, coming from afar, makes me hunger to kiss
> the singer's muffler,
> whoever suffers, to kiss him on his frying pan,
> the deaf man, fearlessly, on his cranial murmur;
> whoever gives me what I forgot in my breast,
> on his Dante, on his Chaplin, on his shoulders.

Everything the speaker seeks to kiss disrupts literal logic, but does not become nonsense. To kiss whoever suffers on his frying pan, suggesting that the sufferer is hungry, implies that the kiss would be a kind of food. To kiss a deaf man on his cranial murmur is even more dense, but intelligible: is the deaf man unaware that his skull, in effect, "speaks?" And by kissing him on his "cranial murmur," does not a mystical reciprocal communication take place? Each of these two prepositional phrases not only re-routes the direction of the sentence but adds elements of human compassion. What is literally contradictory fills cubistically with metaphorical meaning. Via translating Vallejo I came to self-contradiction in the spirit that Whitman had proposed, though not necessarily with his "multitudes" in mind.

After returning to the States in the summer of 1964, I continued to work on my translation of *Poemas humanos*. Writing "The Book of Yornomado" had given me permission to imagine Vallejo, to regard him not only as a text, but as material to draw upon in my own poetry. I was building up a kind of "Vallejo file" of tangential notions and sensations. My view of apprenticeship expanded, and deepened, from that of the bitter struggle in "The Book of Yorunomado" to passages like this from my 1965 poem, "The Book of Niemonjima":

> he approached
> the casket of Vallejo as a book is closed,
> toward the heavy box of flesh blowing
> by the sea, seeing a man crouched
> moving behind, who he feared was himself.
> Los stood naked with his hammer behind
> the casket of Vallejo smiling at Yorunomado;
> he put his hand upon the beaten
> lid as the wanderer approached, smiling,
> for he alone knew what I must do, & stepped

back as I knelt by the box in dignity, in prayer
to Vallejo. Los stood & watched,
& Yorunomado saw how those who weep in
their work cannot weep, how those who
never weep are the weak, the fake
sufferers. To be a man. That suffering
is truer to man than joy. These were
the lines in the heavy pocked face of Vallejo,
trinities of intersections &
heavy lines, a village of nose & lids;
Vallejo never left home, it was home
he always begged for even in the taking on
of the suffering body of man. I stood for
7 years & looked at him there, observing
the Quechuan rags & shreds of priest cloak,
the immense weight in his mind,
& lifting his rags I saw his female gate,
bloodied & rotten, hopelessly stitched
with crow feathers, azure, threaded with
raw meat, odors of potatoes & the Andes,
& how the priest roaches had gotten into
the gate, yet the edges of his gate were
sewn with noble purple velvet & I pondered
my own course, what was in store for me
given the way I was living, how the female
gate in a man must open, yet the horrible
suffering if it opens & something else does
not open! But there was no cure or cause
for who Vallejo was, perhaps it was the enormity
of what he took on, the weight of his people
to utter, & I shuddered to think of Indiana,
of what it would be to cast Indiana off.
Yorunomado sobbed when he saw the extent
of contradiction in Vallejo's body, how
could he have lived even one day, he thought;
this was the agony in the lines, the fullness

& the dark beauty of Vallejo's face horizontal
to sky, long black hair flowing back
into the sand, & Los likewise moved bent
& rested his hammer for one day in tribute
to the fierce & flaming profile contoured
to the horizon...

How long had he been left there? Yornomado
stood & with Los helped the casket off
into the sea of another language.

Los is Blake's figure of the poet, or the spiritual revolutionary who reveals basic truths. Having freed Yorunomado from my solar plexus (or, to put it another way, having transformed my working place into a figure of instruction), he could occupy dramatic space with Los, in the same spirit that I had engaged Los via Blake.

One point I would like to get across here is how translating Vallejo encouraged me to give priority to imagination over memory and to trust in creative presence. Not only was he instructive regarding contradiction (and "the logic of metaphor") but his work also enabled me to begin to confront ambivalence. The fact that one is drawn to the world as one is repulsed by it is an aspect of the larger forces of affirmation and negation that I came to see as core values in the making of an art. I think it was Rilke who wrote "to praise is all," sensing such as the key mission of the poet. I think he is close to being right: affirmation is wonderful, but it is only real when it is constantly tested against negation. Over the years, I have tried to always hold my affirmation to the fire, as it were, believing that only that which survives the fire counts.

In the mid-1980s, and again last year, I wrote two poems that are hard to describe. Both are based on my translations of two Vallejo poems, and are, in a way, translations of translations, though that is not quite right. Both follow to a considerable extent the formal procedures of the translations in such a way that I would think that a person familiar with either the original or the translation would hear them as ghosts inhabiting my own poems. I am also reminded of the palimpsest, or a text that has been written over earlier texts, so that both show through the third or most recent text.

Here is the first of the Vallejo translations, "The Book of Nature," from *Human Poems:*

> Professor of sobbing—I said to a tree—
> staff of quicksilver, rumorous
> linden, at the bank of the Marne, a good student
> is reading in your deck of cards, in your dead foliage,
> between the evident water and the false sun,
> his three of hearts, his queen of diamonds.
>
> Rector of the chapters of heaven,
> of the burning fly, of the manual calm there is in asses;
> rector of deep ignorance, a bad student
> is reading in your deck of cards, in your dead foliage,
> the hunger for reason that maddens him
> and the thirst for dementia that drives him mad.
>
> Technician of shouts, conscious tree, strong,
> fluvial, double, solar, double, fanatic,
> connoisseur of cardinal roses, totally
> embedded, until drawing blood, in stingers, a student
> is reading in your deck of cards, in your dead foliage,
> his precocious, telluric, volcanic, king of spades.
>
> Oh professor, from having been so ignorant!
> oh rector, from trembling so much in the air!
> oh technician, from so much bending over!
> Oh linden, oh murmurous staff by the Marne!

Before presenting my "translation" of this translation, since it concerns the fate of the French poet and metaphysician of the theater, Antonin Artaud, I should say a few things about Artaud that are relevant to my poem. Artaud was incarcerated in insane asylums from 1937 to 1946, where he underwent fifty-one electro-shock sessions. In the last two years of his life—he died in 1948 outside of Paris—he created some of the strangest writing in the 20th-century, texts that at once are profoundly disturbed and uniquely coherent. Many facets of his life—his vision quests to northern Mexico and southwestern Ireland, use of a magic dagger and cane, loss of identity, possession by doubles, glossolalia, the projection of magical daughters from his own body, and his imaginative resurrection in Rodez asylum—have more to do with shamanism than with the lives of 19th- and 20th-century men of letters.

Here is my "translation" of my translation of Vallejo's "The Book of Nature":

The Excavation of Artaud

Shaman of obsession—I said at his tomb—
excavated in electricity, opened between
anus and sex. In the Australian outback of the soul,
3 dead men are fingering your anesthetized root
support
shining like a chain of sputtering lights, for the
key to creation,
between the bone they've drawn out and your
bone they so desire.

Priest of lethal phallic rites, of sparkings
in foetid material, of remaining in antithesis
with no hope of synthesis, priest of a genuine
melée—
3 dead men are fingering your Muladhara
Chakra, your amphimixis,
as if, under the Christian gunk that clogged your
focus,

they could plug into your triangle and its twisting
    tongue of flame.

Pariah in silence, coprophilially
squatting in the corner of your cell for years,
sealed open, who only came when called by your
    mother's name—
repressing their way in, to the point of anal cancer,
3 dead men, licking your electroshock-induced
    Bardo, have found
your atomic glue, the Kundalini compost they
    must eat to speak.

O shaman, from having been so masterfully
    plundered!
O priest, from having been fixed in antithesis!
O pariah, from having been so desired by the
    dead!

Structurally speaking, Vallejo's poem is an apostrophe, in which
a tree is addressed metaphorically in the first three lines of each of
the first three stanzas. In the last three lines of these stanzas, a student attempts to tell his fortune via "the book of nature" present as
a deck of cards in the pedagogical tree. In the final stanza, the pedagogical tree is again apostrophized and in a quick series of contradictions defined.

I have no idea if this is a Spanish verse form, or whether it has
ever been used by anyone other than Vallejo. I thought it would be
a cogent structure to use in apostrophizing Artaud, who claimed he
had been attacked between anus and sex (the location of the Tantric
Muladhara Chakra) by God. I borrow an Australian aboriginal lethal phallic rite from the research of Géza Roheim in an attempt to
dramatize Artaud's plight.

The second of my "translations" of my translations is a poem
that concludes a longer work in prose, "One If By Sea, None If By

Land," and it is spoken by a spider, or my vision of the poet as a spider, based on my reading of the labyrinth.

I see the labyrinth as a three-fold image: the model for the Cretan labyrinth in which Theseus engages and destroys the Minotaur, at the center is the orb-weaving spider web across which a male must make his way to mate at the center with the female builder of the web, and then exit before he is eaten. Writing a poem involves, in my sense of it, the poet symbolically entering this labyrinthian constellation where his activity is transformed into a spider writer (*Argiope*, the "golden orb-weaver," is also known as the "writing spider") devouring his/her material. That is to say that the bitter combat at the center (arachnoid mating, Theseus–Minotaur conflict) is, in the poem's terms, the poem's realization of itself where it simultaneously feeds on itself and gives its heart to itself.

The Vallejo translation I chose to "translate," or re-envision, begins "Chances are, I'm another; walking, at dawn…" Such a phrase evokes, of course, Rimbaud's "*Je est un autre*," I is another. In my piece, Vallejo's "other" becomes a "Minotaur surrogate."

Here is my translation of "A lo mejor, soy otro..":

> Chances are, I'm another; walking, at dawn,
>   another who proceeds
> around a long disk, an elastic disk:
> a mortal, figurative, audacious diaphragm.
> Chances are, I remember while waiting, I annotate
>   marble
> where scarlet index, and where bronze cot,
> an absent, spurious, enraged fox.
> Chances are, a man after all,
> my shoulders anointed with indigo misericordia,
> chances are, I say to myself, beyond there is nothing.
>
> The sea gives me the disk, referring it,
> with a certain dry margin, to my throat;
> nothing, truly, more acidic, sweeter, more Kantian!
> But somebody else's sweat, but a serum

or tempest of meekness,
decaying or rising—that, never!

Lying down, slender, I exhume myself,
smashing my way into the tumefied mixture,
without legs, without adult clay, nor weapons,
a needle stuck in the great atom…
No! Never! Never yesterday! Never later!

Hence this satanic tuber,
this moral plesiosaurian molar
and these posthumous suspicions,
this index, this bed, these tickets.

And here is my version:

Chances are I'm a Minotaur surrogate,
weaving, at night, an arachnoid adept who jigs
about a cordate void,
an anomalous void, orbicular labyrinth.
Chances are, I behead upon being impregnated,
nourishing the just conceived with my brain marrow lunch.
Chances are, I spin-say to myself:
mental war takes place on husk-strewn thread.

The air advertises reality, connecting it,
via respiration, with non-being—
nothing, truly, more noumenal, more depth-
resplendent!
But a religious grid, or gradient, an oasis
beyond this worktomb,
verdant, eternal—that, never!

Abdomen-tentacled, I snag
etymological drift, injecting it with literal

breakdown, so as
to turn it, as a threadbaled Thesean,
into drink.

Hence this spider mind,
this forever warp woof-crossed by never,
this spectral Tenochtitlan,
this Jurassic chandelier.

The initial Jacob/angel combat with Vallejo that produced, instead of a realized translation, an imaginary third figure, enabled me to understand that the translation process was dual: it involved an imaginal reality as well as a linguistic one. From my point of view, these two realities are not in conflict—in fact, I would argue that acknowledging the imaginal realm, and working with it, has enabled me to produce translations that are free of a translator's ego.

In "The Book of Yorunomado," I cast Vallejo as an actor in my drama of self-transformation. In "The Excavation of Artaud," I generated a vision of Artaud's terrible and grotesquely stunning condition and drew upon one of Vallejo's poetic forms to articulate it. And in "Chances are I'm a Minotaur surrogate," I turned my translation into another poem of my own, making use of my totemic figure, the spider. To some extent, I would argue, I have incorporated Vallejo's poetry in translation as an element in my own poetry, and thus reversed his influence. Metaphorically speaking, who I served is here serving me.

NOTES:
[1] This piece was written for Michael Heim's translation seminar at UCLA, and was published in *Rain Taxi*.

WIND FROM ALL
COMPASS POINTS

Not long ago in an issue of the politically liberal *New York Review of Books*, the poet/reviewer Charles Simic praised as a major achievement a poem by the then Poet Laureate Billy Collins which basically expressed Collin's "sensitive" surprise that cows actually moo. In a separate article, Simic dismissed Robert Duncan's inspired confrontation of the American destruction of Vietnam in 1967 in his poem "Uprising" as "worthless." This downgrading of Duncan's imaginative engagement with power, and the extoling of Collin's work, which is hardly even sophisticated entertainment, sadly exemplifies much of what is supported these days by editors, reviewers, and judges as endorsable American poetry.

Some years ago, in *Sulfur #10*, Charles Bernstein defined the officially sanctioned verse of our time as characterized by "a restricted vocabulary, neutral and univocal tone in the guise of voice or persona, grammar-book syntax, received conceits, static and unitary form." This definition is still good today, some twenty years later. In the academic writing programs, the post-confessional and language poetries of the 1970s have fused to produce, in the main, a poetry that is an abstract display of self-sensitivity, the new "official verse." Such programs produce hundreds of young writers each year eager to be accepted, get jobs, and win prizes (virtually the only way a poet can get a first book published today is by winning a contest judged in most cases by a well-known conventional writer; poetry editors who actually edit hardly exist any longer, especially in the service of first books). To my knowledge, few writing programs back a genuinely international viewpoint, exposing novices, for example, to the range of materials one finds in the two volumes of *Poems for the Millennium* (ed. by Jerome Rothenberg and Pierre Joris). More commonly, student-poets are taught material by the same names that reappear with deadly regularity as featured writers at summer retreats, as judges, as grant recipients and as those invited to festivals as key-note speakers.

The extent that Harold Bloom's pronouncements have had a direct effect on contemporary American poetry is hard to determine, but given the extent that poetry readership is oriented to critical admonition, a case can be made that Bloom's and Helen Vendler's failure to back the innovative push at the end of World War II—I mainly have in mind here such poets as Louis Zukofsky, Charles Olson, Robert Duncan, Muriel Rukeyser, George Oppen, and Jackson Mac Low—has skewed readership to several generations of basically conventional writers. While Bloom has brought his considerable erudition to bear on Blake and Shakespeare, his role in the evaluation of several decades of American poetry can be summed up in a statement he made on the poetry of Jay Wright: "His most characteristic art returns always to that commodius lyricism I associate with American poetry at its most celebratory, in Whitman, in Stevens, in Crane, in Ashbery."

Bloom's primary position is that we are at the tail end of a great English tradition, with Wallace Stevens as the last major Romantic figure, trailed by John Ashbery as his radiant ghost. The implication of Bloom's position is that English language poetry has culminated and that what is occurring now, or has been for the past one hundred years, with the above-cited exceptions, is a belated and fractured caricature of it. Such thinking is Koranic, as far as I am concerned, in as much as it treats a great complete tradition (five hundred years of English poetry) as the Koran is treated by its disciples: as a sacred incomparable text. The upshot of such a position is to tell the young poet that he would be better off doing something else, that all his language tits are dry. There is a powerfully-repressed Urizenic poet in Bloom that must account for some of the respect given to his pontifications. Of course if the young poet can be defeated by the likes of Harold Bloom, he would clearly be better off doing something other than writing poetry.

Ever since I discovered the poetry of César Vallejo in the late 1950s, I have intuited that poetry is at a very early stage in its potential unfolding. The depth of "I" has only been superficially explored. Ego consciousness is inadequate to write innovative poetry. Rather than the Freudian hierarchical model, a kind of totem pole consisting of super-ego, ego, and unconscious, I would propose the antiphonal swing of the bicameral mind, which in a contemporary way, relates to shamanism, the most archaic mental travel. While the idea of poetry as a spiral flow, with simultaneous interpenetrations of what we call perception, intuition, feeling, and imagination, is too demanding for most writers, I think it may be one key in enabling a poet to write a poetry that is responsible for all of his experience.

Many poetries prized in any particular decade perform conventional pieties and thus unwittingly bolster the position of someone like Bloom. Given what the American government has been doing throughout the world from the end of World War II on, the American subconscious, into which news spatters daily, is now, more than ever, a roily swamp, at once chaotic and irrationally organized. The fate of American Indians and African-Americans is at the base of this complex. There is a whole new poetry to be written by Americans that pits our present-day national and international situation against these poisoned historical cores.

There are, in 2006, a significant number of poets doing inventive work in their mature years and young poets who look as if they are capable of contributing a fresh body of work. The first names who come to mind in this regard are Adrienne Rich, Robin Blaser, Gary Snyder, Jerome Rothenberg, Jayne Cortez, Robert Kelly, Rachel Blau du Plessis, Ron Silliman, Ron Padgett, Paul Hoover, Nathaniel Mackey, Michael Palmer, Lindsay Hill, John Olson, Pierre Joris, Andrew Joron, Forrest Gander, Will Alexander, Wang Ping, Christine Hume, Linh Dinh, Jeff Clark, Cathy Wagner, Susan Briante, Kristin Prevallet, and Ariana Reines.

I should also mention the poetry of the late Tory Dent and Gustaf Sobin, and the extraordinary English poet, Peter Redgrove, who died at 71 in June 2003, whose writing is hardly known here. In France, the poet Michel Deguy continues to expound a multi-faceted, philosophical poetics (a recent translation of a major Deguy work, *Recumbents*, by Wilson Baldridge, received the 2006 PEN Poetry Translation Award). Recently, I discovered the writing of the Spanish transplant, Gerardo Deniz, who has lived in Mexico City for many years (in Monica de la Torres' fine translation, *poemas / poems*). Also recently Joannes Göransson sent me his translation of a young Swedish poet, Aase Berg (*Remainland*), some of whose linguistic deftness evokes the late poetry of Paul Celan.

Civil poetry in the 20th century is associated with the poetry of Pier Paolo Pasolini. In his Foreword to a selection of Pasolini poems translated by Norman MacAfee (Vintage, 1982), Enzo Siciliano writes: "Civil poetry is poetry in which abstract subject matter—'moral' and 'religious' in Dante's case, and as we know, these can also instantly turn 'political'—becomes fused with an entirely personal sensibility, which absorbs every detail, every shading of inspiration into itself and into the transformation of its content into poetic language."

Without the qualifying clause, Siciliano's statement could refer to Stevens or Ashbery as well as to the Pasolini of "Gramsci's Ashes" (recently retranslated by Michelle Cliff in *NO: A Journal of the Arts #4*). As I see it, the "fusion" involves the figure of the writer against the ground of society. Or the figure of the writer as a kind of moving target in relentless evasion of those forces society uses to disarticulate him: self-censorship as well as editorial censorship, the shying away from materials that disturb a predictable and aesthetically-acceptable response.

For example, I wanted, in my poem "The Assault," to get the possible government conspiracy on 9/11 into the poetic record. Beyond that, I seek to build an atmosphere of political awareness into much of what I write—to write a civil poetry as a citizen–writer, something I have done for several decades. I want a sense of my own time, on a national/international register, to permeate my language. One way that the American poem can remain human, in a social sense, as our government expands its imperialist domination in the world (and space) is for the poet to assimilate and imagine the monstrous interventionist framework within which, as a tiny and impotent god, he mixes his "potions" and proceeds. Siciliano's "fusion" also involves, in my sense of it, not only a porous mixing of perceived and imagined materials, but keeping an experimental poetics intact when addressing civil concerns. The European poetry of César Vallejo reverberates with a social awareness contoured and spiked with associationally arresting metaphors.

In the fall of 2004, I spent a month at the Rockefeller Study Center on Lake Como, Italy, studying a large reproduction of Hieronymus Bosch's triptych, *The Garden of Earthly Delights*, the most challenging painting I have studied. My 60-page improvisations on the triptych, in prose and poetry, tip it, at points, into the 21st century so that, for example, the American assault on Fallujah is there as a disaster of Bosch's Apocalypse. In a section called "Improvisation off the Force of Bosch," I sense the presence of Bush and Rumsfeld in the apocalyptic mayhem to be found in the triptych's right-hand panel:

> The intoxications of immortality
> light up the switchboards when
> another is killed, for the furnaces of "immortality"
> are fed with the bodies of people who look a little
>   different than us.
> How does this work, Donald Rumsfeld?
> Does your Reaper retreat an inch
> for each sixteen-year-old Iraqi boy snipered
> while out looking for food?
> Men in power are living pyramids of slaughtered others.
> Bush is a grinning mountain of carnage.
> The discrepancy between literal suit and
> psychic veracity is nasty to contemplate.
> Imagine a flea with a howitzer shadow
> or a worm whose shade is an entire city ablaze.

Reading these lines today, I realize that "living pyramids of slaughtered others" evokes the tortured body piles of Abu Ghraib.

Being caught up in an agenda can be as undermining to imagination as self-censorship. Traditionally, so-called "political poetry" tends to express a formed, and thus predictable, viewpoint that the writer locks in place as a poem. Such in effect displaces an imaginative openness to spontaneity and notions, images, associations that come up during writing. If I am going to use George Bush in a poem I have to figure out ways to imagine him and to absorb him into my sensibility. This is close to thinking of him as a text that must be translated. Bush creates his own reality (at odds with what we might call real reality) which millions of Americans induct at the same time its repercussions undermine their lives. Bush's "language" is the collision between what he proposes to be and what he actually legitimizes.

Or let me put the problem this way: how to get Colin Powell's language odor into the poem? How layer the lies, the distorted research, the sighs and implications, the black uncle in a My Lai stained uniform, his heil-thin integrity, his good duped intentions, the extent to which slavery is still in his saliva—how ladle all of this, not into proclamation, but into the poem's very climate, into its feelers, its tonalities?

Visually, Botero's recent bringing of tortured Iraqis in the Abu-Ghraib prison into his invented pantheon of the obese (which is starting to look like "real reality" in America) strikes me as a valid example of such translation. And of course, for several decades, until his death in 2004, Leon Golub had been envisioning American power as the dirty work carried out by mercenaries and "white squads" in Central America.

Another of the responsibilities of the poet is to believe that writing remains significant, that significance is not the enemy. The enemy is the eternal game of sticking our heads in the sand and pretending not to know what is going on. In an essay in *American Letters and Commentary*, Ann Lauterbach stated that her response to 9/11 was to stop watching television—a doubly curious statement, since mainstream television has stopped watching life as we know it to be. 9/11 opened up not merely a can of worms but a silo of hydras, and the event itself should drive every artist crazy with curiosity not only about the "official" account of the destruction of the World Trade Center but about what has been done in our name to make *them*, apparently, *assault* us. I think these are the initial commands. One then might ask: why do we now have people in our government who would sacrifice thousands of American and Afghan and Iraqi lives for greedy, global ambitions the repercussions of which they themselves do not understand? I think that one has to face such commands and to risk being overwhelmed by what one finds out during one's investigations. Then one must assimilate them, and, as Vallejo writes, "see if they fit in one's own size."

It is wrong to believe that an event like 9/11 provides justification for a poetry that avoids meaning, or to believe that 9/11 changed the world just because it happened to us. Of course those directly impacted by the assault on the WTC and the Pentagon must grieve and work through their grief, but the rest of us should not feel sorry for ourselves. If anything 9/11 should make us investigate our foreign policy of the past fifty years. Relevant to the Middle East: over the past twenty years, we have shot down Libyan and Iranian planes, bombed Beirut, created a Vietnam situation for the Russians in Afghanistan, aided both Iran and Iraq during their war in the 1980s so as to maximize the damage each side could inflict on the other, bombed Iraq, imposed grueling sanctions upon its population, blown up a pharmaceutical plant in Sudan (that as I understand it provided half of that impoverished nation's medicine), established a hi-tech military presence in Islam's holiest land, Saudi Arabia, and given ten million dollars a day to Israel. The quality of life in Palestine has been so ruined that it is no wonder that many of the humiliated and the abject young there, as well as the educated, can only think of themselves as ammunition.

9/11 aside (if that is possible, at this time), responsibility has to involve responsible innovation, a poetry that pushes into the known and the unknown, making not non-sequitur nonsense but uncommon sense. Wyndham Lewis's view of the basis of art is still true: that of clearing new ground in consciousness. Blake's "Without contraries there is no progression" likewise still holds. Unless poets stave off and admit at the same time, keeping open to the beauty and the horror of the world while remaining available to what their perceptivity and subconscious provide them with, one is pretty much left with an unending "official verse culture." Here I think of a statement by Paul Tillich: "A life process is the more powerful, the more non-being it can include in its self-affirmation, without being destroyed by it." Affirmation is only viable when it survives repeated immersions in negation. At the point one says: "I am an American artist," one finds oneself facing the news in which what is true and what is untrue, what is necessary and what is human, blur into an almost imponderable palimpsest. Such is outer negation with its acidic rivulets of guilt. Inner negation, far more complex, plays the abyss off against one's own hedged gestation and decay.

Poets do not lack an audience because what they write is difficult and demanding—they lack an audience because the poetry that is published and reviewed in mass media publications is often superficial and seldom innovative. People who read *The New Yorker* for its terrific investigative reports, its witty movie reviews, and its often excellent fiction, must find much of the poetry in its pages boring, rococo entertainment. My notion here is that very few readers of complex fiction and commentary seek out poetry because they have a limited view of what it can be, based on examples or reviews of it in publications like *The New Yorker, The New York Review of Books, The New York Times,* or *The Nation*—which often publish sophisticated and pertinent material in other areas they address but not poetry.

In response to my complaint about the pathetic poetry reviewing policy of *The New York Review of Books*, a young poet friend wrote to me: "But who reads it for poetry reviews?"

Indeed, since there is so little real news there, as far as poetry goes. This raises the question, however, of what to read for news of or incisive commentary on complex collections of contemporary poetry. First-rate poetry magazines today, like *New American Writing* and *No: A Journal of the Arts,* do not publish reviews. *The Amer-*

ican Poetry Review, with its huge circulation, publishes some commentary on books and authors, but no reviews. Ron Silliman's blog and John Trantor's online *Jacket* magazine (based in Australia) review a range of books, including contemporary poetry. Silliman's Argus-eyed daily also includes whatever dance, music, and films the editor is attending to, and his daily bulletins and commentaries remind me more of an arts newspaper than a journal. While I find things to gripe about in the way that Silliman categorizes, extols, and dismisses (he tends to peck about the edges of contemporary poetry, sniffing out small issues to dispute or affirm, rather than offering in-depth perspectives on accomplished and demanding works) his blog is the best vehicle we have at this point for news on what is new. And he is a more engaged editor than John Trantor. While I appreciate the international range of *Jacket*, the magazine lacks an argued vision of poetry as well as a core group of savvy reviewers. Saying this I recall the excitement with which I would open new issues of *Kulchur* in the 1960s, eager to see what Gilbert Sorrentino or Leroi Jones had to say in their pungent reviews, which included bristling polemic as well as praise.

Earlier I spoke of the increased irrational turmoil in all of our minds. There is palpable guilt everywhere, and we poets must make ourselves conscious of it. If we feel that we must express it, we should work such out in our poetry and not thoughtlessly take it out on others in vicious literary commentary. Not too long ago, Peter Campion, in *Poetry* magazine, ended a trashing of Jeff Clark's book, *Music and Suicide*, with the following: "Clark writes and publishes these poems for the same reason that Kim Jong Il shoots missiles over Japan: simply because he can." It is of course outrageous that *Poetry* would publish such crap, in which a writer with whom the critic disagrees is compared to a Stalinist dictator. Of course, who knows, Mr. Campion might say the same thing under any circumstances. But the times are ripe for a lot of projected, misplaced bile...

We might ask, with Nietzsche: "Are we forced to be conquerors because we no longer have a country we want to remain in?"

Writing on Henri Michaux's art in 1977, Octavio Paz stated: "His paintings are not so much windows that allow us to see another reality as they are holes and openings made by powers on the other side." At seventy now, I continue to work on accessing one kind of the language I hear in dreams, a kind of magnificent nonsense, non-English English which, in the dream, makes perfect uncommon sense! Such language is super-egoless, and potentially the presence of that "other side" that Michaux seems to have visualized. I believe this language relates to the language-twisting of shamans, and that it is still writhing, in our subconscious, on the ground floor of poetry. However, like all dreams, it does not transfer directly, effectively, into writing. The dream mind is a rapt spectator which does not reflect on the meaning of what it is beholding or hearing. The same can probably be said about shamanic trance. Thus, if in trance, the poet has to keep a shit-detector active, a bird's-eye critical view, that injects invention with responsibility.

When not dreaming these days, the American artist is confronted by a plethora of new information daily on the misdeeds of the Bush administration at home and abroad. Unlike the Vietnam era, there are no artistic mobilization units like "Angry Arts." One is on one's own. To really follow the news as the writers Eliot Weinberger and Mark Crispin Miller have done is a fulltime job. Aesthetically, one of the most vexing aspects of the present administration is that an artist is forced to give up a lot of traditionally creative time just to keep up on new revelations about the war, torture, renditions, the Patriot Act and the 2004 national election (with probable voting irregularities in 2008 now on the horizon), or to disregard this political nightmare completely, and subsequently live as an artist in one's own little bubble. And if one does not go the bubble route, the more roguery one uncovers or tunes in to, the more one may confront extreme emotions of rage, despair, and bafflement. The news has become an unfollowable roadmap of facts crisscrossing opinions. For every uncovered so-called "fact" one suspects there is a host of supporting and contradictory ones in the shadows. I realize that one reason that I have written poems about art and artists over the past decade is that, complex as Bosch, Caravaggio, and Golub may be, one is at least on firm ground facing their imaginative elaborations.

It would now seem that with the 20th-century re-discovery of the Ice Age painted caves in Europe, we have made contact with what could be thought of as the back wall of image-making which, especially in its hybrid aspects, evokes mental travel and thus the roots of poetry. While it is possible that there are even older imaginative materials in Africa and Australia, the chances are that researchers will not uncover on these continents the ancient creative range and quality to be found in such caves as Lascaux and Chauvet. While it is thrilling to know where one is ultimately based as an artist, it is equally horrifying to realize that one may also be witnessing the ecological destruction of the fundament that made art possible in the first place. As these massive vectors shift into place and cross, a disturbance in my mind challenges the convictions that I held as a young man: that the most meaningful way I knew of to deal with myself and with the world was to explore poetry and to write it. This is not a back-handed way of suggesting that poetry or art at large is dead, but a recognition that I may be of the first generation to be witness to one of the recuperations of the roots of culture *and* to the devastations that may make culture as we know it today a thing of the past. Rather than resonating with the magnificent aurochses of Lascaux, the abyss that opens before us today declares itself through the potential extinction of frogs and honey bees, and the accompanying sensations of the empty and lifeless space that humankind has always suspected fueled depth and its analogues of loss.

SHADOW MATTERS: AN INTERVIEW WITH CLAYTON ESHLEMAN[1]

January 2007

by John Olson

Olson: In the preface to *An Alchemist With One Eye On Fire*, you remark that poetry "is about the extending of human consciousness, making conscious the unconscious, creating a symbolic consciousness that in its finest moments overcomes all the dualities in which the human world is cruelly and eternally, it seems, enmeshed." This is a provocative statement. It suggests that poetry is something more than a cognitive titillation, more than intellectual candy, but a powerful agency, a transcendent force. D.H. Lawrence describes this phenomenon as "the soul and the mind and the body surging at once, nothing left out." You would think people would hunger for poetry as they do food and sex, yet very few appear able to make this connection; it is as if there were some sort of stranglehold on people's consciousness. Artaud goes so far as to suggest it takes something as catastrophic as a bubonic plague to wreak havoc and delirium and break down social order so that those who survive are able, at last, to discover a much more intense experience of life. I was wondering if you could identify some of the obstacles we face now, at the beginning of the 21st century, and how someone attempting to write poetry of this nature might best go about it.

Eshleman: The opening part of your paragraph evokes Wyndham Lewis' little essay of 1926, called "Art and the Unknown." In it he makes a distinction between cleared and uncleared space. He likens consciousness to cleared space. He doesn't say much about uncleared space other than to identify it with "the unknown." I think we could call it the subconscious as well as the unconscious. From Lewis' viewpoint, artists who work in cleared space produce entertainment and education. "The total addition made to the cleared space is the measure of greatness as an artist—*at the time the addition is made*," he writes.

I would say that very few people can appreciate art that is clearing new space in their time. I don't see how this will ever change. A further question might be: does this make any difference?

People do not "hunger for poetry," as you put it, because reading poetry that is not a form of entertainment takes a lot of effort. Billy Collins vs. Robert Kelly. A real poem is a half poem, the second half of which is completed by the reader.

Regarding Artaud and the plague: Artaud wrote: "The plague takes images which are asleep, a hidden disorder, and suddenly pushes them toward the most extreme gestures; and theatre too takes gestures and pushes them to their final point: like plague, it remakes the chain between what is and what is not, between the hidden potential of the possible and that which exists in materialized nature."

In response to your last sentence several things come to mind. As always, humanity is attempting to attain a state of pre-birth, with the new virtual world replacing paradise. Such words as Democracy, Justice, Human Rights, and yes, Terrorism, have been turned inside out, and have become just more slag, junk, which of course evokes shooting up—politicians and even well-meaning citizens shooting themselves up with Terrorism.

God is the Lie that opens the horror-gate of permission; I fear that many of those who contest global warming or are indifferent to it have either conscious or unconscious evangelical desires for the end of the world.

There is no "best" way to go about writing poetry today.

Olson: Rimbaud's solution to liberating the mind from western civilization's stranglehold was to make oneself a visionary by way of a "long, immense and systematic derangement of all the senses," ostensibly with alcohol and drugs. This seems a little drastic, and not particularly healthy. Are there other ways? Meditation, for instance, or Native American sweat lodge ceremonies? Is it possible to make oneself a seer without recourse to Wild Turkey, psilocybin, or absinthe? Do you think Wordsworth was on to something when he said "the human mind is capable of being excited without the application of gross and violent stimulants...to endeavor to produce or enlarge this capability is one of the best services in which a writer can be engaged"? I find this an encouraging statement, but futile, if you can't open people's eyes to the light shining through the words of a line like "Noh-ghosts on a bridge between worlds," or "these chess words, slippery with blood, / they are my pistons, my petrol, the fits of memory scrawled in a hulk log."

Eshleman: The roots of poetry are buried in proto-shamanism, which I suspect is of Upper Paleolithic antiquity. The shaman, as a novice, must rid himself of his given body, for a new and magical body, which is capable of mental travel. The main difference here between shamans, say, in 19th-century Siberia, and poets in America today, is that the shamans were central to their communities, they belonged in a way no American writer, even those with huge audiences, belong today. Whatever one must do to make the move from the given life to a creative one—well, that is up to each of us. The poetry scene today is flooded with young, talented, unoriginal writers who are trying to write significant poetry based on their given lives; they adhere to the given because most are part of the educational system, and thus they belong to their parents, and are without what I would call a viable self-initiation.

Olson: What does Rimbaud mean by "I is an other?"

Eshleman: Rimbaud is extraordinary in several ways: as a teenager he immediately made use of everything he was learning about poetry, and determined that to present common experience (based on the given life) in a special wrapping was a mockery of true poetry. True poetry involved altering the nature of reality, and to do this, one had, for starters, to discover the nature (or anti-nature, really) of one's inner world—the other or unknown person partially hidden in dreams, impulses, the realm of the subconscious.

Rimbaud thus became obsessed with self-transformation in somewhat the same spirit that Indian and Eskimo medicine men and women, or shamans, are. Note the difference between writing "I is another," as Rimbaud did, and "I am another." "I am another" suggests that my customary "I" is still present and that it has something mysterious about it. "I is another" (or "I is somebody else") suggests that "I" is an unidentified actor, or personality, about whom my ordinary (given) "I" knows very little. Furthermore, Rimbaud states that the soul must be made monstrous. In less febrile words, the subconscious must be made available to consciousness. Fasten your seat belts.

The most important word in Rimbaud's "program" that you quote is "systematic" (or to my reading, "rational"). A rational disordering (or "derangement") is programmatic, an apprenticeship, in which the novice sets up some near-impossible hoops to jump through. In 1962, in Kyoto, Japan, I committed myself, as my apprenticeship to the art of poetry, to a translation of César Vallejo's *Poemas humanos.* That was my "rational disordering," or the crowbar I used to break up the floorboards over my sealed, irrational strongroom.

Olson: What does André Breton mean by "Existence is elsewhere?"

Eshleman: I do not know the context in which Breton made that remark. But I will take a stab at an answer. Existence is not in the here and now, but in an "alternative world" that can be tapped in dreams and through visions. I would prefer to replace "existence" with "being" in Breton's remark, since the latter, for me, pertains more accurately to dreams and visions than existence does. The existent is the core of our materiality, of life itself, and facing the virtual/Monsanto take-over, it is more precious than ever. I wonder what Breton thought of the paintings of Chaim Soutine, which are a testimony to the precious, un-elsewhere beauty and grotesqueness of the existent.

Olson: If you could be a tool, what kind of tool would you be?

Eshleman: Since I allow myself to be, in part, manipulated by my subconscious, when writing poetry, I suppose that I am a "tool" in that sense. I would also like to be a tool in a surgeon's hand saving someone's life.

Olson: In *Les Chants de Maldoror*, Isidore Ducasse (a.k.a. Comte de Lautréamont) states, "it is rather difficult to distinguish buffoonery from melancholy, life itself being a comical drama or dramatic comedy." I see a lot of humor in your work, often mixed in with some rather horrific observations of modern life. I was wondering if you could comment on this.

Eshleman: Comic strips in newspapers and comic books were my introduction to imagination and literature as a child growing up in Indianapolis in the 1940s. So that is probably one source of the humor in my poetry, though not the most important, which, as I understand it, relates to Mikhail Bakhtin's sense of "grotesque realism." That is, for me, events are often hybrid, as are people, and emotions, packed with the serious, the absurd, the horrifying, and the ridiculous. Another way to say this would be (from my poem "Cemeteries of Paradise"):

> To get at the round,
> the jagged round of any situation,
> how we fence with the udders of snow!

Olson: Writing on the sublime, Edmund Burke argued that, in nature, dark, confused, uncertain images have a greater power on the imagination to inspire grander passions than those that are more clear and determinate. Would you agree with this?

Eshleman: The sublime, or the lofty, implies an underlying depth, which includes loss, bottomlessness, and our inability to encompass the soul. Burke's observation may drift all the way back to the Ice Age caves, where grotesque figures scratched onto the wall occurred as a result of the combined pressure of sensory isolation, darkness, stone, and the feeling that certain "entities" were present.

This is not to knock clarity that, when earned, when arrived at against the unending impasses of ignorance that surround us, can be, to jump ahead with your questions, "the pearl of great price."

Burke may also have had dreams in mind, or opium visions in which vast, murky, architectural abyss-scapes are said to appear.

Grandeur is tricky. The lofty can also be infested with haughtiness and bogus solemnity.

Olson: The idea of a regenerative abyss, a redemptive darkness, is a critical factor in your writing. Could you further elaborate on this?

Eshleman: I would first mention metaphor, always, very old and of the root of the hybrid figures to be found in the Ice Age caves. When someone gouged the outlines of a horse head in limestone and then gouged a vulva (same size as the horse head) across the neck of the horse (at, we think, around 30,000 B.P.), we have the Upper Paleolithic equivalent of Allen Ginsberg's "hydrogen jukebox" (which also qualifies as an image, in Reverdy's sense of it).

What is the abyss? It is the Deep each one of us carries around inside. But how did this Deep get there? One possibility is out of the seemingly infinitely elastic crisis of therio-expulsion, our separating the animal out of our to-be human heads. I feel this "act" is tied into the origin of image-making.

Out of non-being, being.

Shadow matters.

Abyss as the unconscious, the primordial cornucopia, paradise and Pandora's box.

Olson: In 1974, you made your first trip to the caves of the Dordogne to view prehistoric cave art. You have been returning almost annually to these caves since then. These journeys have played a crucial role in shaping your poetic philosophy. You once remarked that "going into the earth for my poetry" was performed in the belief "that there is a light and intelligence there that I am to penetrate, a new sort of den, not the lair I was dropped in." I believe that "lair" was an upbringing, by German parents, in Indiana, was it not?

Eshleman: My figure of the imagination, Yorunomado, told me, at the end of the poem "Coils" (in the book, *Coils*, 1973): "From this point on… / your work leads on into the earth." I think that last line points directly into Caryl's and my "discovery" of the Ice Age underworld in 1974.

By the way, Caryl is my editor, and my work would not be what it is without her attention over the years.

I forget where "the lair I was dropped in" comes from, but it is certainly a sardonic comment about being brought up in Indianapolis by, for the most part, clueless parents. German? I don't know. I have never had any interest in genealogy. I was told my mother had Spanish blood, and once, I recall, as a child, I was told by an uncle on my father's side that the Eshlemans embarked from Amsterdam at the beginning of the 19th century. But I don't know how they got to Amsterdam, so I could be, on my father's side, German, Dutch, Swiss, or Austrian. "Eshleman" can be spelled many ways and ours is one of the least common spellings.

Olson: In *Dream and Underworld,* James Hillman states: "To know the psyche at its basic depths, for a true depth psychology, one must go to the underworld." Where might we find that underworld? How do we access it? It appears to be the mental equivalent of the prehistoric art in the caves of the Dordogne. How do we get there? Is a poem the equivalent of animal fat & burning wick?

Eshleman: Your question brings back some material that has come up before. The underworld is a pre-pagan concept and not, in its visionary sense, related to hell. In *The Odyssey*, in Book XIII, it is a place of instruction, where the seeker, via sacrifice, acquires visionary information. I think that the earliest underworlds, undoubtedly the decorated, or ensouled, Upper Paleolithic caves, carried the initial vibrations of paradise. This is an extraordinary thing to think about. In deep, anti-natural recesses, filled with rock foliage, which looked organic, but was not, our ancestors realized, for the first time, that an alternative "world" existed. They probably had no "idea" of what it was, but they recognized it, and, in effect, created it out of their recognition. Extraordinary! I think of such caves today as the cemeteries of paradise.

The Greek word for the Pit was *abaton*, which the Jews called *Abaddon*. There is a swirl of meanings here for this place was also an earth-womb, which Barbara G. Walker tells us novice priests went down into for long "periods of incubation, pantomiming death, burial, and rebirth from the womb of Mother Earth."

How do we access it today? In my book *Juniper Fuse*, I quote a long passage from an essay by Barbara MacLeod who in the 1970s did some long (48-hour) sits in deep caves in Belize and Guatemala. She had some experiences that illuminate to your question.

Allen Ginsberg had contact with the underworld via ingesting yagé. Others have fasted, or gone on vision quests in the wilderness.

I don't sense the poem as the equivalent of an Upper Paleolithic hand-lamp, though if you think of certain incised, carved hand-lamps as proto-tjurungas, I guess you would be in the archaic vicinity of a poem!

Olson: Contemporary artists such as Francis Bacon, Nora Jaffe, Chaim Soutine, John Register, and Willem de Kooning have all had an influence on you. What in particular has drawn you to the work of these artists?

Eshleman: I am interested in what I see in paintings as well as what the paintings see in me. For many years I have tried, facing works of art, to inhabit a "between" in which a reciprocal distillation could occur. I have been drawn to all of the people you mention, and many others, for specific reasons, and I suppose the best response I can make to this question is to refer the reader to *Reciprocal Distillations* (Hot Whiskey, 2007), which has a selection of my poems on art and artists.

Soutine probably had the greatest impact on me, of the people you mention: I discovered one of his *Hanging Fowl* in a Japanese museum in 1963 and it is still as vivid in my imagination today as it was then.

Nora Jaffe, a kind of abstract erotic formalist, was a dear friend who died of lung cancer in 1994. I have two major pieces on her, "Nora's Roar" and "Nora's Transmission."

I adore Bacon's portraits and have written about the semen, blood, and soot that seem to be impacted in them, or whirling about and through them, in "Spirits of the Head."

John Register's concept of "The waiting room for The Beyond," worked out in paintings that seem hyper-realistic, but are also eerily dream-like, made a lasting impression.

As for de Kooning, his abstract canvases, upon scrutiny, often seem alive with what I'd call image babies, or near-images (such as one discovers in Henri Michaux's drawings). I like to work with these in language, to try to find constructions that are equally dense and mysterious.

Olson: In *Blue Fire*, James Hillman states, "a goal of the alchemical process was the pearl of great price." What is the pearl of great price?

Eshleman:

> A poem without subject,
> all parts of which surprise and interlock, a poem
> with twenty centers,

all muscular and avid, each word dense, full in
    itself, a nest,
a sound of wood crackling in the fireplace, a shiver
    without skin,
each word an outpost, a courier, monkey words
feeling the earthquake coming before I do...

(from "Combined Object" in *An Alchemist with One Eye on Fire*)

NOTES:

[1] This interview appeared in the *The Seattle Review*.

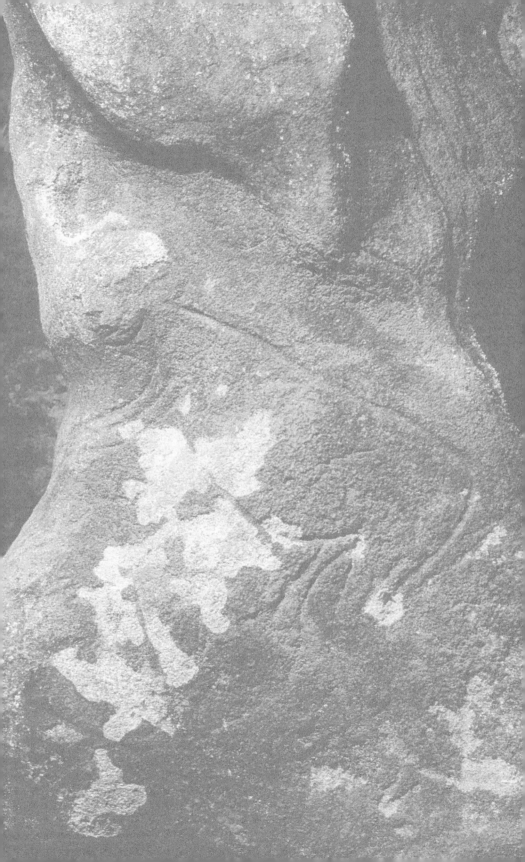

ACKNOWLEDGEMENTS

Cover: Grotte de Saint-Cirq (Dordogne) ©Michel Lorblanchet

St Cirq is a small cave a few kilometers from the village of Les Eyzies in the French Dordogne. The Upper Paleolithic engravings in it are thought to be from the Middle to Late Magdalenian period. The naked, male figure has a prominent belly, and possibly a long penis. I say "possibly" as his placement on a rock that strongly evokes a woman's belly (with breast-like rock protrubences above) locates him in the position of a foetus if his female background shape is acknowledged. Thus what looks like a long penis might be an umbilical cord. The man's face, with its slightly smiling, sleepy expression, can also be seen, which is quite unusual in the Upper Paleolithic portrayal of males, nearly all of which are masked.

ABOUT THE AUTHOR

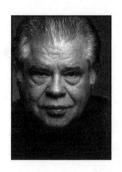 Clayton Eshleman was born in Indianapolis, Indiana, in 1935. The author of more than twenty-five books, including fifteen collections of poetry, Eshleman is the recipient of the National Book Award, The Landon Translation Prize from the Academy of American Poets, a Guggenheim Fellowship, and several fellowships from the National Endowment of the Arts and the National Endowment for the Humanities. He is also a masterly translator, especially from the Spanish of Neruda and Vallejo, and the French of Artaud and Césaire. In 2003, Wesleyan University Press published Eshleman's *Juniper Fuse: The Upper Paleolithic Imagination and the Construction of the Underworld*, the fruit of a thirty-year investigation into the origins of image-making and poetry via the Ice Age painted caves of Southwestern France. This past year saw the release of his translation of *The Complete Poetry of César Vallejo*, the accumulation of forty years of study and interaction with Vallejo's poetry, and a book of his own poetry, *An Alchemist With One Eye on Fire*. Both titles have been widely praised. In 2008, a comprehensive anthology of Eshleman's various writings, translations, and poems of the last forty years will be published by Black Widow Press. His writings, translations, essays, and reviews have appeared in hundreds of literary magazines and newspapers throughout the world. A professor emeritus of English at Eastern Michigan University, Clayton Eshleman continues to live in Ypsilanti, Michigan, with his wife, Caryl.

TITLES FROM BLACK WIDOW PRESS

TRANSLATION SERIES

Chanson Dada: Selected Poems by Tristan Tzara
Translated & edited by Lee Harwood

Approximate Man & Other Writings, by Tristan Tzara
Translated & edited by Mary Ann Caws

Poems of Andre Breton: A Bilingual Anthology
Translated & edited by Jean-Pierre Cauvin and Mary Ann Caws

Last Love Poems of Paul Eluard
Translated with an introduction by Marilyn Kallet

Capital of Pain, by Paul Eluard
Translated by Mary Ann Caws, Patricia Terry, and Nancy Kline

Love, Poetry (L'amour la poésie), by Paul Eluard
Translated with an introduction by Stuart Kendall

The Sea & Other Poems, by Guillevic
Translated by Patricia Terry with an introduction by Monique Chefdor

Essential Poems & Writings of Robert Desnos: A Bilingual Anthology
Edited by Mary Ann Caws   [forthcoming]

Essential Poems & Writings of Joyce Mansour: A Bilingual Anthology
Translated with an introduction by Serge Gavronsky   [forthcoming]

Eyeseas (Les Ziaux) by Raymond Queneau
Translated with an introduction by Daniela Hurezanu & Stephen Kessler   [forthcoming]

Poems of A. O. Barnabooth by Valery Larbaud
Translated with an introduction by Ron Padgett and Bill Zavatsky
[forthcoming]

Art Poetique by Guillevic
Translated by Maureen Smith   [forthcoming]

MODERN POETRY SERIES

An Alchemist with One Eye on Fire
Clayton Eshleman

Backscatter
John Olson   [forthcoming]

Crusader-Woman by Ruxandra Ceseraneu
Translated by Adam Sorkin. Introduction by Andrei Codrescu
[forthcoming]

The Grindstone of Rapport: A Clayton Eshleman Reader
Clayton Eshleman   [forthcoming]

NEW POETS SERIES

Signal from Draco: New and Selected Poems
Mebane Robertson   [forthcoming]

LITERARY THEORY/BIOGRAPHY SERIES

Revolution of the Mind: The Life of Andre Breton
(Revised and augmented edition)
By Mark Polizzotti   [forthcoming]

www.blackwidowpress.com